www.brookscole.com

www.brookscole.com is the World Wide Web site for Thomson Brooks/Cole and is your direct source to dozens of online resources.

At www.*brookscole.com* you can find out about supplements, demonstration software, and student resources. You can also send e-mail to many of our authors and preview new publications and exciting new technologies.

www.brookscole.com
Changing the way the world learns®

Explorations in Privilege, Oppression, and Diversity

SHARON K. ANDERSON
Colorado State University

VALERIE A. MIDDLETON
Colorado State University

THOMSON
™
BROOKS/COLE

Australia • Canada • Mexico • Singapore • Spain
United Kingdom • United States

THOMSON
BROOKS/COLE

Executive Editor: Lisa Gebo
Senior Acquisitions Editor: Marquita Flemming
Assistant Editor: Shelley Gesicki
Editorial Assistant: Amy Lam
Technology Project Manager: Barry Connolly
Marketing Manager: Caroline Concilla
Marketing Assistant: Mary Ho
Advertising Project Manager: Tami Strang
Project Manager, Editorial Production: Candace Chen
Art Director: Vernon Boes

Print Buyer: Barbara Britton
Permissions Editor: Stephanie Lee
Production Service: Janet Kiefer, Carlisle Publishers Services
Copy Editor: Pat Eichhorst
Cover Designer: Paula Goldstein
Cover Image: © Photodisc/World Portraits
Text/Cover Printer: Webcom
Compositor: Carlisle Publishers Services

For more information about our products, contact us at:
Thomson Learning Academic Resource Center
1-800-423-0563
For permission to use material from this text or product, submit a request online at
http://www.thomsonrights.com.
Any additional questions about permissions can be submitted by email to
thomsonrights@thomson.com.

Library of Congress Control Number: 2004102037

ISBN 0-534-51742-0

Thomson Brooks/Cole
10 Davis Drive
Belmont, CA 94002
USA

Asia
Thomson Learning
5 Shenton Way #01-01
UIC Building
Singapore 068808

Australia/New Zealand
Thomson Learning
102 Dodds Street
Southbank, Victoria 3006
Australia

Canada
Nelson
1120 Birchmount Road
Toronto, Ontario M1K 5G4
Canada

Europe/Middle East/Africa
Thomson Learning
High Holborn House
50/51 Bedford Row
London WC1R 4LR
United Kingdom

Latin America
Thomson Learning
Seneca, 53
Colonia Polanco
11560 Mexico D.F.
Mexico

Spain/Portugal
Paraninfo
Calle Magallanes, 25
28015 Madrid, Spain

To my parents (Joanne and Lawrence), who are one in a million; to my wonderful son,
Bobby, and awesome daughter, Taya;
and to God, who gives me all my worthwhile ideas.

Sharon

Keeping thoughts of you on my mind helped me to persevere—
God, Bobby, Taya, Kia, Doreen, Ma, Mudea.

Valerie

Contents

Preface

VALERIE MIDDLETON AND SHARON K. ANDERSON

VAL'S STORY

Relying on 8 years of public-school teaching experience in the Chicago area, I smiled confidently upon entering my first university classroom as a teacher educator, in spite of the fact that nearly every student in the room sat before me with mouth agape. I turned my back to them to write identifying information on the board while I subtly checked to make sure I was buttoned and zipped. When I realized that I was appropriately secured, I assumed that the shocked expressions were a result of my being a Black female in a classroom of all White students. At my about face, the students had corrected their posture and were awaiting my delineation of the syllabus for a course on diversity. That was the first time I taught a university course. That scenario is similar every semester and lends itself to teaching about issues of diversity, privilege, and oppression in my role as an associate professor in the School of Education at Colorado State University.

My previous teaching experiences were in Chicago-area, K–12, public-school settings, where students came from a variety of racial, ethnic, religious, and socioeconomic backgrounds. In contrast, my current experience is as an associate professor at Colorado State University, teaching predominantly White, Christian, middle-class students who are in training to be teachers, counselors, social workers, and the like. I, a Black American, female college professor, am an anomaly. Typically, I am the only teacher of color many of my students have had, the only Black teacher they have had, or the only Black professor they have had. As a result, I find I must carefully and purposefully establish a level of credibility and authority that would typically come with the position, as it does for many of my White American male counterparts—a privilege they automatically have.

Sharon and I, the coeditors of this book, are both instructors—one White and one Black, working in a predominately White university setting, in a predominately White city, with graduate and undergraduate students in counseling and education who are predominately White. Most of our students come from mono-racially White suburban or rural settings in Colorado or other states across the country, while a few come from areas such as Denver, Chicago, or Los Angeles.

Within the context of teaching about multiculturalism, many of our students say they support issues of diversity and multiculturalism; however, closer inquiry reveals that they mean "I am not a racist." They then go on to share scenarios of how they have a Black or Mexican friend, have dated someone outside of their race, listen to rap music, or attend Native American Pow Wows. When the "burden of proof" regarding the validity of their claims is placed at the forefront, many of the students become agitated, defensive, or resistant. However, rather than shy away from these reactions, we believe that they are a necessary and critical step in deconstructing and reconstructing a belief system that supports multicultural understanding. This book contributes to other works in the area of privilege, diversity, and oppression by encouraging readers to look inside themselves rather than claim "I'm not" and place the blame elsewhere.

FOCUS OF THE BOOK

The title of this book is *Explorations in Privilege, Oppression, and Diversity* because of the elusive nature of privilege, its resulting oppression, and the diversity of positions in which it is manifested. Privilege, though complex, is generally defined as the invisible knapsack of unearned assets to which one is oblivious (McIntosh, 2000). Discussions of privilege aimed at surfacing beliefs about diversity generally have an impact on students in the same way they bring to the surface their fear of being labeled a racist. Denial and resistance often are manifested in statements such as "I've had to work hard for everything I have," "I grew up poor," "I'm just a poor college student," "Anybody can achieve if they just work hard enough," or "Both of us help around the house." Moving individuals beyond defensiveness and cliché and toward a truer understanding of self-relative beliefs about race, class, gender, ability, and sexual orientation, by their reading and reflecting on the struggles and transformations of others, is the focus of this book.

This collection of narratives is designed to help readers understand that privilege has many faces and many statuses, and individuals are subject to it as either agents of discrimination, targets of discrimination, or both. Agent status groups (that is, White, male, heterosexual, able-bodied) benefit from the inequality of privilege, while target status groups (that is, people of color, female, homosexual, people with disabilities) are oppressed. Reading, critically examining, and using self-reflection prompted by the "coming to consciousness" stories of others is a way to come to terms with one's own beliefs and actions.

We want our readers to analyze and dismantle privilege by acknowledging that privilege exists, that oppression exists because of privilege, that we participate in such oppression either consciously or unconsciously, that we benefit from privilege regardless of the other oppressions we experience as target groups, and that privilege is reinforced at institutional and societal levels. We also want it recognized that knowledge is nothing without personal action, and that choosing not to take an action is an action.

The authors of the chapters in this book represent "real people" involved in their struggles with privilege. Each chapter represents the authors' own voices, and their own way of sharing their stories. The authors use various means to describe their own positionality relative to ability, socioeconomic class, gender, race, and sexual identity, and that of others. Although it is recognized by all of the authors that the concepts discussed here are socially, politically, ideologically constructed, it is also recognized that these are the categories by which we call ourselves and others, and the categories that make the meaning of the narratives clear and accessible to the reader. Our hope is that classes and training sessions, in the process of reading stories, telling stories, and critically reflecting on those stories, will use student and participant voice to co-construct their own narratives toward engaging the learner and making learning relevant by exploring issues from both privileged and oppressed positions.

EMERGENT NARRATIVES

The process by which the book took shape was emergent. That is, although a fairly structured and descriptive call for papers went out, the manuscripts that came back were varied in style, different from what we had imagined, but nevertheless thought-provoking in content. At the time, we thought it important to be as inclusive as possible, knowing firsthand about the "publish or perish" paradigm of higher education. As a result of these unanticipated circumstances, we had to work through our differences over the goal of the book, what should be included or not included, and what to do about manuscripts that did not "specifically" fit the focus (that is, "Is this privilege, or something else?"). We also wanted to provide balance and equity, but we were restricted by the types of submissions we received—many were related to white privilege, one was on sexism related to men, two were on ableism, two were on heterosexism, and several did not fit into our prescribed categories. In the end, we tried to provide for more representation by soliciting manuscripts in those areas. Overall, we believe that we selected accessible narratives, including some of "questionable" contexts relative to privilege, but we believe that all would allow for challenging thinking around the issues and informing the transformative process of our students, ourselves, and others.

ORGANIZATION OF THIS BOOK

This book has two major parts that are further divided into topic-area sections; these sections contain chapters written by individual authors. "Part I" addresses the concept of privilege and privileged statuses via five sections: "Stories of White Privilege," "Stories of Socioeconomic Privilege," "Stories of Able-Bodied Privilege," "Stories of Heterosexual Privilege," and "Stories of Sexism." In the chapters within these sections, the authors share their personal histories and their journeys of recognizing and acknowledging their privilege. In instances in which the authors addressed more than one privileged status, the chapter has been placed in the section that represents the most prominently described journey.

Some authors share stories of privilege that occurred as part of their circumstances at birth, such as White, heterosexual, or gender privilege (for example, see Zetzer's "White Out: Privilege and Its Problems"). Other authors describe being born into one context (for example, low income), but, due to life's events, they moved into a more privileged context (for example, see Tuason's "Deprivations and Privileges We All Have"). These authors take the reader through interesting journeys in which one becomes aware of the authors' discordant experiences and how, in one context of time, they were oppressed and, in another, privileged. A third group of authors describes the phenomenon in which they almost simultaneously experience oppression (for example, as a person of color), and privilege (for example, as able-bodied) (see Lo's "Seeing Through Another Lens"). This mix brings to light the reality that we all have multiple identities, and as Liddle (in the ". . . Personal Compassion and Being Allies" section of "Part II") suggests, such multiple identities can give one "mental whiplash, alternating as it does between disadvantaged and privileged group memberships." (p. 171)

"Part II" of the book includes three sections, which focus on issues related to privilege, including "Stories of Assumed Privilege," "Stories of Internalized Oppression, Acculturation, and Assimilation," and "Stories of Personal Compassion and Being Allies." In each of the stories within the "Stories of Assumed Privilege" section, the authors are assumed by others to be different (for example, heterosexual, White) from whom they really are and/or how they identify (for example, see Barsky's "Assumed Privilege: A Double-Edged Sword" and Deines's "Who, Me? White?: The Process of Acknowledging and Challenging Racial Privilege"). These authors talk about having a "choice" to share or not to share their "real" or "true" identity of being gay or "looking White"—a choice that plays into having or giving up privilege. In the "Stories of Internalized Oppression, Assimilation, and Acculturation" section, the authors (most of whom are people of color) present their stories about the impact of internalized oppression and the subtle nature of assimilation and acculturation in different contexts. Choudhuri, in her chapter "Oppression of the Spirit:

Complexities in the Counseling Environment," graciously offers the reader an opportunity to see the power of oppression when a counselor of color (from India) fails to assess the background differences between herself and a client of color. Gonzalez ("Acculturation and Identity: Intra-Ethnic Distinctions Among Mexican Americans") shares his perception of psychological and economic privilege as it relates to Mexican American students who distance themselves from the Mexicans across the border and who exchange or try to exchange components of their culture, such as the values of their parents and their native language, to obtain the benefits of the dominant White culture. The chapter by Lichaw and Howell-Carter ("Unmasking Within-Group Prejudice: A Case Study") addresses the sometimes subtle nature of assimilation and its impact in the counseling relationship between a counselor of color and clients of color.

The authors in the last section, "Stories of Personal Compassion and Being Allies," share their insights into the process of connecting with someone different from oneself through compassion (see Mock's "Personal Compassion and Alliance Building: Observations of an Asian American Professor") and being a person of color counseling a White client (see Chao's "Going Through Cultural Barriers in Counseling"). Liddle ("Tales from the Heart of Dixie: Using White Privilege to Fight Racism") shares her journey of addressing racism in the community and classroom. MacPhee ("Yes, I See You're Committed to the Cause . . . But Where's Your Credibility, and Why That Angst?") tells of his first experiences with colleagues and students when he infused multicultural material into the curriculum. And Gormley ("A Multiracial Unity Group for Graduate Students") shares her story of attempts to bring students of color and White students together to begin a dialogue and bring about greater understanding.

The difficulty in uprooting systems of privilege is privilege's invisibility and the power it has to provide advantages to its beholders—advantages many do not want to lose. However, the consequence of maintaining this system of advantage is that it serves to disadvantage and oppress others. The uprooting process comes with recognizing our own points of privilege, which is the forerunner of true cultural sensitivity and cultural competence. We hope that the contributions in this book will serve to uproot the elusiveness and power of privilege and bring about less discrimination, intolerance, and judgmental attitudes, and bring about more understanding, compassion, and equality.

Acknowledgments

We would like to thank all of our contributors for their willingness to share their stories, and their hard work in making this book become a reality. You have been an awesome group to work with. Thank You!

We would also like to thank the following reviewers who carefully read the manuscript and offered valuable suggestions for improvement: Deborah McGriff, University of Wyoming; Beth Rienzi, California State University, Bakersfield; Barry Feldman, MSW, Ph.D., University of New Hampshire; and Thomas Scofield, University of Nebraska, Kearney.

Sharon Hamm assisted us with word processing and editing issues. Thank you!

Finally, we would like to thank our editors, Julie Martinez and Shelley Gesicki. You both were a pleasure to work with! Thank you for believing in this idea and helping us along the way!

About the Contributors

Sharon K. Anderson

Sharon Anderson, Ph.D., grew up on a farm/ranch in Wyoming. Being the youngest of three, she has fond memories of playing football, softball, and basketball with her older brothers; helping her mom with indoor responsibilities; occasionally getting to drive a tractor with her dad; and attending a very small public school that held K–12 grades in the same building. After graduating from high school, she attended the University of Wyoming and received her bachelor's degree in English education in 1978. She taught junior high for 1 year and then returned to the University to work on a master's degree in counseling. She then worked for the TRIO programs at UW. This is where her first experiences with people really different from herself began. Anderson worked with TRIO for several years, and then decided in 1988 to pursue her doctorate in counseling psychology through the University of Denver. She graduated in 1993 and obtained her current faculty position at Colorado State University in 1994. As an associate professor, she teaches professional ethics, practicum, and internship classes in a master's counseling and career development program.

On the personal side, Anderson is a single mom of two awesome children, Bobby and Taya. She spends a lot of her free time with them playing outside, watching children's movies, and reading them stories. She loves to travel and see new scenery, as well as spend time in the Rocky Mountains.

Valerie A. Middleton

Val Middleton, Ph.D., is currently an associate professor at Colorado State University teaching and researching courses on diversity, exceptionality (special needs), and educational methodology using both service-learning and school-university-community partnership (Professional Development School Partnership) delivery systems. She holds a bachelor's degree in Special Education from Illinois State University, a master's degree in Special Needs from Colorado State University, and a doctorate in Teacher Education/Staff Development from Colorado State University. Previously she taught students in grades K–12 in Chicago-area public schools.

Heidi A. Zetzer

Before and during college, Heidi Zetzer, Ph.D., worked as an instructor for the Institute for Creative Living, an outdoor school located in Cleveland, Ohio. She earned a bachelor's degree in Psychology from Denison University in 1983. Although effective as an outdoor education instructor, she wanted to learn about the science and practice of psychotherapeutic change, so she entered the doctoral program in Counseling Psychology at Ohio State University. In 1986, Zetzer earned a master's degree from Ohio State, left Columbus, Ohio, and moved to Santa Barbara, California. She earned a doctorate in Counseling Psychology from the University of California, Santa Barbara, in 1990.

From 1992–1995, Zetzer served as the Project Coordinator for the Couples Alcoholism Treatment Project at the University of California, Santa Barbara. She became licensed as a psychologist in 1995. In 1995 and 1996, Zetzer served as a staff psychologist at Child Abuse Listening & Mediation, in Santa Barbara, California, where she provided treatment services to child abuse victims and their families as well as adult sex offenders.

Zetzer has been a core faculty member in the graduate psychology program at the Santa Barbara campus of Antioch University, Southern California since 1996. She teaches Multicultural Awareness, Multicultural Clinical Skills, Clinical Skills I, Feminist Theories of Psychology, and Psychopathology. She is also the Coordinator of the AUSB Professional Development & Career Counseling Program. In addition to teaching, Zetzer and her colleague, Muriel Shockley, MFT, co-direct Antioch's component of the Multicultural Mental Health Access and Services for Family Violence Prevention & Demonstration Project. The main goal of the three-year collaboration is to develop a process model of multicultural organizational development. The model is the focus of a handbook, designed to help agencies enhance the cultural competency of their organizations.

Zetzer has been rock climbing in locations throughout the United States and Canada for the last 30 years! She climbs with her two sons and her husband, who is a cognitive neuroscientist at the University of California, Santa Barbara. Joshua Tree and Red Rocks National Parks as well as Squamish, British Columbia, are the family's favorite climbing spots. Zetzer took up golf three years ago. It is a notoriously difficult game, wrought with moments of beauty and pleasure and the constant possibility of trouble and humiliation. When asked why she plays, she said, "I play because it teaches me about myself."

Deborah Megivern

Deborah Megivern, Ph.D., is an assistant professor of social work at Washington University in Saint Louis, Missouri. She earned her undergraduate degree at Luther College in Decorah, Iowa, and her master's degree in social work and psychology from the University of Michigan. Prior to entering academia, Megivern worked as a residential counselor in mental-health programs and probation officer in adult corrections. In 2001, Megivern completed her doctorate in social work and psychology at the University of Michigan; her dissertation focused on the college experiences of students who have a mental illness. Megivern accepted a two-year position as a postdoctoral research fellow with the National Institute of Mental Health's Center for Mental Health Services Research at Washington University.

Megivern's research interests include economic and social disadvantage as factors for the development of mental illness, access to social/economic capital (especially higher education) for people with mental illnesses, and early intervention and recovery from mental illness. She is participating in a National Institute of Health program to encourage researchers to study disparities in the mental-health system based on race and socioeconomic status.

Megivern teaches social policy, mental-health policy, and human diversity at the George Warren Brown School of Social Work. Her courses focus on social justice, and the application of multiculturalism to public policy and social problem resolution. She is married and has two stepsons. The sister that Megivern assisted in parenting graduated from college in 2004, becoming the second child from the Megivern family to complete a bachelor's degree.

Rich Furman

Rich Furman, Ph.D., is an assistant professor in the School of Social Work at University of Nebraska, Omaha. He previously was an assistant professor in the School of Social Work at Colorado State University, Fort Collins, Colorado. He has taught throughout the social-work curriculum but currently teaches mostly clinical courses.

Furman has worked in various roles in social-work practice and education for 15 years. He was the founding director of Children's Outreach Services Programs, Resources for Human Development, Philadelphia, Pennsylvania. He also founded and directed an early intervention program for the same agency. He has been a clinical social worker conducting individual, group, and family therapy with adults, children, and families in the various communities. He was the supervisor of group therapy for a substance-abuse program in the Puerto Rican community in Philadelphia. Furman was also previously the Director of the Youth Work Certificate Program at Community College of Philadelphia, and a member of the faculty in the department of Behavioral Health and Human Services.

Furman has published numerous articles on social-work practice and ethics, managed care, youth services, social-work education, friendship, and poetry as a tool in social work practice, research, and teaching. He has published a workbook on group practice.

He is also an internationally published poet. His poetry has been published in *Hawai'i Review, The Evergreen Review, Black Bear Review, Red Rock Review, Sierra Nevada Review, Penn Review, Free Lunch, Colere, Pearl, The Journal of Poetry Therapy, Impetus, Poetry Motel,* and many other publications. He has performed his work throughout the United States, and in Nicaragua, Mexico, and Guatemala. His work has been described as "neither street nor beat nor meat nor academic, but an emotionally evocative mix of styles that can be brutally imagistic or powerfully terse." Snorting Dog Press published two of his chapbooks, *of only average intent, 2002* and *Gleaming and Faded, 2003*. He also has an e-book on the Internet Poet's Cooperative Web site. Legitimate Press will be releasing a CD of Furman's and James L. Smith's poetry.

Colleen Loomis

Colleen Loomis, Ph.D., spent most of her youth barefoot and swimming in Florida lakes, springs, and the Atlantic Ocean. At home with alligators, water moccasins, and jellyfish, Loomis's sense of adventure developed early and continues in both personal and professional aspects of her life.

Loomis is recognized as a "Trailblazing Woman" in community psychology by the Society for Community Research and Action. An assistant professor of psychology at Wilfrid Laurier University in Ontario, Canada, Loomis's research examines the meaning of *sense of community* and its relation to preventing alienation and promoting social responsibility. She also investigates how sense of community relates to positive and negative educational (for example, literacy and numeracy) and health consequences for youth in the United States, Canada, and Cameroon. She has published on these and related subjects, including self-help groups, gender and power, socioeconomic class, mentoring, and bilingual education in the United States. Loomis also serves as a consultant to the U.S. Centers for Disease Control for the *Legacy for Children*™ project and collaborates in psychosocial research on HIV prevention and AIDS care in Cameroon. In 1994, Loomis completed a bachelor's degree in psychology at the University of Tulsa. She earned her doctorate in human services psychology from the University of Maryland, Baltimore County in May 2001 and was a Postdoctoral Scholar at Stanford University Medical Centers for the following 2 years.

Loving both solitude and companionship, Loomis takes long walks, enjoys sharing an evening with friends over dinner and conversation, watches independent films, reads, and travels. She says, "I want to go anywhere I haven't been, and there are many places where I would go again." She focuses on the journey as well as the destination. Often she is found near water, whether a fountain, ocean, lake, or mountain stream. At the publishing of this chapter, Loomis began taking piano lessons for the first time in her life.

Ma. Teresa Tuason

Ma. Teresa Tuason is currently an assistant professor in the Psychology Department of the University of North Florida in Jacksonville, Florida. Tuason (or Tes, as she is fondly called by family, friends, and colleagues) came to the United States for her graduate degree. She was born and raised in the Philippines.

Before coming to the United States, she taught for four years in the Psychology Department of the Ateneo de Manila University. During that time, she also had an active clinical practice at the Greenhills Creative Child Center and in the Psychology Department of the Ateneo de Manila University.

When she went to Albany State University of New York for her Ph.D., it was her first time to live outside of the Philippines. This was where she had meaningfully experienced being different (that is; as a Catholic, heterosexual, poor, Asian woman). It was also in Albany that she learned to discover and love Counseling Psychology. After completing her dissertation, she did her internship and postdoctoral fellowship at the University of Utah, Salt Lake City. It was there that she experienced the nurturance and generosity of her Caucasian American supervisors and colleagues and learned how White people can be multiculturally competent and sensitive, too.

As part of her love for the Philippines and her emotional obligation to share what she had learned here in the United States, Tuason went back to the Philippines. She taught and was Clinical Director of the Ateneo Wellness Center, a clinic for practice and training of graduate students. Within eight months she realized that the country's economic and political instability, and the institution's inadequacy to welcome what she wanted to teach were both inhibiting her commitment to her country. It became clear that she could help her country in service and advocacy more from the outside (that is; people are people wherever you go). She then applied for a counseling-center job in Illinois.

Her research interests include differentiation of self in Bowen's Family Systems theory applied to Filipinos, poverty's psychological correlates and processes, and Filipino-American ethnic identity. Tuason lives with her husband in Jacksonville, Florida. In her free time, she sings and dances to karaoke, watches sea turtles hatch on the beach, and visits her family on the other side of the world.

Kaying Lo

Kaying Lo grew up in Wisconsin and currently resides in Minnesota. She has a master's degree in marriage and family therapy and currently practices with a nonprofit mental health agency. Her graduate studies have included topics of immigration, assimilation, and gender classification. She has aspirations to continue her education and teach at the collegiate level. Lo is working to expand her professional experience before returning for her doctorate degree.

Being the oldest daughter in her family, Lo seeks to define herself in both the mainstream and Hmong culture. During most of her childhood, she lived with two brothers in a single-parent home. Her biological father died in Thailand. As a refugee growing up in America, Lo has faced the many challenges of poverty, prejudice, isolation, discrimination, acculturation, privilege, loss, and redefinition. Lo's history influences her commitment to defining herself and how she relates to others in a culture of privilege and bias.

Paul E. Priester

Paul Priester, Ph.D., is an assistant professor in the Department of Educational Psychology at the University of Wisconsin, Milwaukee. He completed a master's degree in rehabilitation counseling at the University of Iowa and a doctorate in counseling psychology at Loyola University, Chicago. Priester's research interests include the substance abuse counseling process, 12-step-based recovery from addictions, the integration of spiritual/religious issues in psychotherapy, meta-analysis as a research tool, and the cross-cultural counseling process. He has a wife (Kathy), three kids (Caiti, 10; Paul, 4; and Margie, 2) and a black and tan coonhound (Buddy, 90 pounds). His hobbies include morel mushroom hunting, gardening, old cars that don't run, fantasy football, and taking his kids fishing. His dream is to run a small farm, growing heirloom apples and berries.

Allison L. Cashwell

Allison Cashwell grew up in the quaint town of Mount Airy, North Carolina, hometown of actor Andy Griffith, and better known as the inspiration for the fictional TV town of "Mayberry." After graduating from the University of North Carolina at Chapel Hill with a bachelor's degree in psychology in 1992, she relocated to Crested Butte, Colorado, where for 2 years she was the artistic director of the Crested Butte Mountain Theatre, Colorado's longest-running community theatre. She received a master's degree in education and human resource studies from Colorado State University in 1999.

Cashwell is a Licensed Professional Counselor, Certified Addictions Counselor, and an Approved Domestic Violence Offender Treatment Provider for the state of Colorado. Since 1998, her work in the helping professions has focused on educating nonvoluntary clientele in the areas of addictions and domestic violence. A strong believer in co-creating solutions in a therapeutic setting, her theoretical orientation is Solution-Focused Therapy. She strives to take this philosophy into the classroom as well as home from work each day.

Cashwell is a professor of psychology at Front Range Community College in Fort Collins, Colorado. She teaches introductory psychology, human growth and development, and stress management. A proponent of primary prevention, her teachings in the classroom include therapeutic touch as well as didactic discussions. Her motto is "Conflict is inevitable; violence is not."

Additionally, Cashwell teaches aerobics and weight-training group fitness classes 3 days per week at the Fort Collins Club. In the summertime, she works as an experiential counselor/ropes course facilitator for Hands On Resources, LLC. She enjoys hiking, camping, and exploring the majestic Rocky Mountain region she now calls home.

Suzanne Weatherman

Suzanne Weatherman is a lecturer in the Gender Studies program and the Freshman Orientation program at Southwest Missouri State University. She is currently working as part of a multidisciplinary federal grant project aimed at implementing emotional intelligence curriculum into the education system. Weatherman, who is also an artist, makes glass beads that she incorporates into her jewelry designs.

She received her bachelor's degree in agriculture at the University of Missouri in 1976 and her master's degree in counseling from SMSU in 2000. Suzanne's current interests involve gathering women of difference together to discover their mutual concerns for social justice. She hopes to someday provide a permanent gathering space for women in the Ozarks region.

Cherice Sommer

Cherice Sommer received her master's degree in counseling from Southwest Missouri State University in 2003 and has an extensive background in feminist and gender issues. Currently she is in private counseling practice, where her work includes individual, couples, and group therapy, as well as treatment of sexual offenders. In addition, she has presented at multiple conferences on topics including sexuality, stress management, and domestic violence. Her areas of interest at this time involve lesbian identity maintenance and gender socialization. In addition, Sommer feels an urgency and personal responsibility to raise awareness of the connection of all living things in her work, and of the power of creating a safe world for all to share. She and her partner, Sandi Hart, spend their time nurturing creativity and guiding their two teenage boys in finding their own unique paths.

Deborah L. Cox

Deborah L. Cox, Ph.D., is a licensed psychologist and associate professor of counseling at Southwest Missouri State University, where she is also a member of the gender studies faculty. She directs research teams and teaches graduate courses in multicultural counseling, family therapy, and basic counseling skills. Having grown up in a fundamentalist Christian community in the Southern United States, Cox feels particularly grateful for the feminist training she received in graduate school—training that allowed her to question traditional assumptions about things such as cultural difference, good versus evil, and gender or sex roles. She received the doctorate in counseling psychology from Texas Woman's University in 1996 and has extensive clinical experience including individual, couples, and family therapy in mental health agencies, private practice, and the Dallas Public Schools. Cox is coauthor of *Women's Anger: Clinical and Developmental Perspectives*

(1999, Brunner-Mazel), and *The Anger Advantage (2003, Broadway).* Her formal research program involves emotional development, anger, cultural beauty issues for women and men, and gender socialization. Cox values models of teaching and psychotherapy that involve a focus on emotion. She considers it a personal ambition to raise social consciousness in her students and facilitate emotion consciousness in both clients and students. She resides in Springfield with her colleague and partner, Joseph Hulgus, and their son, A.J.

Heather Trepal

Heather Trepal, Ph.D., received her master's degree in education in Community Counseling from Cleveland State University. She graduated in December 2003 with her doctorate in Counseling and Human Development Services from Kent State University. She is licensed as a Professional Counselor in the state of Ohio where she works in private practice. She focuses on individual, child, family, and couple therapy and specializes in the treatment of victims of rape and sexual assault.

In addition to working in the practice, Trepal is the Project Assistant for the Coping, Stress, and Well-Being of Custodial Grandparents project in the School of Family and Consumer Studies at Kent State University. She is a part-time faculty member in the Department of Counseling at Youngstown State University and has taught a number of graduate counseling courses, including practicum, supervision, and group counseling lab. Trepal has also taught both graduate and undergraduate courses at Kent State University and Northeastern Ohio Universities College of Medicine (NEOUCOM).

She has presented and conducted workshops on a number of topics including rape and sexual assault, self-injury, disordered eating and body image, relationships, bullying, and gender. Her publications have been in the areas of sexual assault, self-jury, and reflective thinking in counseling. Trepal's research has focused on subjective perceptions, and she has used Q methodology to investigate children's perceptions of bullying behavior, counselor's perceptions of gender, and adolescents' perceptions of their pregnancies.

Trepal lives in Stow, Ohio, with her husband, Todd, and their sons, Aidan and Mason.

David H. Whitcomb

David Whitcomb grew up in small, picturesque towns in Connecticut at the edge of the New York City metropolis. The oldest of three sons, he comes from a musical family where singing, musical instruments, and a rich variety of recorded music resounded throughout the home. In addition to exploring Connecticut, summers were spent hiking and canoeing in New York's Adirondack Mountains and swimming in the Atlantic waters of Nantucket, while winters were filled with ice skating and downhill skiing.

Even though his interest in psychology began in high school, Whitcomb's career has taken a circuitous route, including a summer as an exchange student in Peru, a year of internships (in mental health, community theater, and public radio), and several years working before starting a doctoral program in counseling psychology. Whitcomb's career has included residential care and vocational instruction for individuals with multiple disabilities; vocational counseling for welfare-to-work clients; crisis counseling at several hospitals; outpatient substance abuse counseling; individual counseling and coming out support groups for gay and bisexual men; psychological assessments for pre-adoptive children; and a predoctoral internship at the University of Maryland Counseling Center.

Whitcomb once helped his partner of ten years build a rustic home "from scratch" in the Berkshires. Now single, he remains equally attracted to big city life and a slower rural pace. Since 1998, he has been on the faculty at the University of North Dakota, where he directs the master's program in counseling, teaches several courses, and generates research from social justice projects such as HIV prevention and human rights pertaining to sexual orientation. Currently, Whitcomb is Chair of the Section for Lesbian, Gay, and Bisexual Awareness within the Society of Counseling Psychology.

James A. Cummings

James Cummings grew up in the small town of Aitkin, in the heart of Minnesota's lake country. Growing up with five older siblings, he enjoyed many of the outdoor activities his home area offered such as hunting, fishing, boating, and biking. After graduating from high school in 1988, he attended Bemidji State University and obtained bachelor's degrees in history and secondary education. After two years of substitute teaching, Cummings left the education field to embark upon a career in sales. Education called him back when his wife's career path led the Cummings family to Grand Forks, North Dakota. He completed a master's program in counseling at the University of North Dakota, and is currently working as a school counselor in the quiet farming town of Finley, North Dakota.

Cummings and his wife of eleven years are proud parents of three children—Megan, 6; Ryan, 4; and Ellie, 3 months. He and his family enjoy family time together watching movies, playing board games, ice-skating, swimming, and visiting relatives. Cummings is still an avid outdoorsman who also enjoys cooking, computers, and singing.

Carol L. Langer

Carol Langer is a lifelong resident of Nebraska. She grew up on a small farm near Dawson, a town so small that people joked, "Blink, and you'll miss it." She attended a consolidated high school, graduating in 1967 with 28 other young people. She attended Peru State College, a state institution whose original and primary mission was teacher education. After graduation, she taught high school for several years. She and her family relocated to a larger town in Nebraska, and after her husband's death, Langer returned to school and received her master's degree in social work in 1985. She was a school social worker and a medical social worker for a number of years. She began teaching college courses in early 1986, and as a result, began work on her doctorate in sociology. Langer completed her doctorate in 2000 and moved to her current position at the University of Nebraska, Omaha in 2002. She is currently an assistant professor teaching a variety of social work courses, including generalist practice, social work with American Indian families, and human behavior in the social environment.

Langer has three married sons—Jason, Justin, and Jeremy—and two grandchildren, David and Alexis. She travels frequently, preferring the Southwest for lengthy stays. Her ongoing commitment to Native American populations is her passion. Reading, writing, and spending time with nature occupy her leisure time.

Allan E. Barsky

Allan Edward Barsky was born and raised in Regina, Saskatchewan, the "Queen City" of the Canadian Prairies. He learned the meaning of compromise and sharing at a very early age, being the third of four sons.

Regina, a city of 180,000 people in an agricultural province, had a small but tight-knit Jewish community whose cultural life centered around its orthodox synagogue. Growing up as part of a religious minority, Allan learned about the challenges of dealing with various forms of bigotry and the importance of pride in oneself and one's heritage. He was instilled with social democratic values, where people worked together for the common good, as Saskatchewan was the birthplace of universal healthcare, farming cooperatives, and no-fault automobile insurance.

At 18 years old, Barsky moved east (to the right side of Canada) to study business at Queen's University at Kingston, Ontario. He studied law at the University of Toronto and was called to the Bar of Ontario. Although law and business education provided Barsky with useful life and career skills, he headed back to school for a course of studies that provided an outlet for his interest in fostering social justice. He received his masters degree in social work from Yeshiva University at New York City, where he worked with heroin abusers in the Bronx and with families in conflict with the law in Brooklyn.

Barsky received his Ph.D. in Social Work from the University of Toronto where his doctoral dissertation looked at the process of mediation in helping families and child protective services work out plans to ensure children were free from abuse and neglect.

His academic career has spanned three universities—Ryerson University in Toronto, University of Calgary in Alberta, and Florida Atlantic University in Boca Raton. Barsky's teaching and research interests include human diversity, conflict resolution, professional ethics, and addictions. His book credits include *Conflict Resolution for the Helping Professions* (2000, Brooks/Cole), *Interprofessional Practice with Diverse Populations* (2000), and *Clinicians in Court* (2002, Guilford), and *Alcohol, Other Drugs and Addictions: A Professional Development Manual for Social Work and the Human Services* (In press, Brooks/Cole).

Barsky and his effervescent partner, Greg, were legally married in Canada in 2003. They live in a progressive area of south Florida, where ironically their same-sex marriage is specifically rejected by state laws. They are currently learning how to be parents from an excellent teacher, their wonderful daughter, Adelle.

Helen G. Deines

Helen Deines, Ed.D., is an associate professor of social work at Spalding University in Louisville, Kentucky. She earned a bachelor's degree in history from Stanford University, then the master of education (counseling in higher education) from Oregon State, master of social work from the University of Louisville, and doctor of education (educational leadership) from Spalding University.

Deines's primary academic interest—and her avocation—is social action that promotes global economic justice. She volunteers with the national Jobs with Justice coalition and works for living wage legislation and trade policies that promote the well-being of all the world's peoples. Deines encourages U.S. students to learn their economics experientially, traveling with groups such as Witness for Peace and Global Exchange to look at the impact of our policies "up close and personal."

She gratefully acknowledges the contribution of Linda Chatmon, M.S.S.W., Director of First Neighborhood Place, in Louisville, Kentucky—the colleague who reminded her that she always had a choice about naming her racial identity.

Edward A. Delgado-Romero

Edward A. Delgado-Romero, Ph.D., is an assistant professor in Counseling Psychology at Indiana University, Bloomington. He is also adjunct faculty with Latino Studies and on the board of the Institute for Latino/a Cultures, known as "La Casa." He is the past-chair of the Section for Ethnic and Racial Diversity of the Society for Counseling Psychology (Division 17 of the American Psychological Association) and is also involved with the Association of Multicultural Counseling and Development (AMCD) of the American Counseling Association. He is currently the treasurer for the National Latina/o Psychological Association. Delgado-Romero is on the editorial board of the *Hispanic Journal of Higher Education* and has been nominated to the editorial board of the *Journal of Multicultural Counseling and Development*.

He teaches Introduction to Counseling, Introduction to Group Counseling, and Practicum in Counseling, and supervises doctoral students in clinical work. He is a licensed psychologist in both Indiana and Florida. Delgado-Romero's research has been published in several journals and books (most recently in the *Handbook of Multicultural Counseling Competence*). His research interests include Latina/o psychology, multicultural counseling competence, ethics, and investigating race and racism in psychotherapy process.

Delgado-Romero graduated from the University of Notre Dame with a doctorate in Counseling Psychology. He spent his internship year at Michigan

State University. From 1997–2002, he was a clinical assistant professor at the University of Florida Counseling Center, and also became the Assistant Director for Clinical Services. While at Florida, he was affiliated with the Counseling Psychology and Counselor Education departments. He was the advisor of the Colombian Student Association from 1997–2002.

Delgado-Romero is married to Dr. Amy Heesacker, who is also a Counseling Psychologist and a Notre Dame graduate. They have a son, Javier Leandro Romero-Heesacker. Delgado-Romero owes a debt of thanks to his mother, Isabel Delgado-Alonso, who immigrated to the United States in the hopes of giving her family a better life.

Dibya Choudhuri

Dibya Choudhuri, Ph.D., is currently an assistant professor at Eastern Michigan University. She received a doctorate in Counselor Education, with a specialization in Multicultural Counseling from Syracuse University, and a master's degree in counseling from the University of Vermont. She teaches cross-cultural counseling, helping skills, counseling theories, and group counseling courses.

Choudhuri is licensed as a Professional Counselor in Michigan. She is a member of the American Counseling Association, the Association of Multicultural Counseling and Development, and the Counselors for Social Justice. She is currently serving on the editorial board of the *Journal of Counseling and Development*. Her research interests are in qualitative approaches to understanding the experience of clients, pedagogical issues in teaching multicultural counseling and counselor supervision, and international issues in counseling.

Choudhuri worked as a counselor with international students for five years as well as with refugee and immigrant clients through a community mental health agency. She also worked through university multicultural affairs in coordinating student programs for ALANA students as well as providing counseling services. Choudhuri grew up in India, an army brat who traveled constantly, leading a nomadic experience across 16 schools. She came to the United States for her undergraduate work and ended up staying. Choudhuri brings multicultural issues to her daily experience as an immigrant, as well as in her marriage with Damian Fermin who is Dominican American. Her activities are a mix of sedentary and active: reading, writing, and dance. The public library of every town she has lived in knows her well.

Genaro Gonzalez

Genaro Gonzalez was born in McAllen, Texas, into a family of farm workers who migrated annually from their border town to northern agricultural areas. He spent two years in the Honors Program at Pan American College but transferred to California when his activism in the local Chicano movement jeopardized his scholarship status. After receiving his bachelor's degree in Psychology from Pomona College, he obtained his doctorate in Social Psychology and Personality from the University of California at Santa Cruz in 1982.

In addition to his publications in psychology, Gonzalez has published three books of fiction with Arte Publico Press (University of Houston). These include two novels, *Rainbow's End* and *The Quixote Cult,* and a collection of short stories, *Only Sons.* He recently completed a novella and short story compilation, *Our Fathers and Other Figures.*

Gonzalez's interest in psychology centers on cultural issues, including collaboration with his wife, Dr. Elena-Bastida-Gonzalez, on an ongoing NIH project that she directs on the Mexican American elderly. He has taught at the Texas Governors School at University of Texas Austin; at The Wichita State University's Minority Studies Program; and at the University of the Americas in Puebla, Mexico, a position that allowed him to enhance his fluency in Spanish and his knowledge of Mexican culture. Gonzalez is currently a Professor of Psychology at the University of Texas, Pan American, the same institution where years earlier he thought it best to leave. His course load includes Social Psychology, Systems and Theories, Cross-Cultural Psychology, and Psychological Issues in the Mexican American Community.

In addition to working on his garden, Gonzalez likes to spend time in his backyard, where he practices target archery and stargazes with his telescope. He also enjoys helping his daughter Mariella care for their delightful Arabian mare, Saffron.

Felice Lichaw

Felice Lichaw received her master's degree in counselor education from the University of Wisconsin, Madison, and was a Licensed Clinical Professional Counselor in the state of Illinois. She worked in private practice in Chicago, in a strengths-based practice, focusing on adolescent and family treatment, individual and couples therapy, and treatment of traumatization and substance abuse/dependence.

Lichaw presented on a variety of topics including Feminism and Multiculturalism, Managing Compassion Fatigue, Treatment Strategies for Families in Recovery, Working with Resistant and Mandated Clients, and Models of Post-Trauma Intervention for Children and Families. She served as a consultant to the State's Attorney of Cook County—Victim Witness Assistance Program. Lichaw's interest in cultural diversity was a byproduct of growing up in a large extended immigrant/first generation family where she had the opportunity to observe, and to be subject to, the intricacies of acculturation and assimilation. A common thread running through her practice was working with clients who live on the margins of the dominant culture based on their ethnicity, income, culture, or survivor status. An abiding interest was understanding acculturation and assimilation as they relate to these populations and accommodation in individuals and groups living outside the dominant culture.

Lichaw was a published poet and essayist, and worked as a volunteer for The Guild Complex, a Chicago Multi-Cultural Arts organization. She performed her work on stage at the Complex and Green Mill, as well as the Publisher's Row Book Festival and Around the Coyote Arts Festival in Chicago. Lichaw traveled extensively through the United States, Canada, the Dominican Republic, and Costa Rica.*

Marya Howell-Carter

Marya Howell-Carter, Ph.D., is a New York State Licensed Clinical Psychologist. She currently serves as Assistant Director for Clinical Services of Counseling, Career Development, and Placement, and as an Adjunct Professor in the Department of Psychology, at the College of New Rochelle in New Rochelle, New York. She received her doctorate from Northwestern University in Counseling Psychology. After completing her dissertation, Howell-Carter began a faculty position at the University of Saint Francis in Fort Wayne, Indiana. At Saint Francis, she was the Director of the Master's Program in General Psychology. After a change in her husband's employment necessitated relocation to New York, Howell-Carter's interest in a position in which she could use and expand her clinical skills, conduct clinical research, and use these experiences to inform her instruction led her to select the position at the counseling center in New Rochelle in the fall of 2002.

Howell-Carter was raised in Detroit, Michigan—her mother is of German descent from a large, rural, farm family and her father is African American, raised an only child in urban-industrialized Detroit. Howell-Carter's experience of being both a member of the White community in a predominately African American city and a member of the Black community in a predominately White nation where racism pervades belief and behavior, sparked her professional interest in investigating issues of diversity, culture, and the nature of group membership and exclusion. She has selected professional opportunities that challenge her ethnocentric thinking by infusing her understanding of race, mental health, and group membership with the dynamics of economic diversity, skin-color privilege, and cultural bias in the helping professions. She attempts to bring this broad perspective to her treatment, research, and teaching.

Howell-Carter is married to a music-industry executive and is the mother of two young children—one a budding performer, the other a gymnast-(or perhaps daredevil) in-training. She finds that neither her education nor her professional experiences were adequate preparation for motherhood, but that motherhood has been an invaluable source of knowledge and illustration for both teaching and clinical practice.

---

* Just after completing this biography, Lichaw's life came to a premature end in a tragic fire. She leaves behind a large extended family, friends, colleagues, and godchildren who all loved her dearly. This article was not only a reflection on a transformative supervision experience; it was a new step in Lichaw's professional career. Writing the article was a synthesis of her passion for writing, years of therapeutic experience and insight, and a 12-year friendship that deepened through the collaborative writing process. She was proud of the work and looked forward to producing more. All who knew her will miss the deep passion, enduring curiosity, and incisive interpretations she shared with us.

Matthew R. Mock

Matthew Mock was born in Santa Monica, California, as one of seven children. He grew up in one of the few Chinese American families in the West Los Angeles community where he lived, and remembers being very Chinese while in the family home and almost anything but Chinese outside the home. His father supported the family financially as a postal carrier, walking the same, exact route for fifty years until he retired. His mother worked very hard tending to the needs of the children, all the while making her own cultural adjustments and adaptations. He has memories of how his family oftentimes had very little in terms of economic resources but a lot in terms of sibling richness and interactions.

Never having seen snowfall, nor for that matter ever having been outside of the L.A. Basin, Mock attended Brown University in Providence, Rhode Island, on a full scholarship, ostensibly to write short stories, poetry, and follow his heart to work as a teacher with children in special education. He received a bachelor's degree with a major in psychology and a minor in special education.

Mock moved to Berkeley, California (where he has since lived) to attend graduate school. While in school, he worked as the mental health coordinator at an Asian American organization. This crystallized his developing awareness of his own identity and significance in addressing all of the differences and cultural shock that he had experienced in his life up to that time. He received his doctorate from the California School of Professional Psychology, Berkeley/Alameda where he also teaches as adjunct faculty.

Mock holds multiple roles. He is a Professor and Director of the Cross-Cultural Program in Psychology at John F. Kennedy University in Orinda, California and Director of the Family, Youth, Children's and Multicultural Services for the City of Berkeley. He also has a private clinical and consulting practice in Berkeley and carries multiple affiliations with several universities. Most importantly, Mock has a twelve-year-old, "full-focus" daughter who is "our gift to life, our jewel" who gently reminds him about social justice and gender issues on a daily basis.

Mock still bicycles, writes professionally and personally, and travels, oftentimes as an invited speaker, consultant, and trainer nationally and internationally. He loves to teach and write and to break stereotypes by demonstrating to his audiences that he is one example of a "passionate, Asian American man!" Lastly, as the more traditional Chinese members of his family who still don't understand what he does for a living remind him, he is humble and grateful to be able to contribute something in his life to personal compassion and social justice locally and globally.

Ruth Chao

Ruth Chao was born and raised in Keelung, the "rain harbor" in Taiwan. Keelung has rain almost the whole year and is well known for fresh seafood and local foods. While Chao was growing up, her homemaker mother would go to the food market to buy fresh fish caught just a few hours before dawn. Her father is a retired sailor, who worked as an engineer on board ships for 30 years. She has two elder brothers and two elder sisters who were her best support in childhood.

Taiwan is a country with diverse cultures. It was governed by Japan for 50 years prior to World War II, then by Chiang Kai Shek and Kuo-Min-Tang (KMT). Taiwan blends Western/American thoughts and foods (for example, McDonald's, Starbucks, Subway) with its native culture.

Since quite young, Chao experienced diverse cultures in life. Her father, brought her American toys and chocolates, which were the envy of her class-mates. When she was in college, she changed her major from literature to psy-chology to understand the human mind. She came to the United States to obtain her doctorate in Counseling Psychology from the University of Missouri Columbia. Being culturally different from others has inspired her reflection as she counsels clients who are almost always culturally different from her (for ex-ample, White or non-Chinese). Being culturally different is one thing, but how one consciously reflects on cultural difference is quite another. She proceeds from the former to the latter, and enjoys the latter.

Chao is now completing a predoctoral internship at the Counseling Cen-ter, Michigan State University. She has 21 publications and presentations to her credit. Her articles include "Integrating Culture and Attachment" and "Toward an Integrative Curriculum," both published in the *American Psychologist*. Some book chapters, including "Integrating Taoism and Western Therapeutic Ap-proaches in the Treatment of Anxiety" and "Integrating Holland's Theory with Tao-te Ching for Career Counseling" appear in *Alternative Approaches to Coun-seling and Psychotherapy,* edited by D. S. Sandhu.

Chao enjoys traveling around the world. She has been to Finland, Denmark, Germany, New Zealand, China, and Japan. She loves cooking and tasting dif-ferent fine foods.

Becky J. Liddle

Becky Liddle, Ph.D., is an associate professor in the Department of Counseling and Counseling Psychology at Auburn University, where she is in her twelfth year of teaching master's and doctoral students in counseling-related fields. Her favorite course is Counseling Diverse Populations. It is rewarding to watch the dawning of awareness of oppression and privilege in a group of Alabamians who have typically never had the opportunity to talk directly about race, class, or sex-ual orientation. Challenging students enough to provoke growth without pro-voking defensiveness is a delicate balance, but one with great rewards. It is a joy to watch good-hearted but somewhat clueless students move from merely toler-ating diversity to becoming allies in the struggle against multiple oppressions.

Liddle received her bachelor's degree from Oberlin College. Nearly 25 years later, Oberlin remains a touchstone for her—a reminder that there are whole communities working together effectively for social justice. She holds a master of education degree in Counselor Education from James Madison University and a doctorate in Counseling Psychology from the University of North Car-

olina. She is licensed in Alabama and in Georgia, where she lives with her partner Kathy Liddle and maintains a small private practice serving the lesbian, gay,
and bisexual communities. She serves on the editorial boards of the *Journal of
Counseling Psychology* and *Journal of Lesbian Studies,* and is editor of the *Newslet-
ter* of the American Psychological Association's Division 44: Society for the Psychological Study of Lesbian, Gay, and Bisexual Issues.

David MacPhee

David MacPhee, Ph.D., is a professor in Human Development and Family
Studies at Colorado State University. His research and teaching focus on parenting, child development, risk and resiliency, and effective prevention programs. Related to diversity issues, he has been actively involved in work on
feminist issues, including CSU's Women's Studies Program; the Multicultural
Curriculum Infusion Project, which has become a national model for teaching
about diversity; and research on families from diverse cultures.

Although he grew up in a fairly homogenous culture in Idaho, MacPhee
has traveled, studied, and worked throughout the United States (particularly the
South and Southeast), Belize, and Australia, all of which deepened his appreciation for diverse cultures. Being the single father of a teenage daughter also has
brought into relief issues of gender development.

Barbara Gormley

Barbara Gormley, Ph.D., was raised in a homogeneous suburb of Detroit in the
1960s and 1970s and was a member of a large, politically active Irish Catholic
community. She provided services to violent families in a rural setting for 12
years before returning to school to get her doctorate in Counseling Psychology
from Michigan State University in 2002, after completing a clinical internship
at Harvard Medical School. Currently, Gormley is a National Institute of Mental Health Postdoctoral Fellow in the Clinical Services Research Training Program in the Department of Psychiatry at the University of California, San
Francisco. Work on this chapter was partially supported by Grant T32
MH18261.

Introduction

An Awakening to Privilege, Oppression, and Discrimination

SHARON K. ANDERSON AND VALERIE MIDDLETON

SHARON'S STORY

A few years ago, a friend told me about an experience she had had at a fast-food restaurant. My friend, an African American woman, was in the front of the line, ready to order, when the cashier looked right past her and asked the next person in line what she would like. I had a hard time believing my friend's story, but I listened to her as though I did. Behind my attentive facade, however, I was thinking, "I'm sure she's mistaken. People aren't that rude. I'll bet she thought you were still deciding on your order."

My blindness to white privilege and other privileged statuses most certainly originates in my social and cultural background. I was born into a family of White European descent and middle-class income, and I was raised in a White, rural community. All of my extended family is White. I attended a school in which almost all students and faculty were White. The people who attended my country church were White. When I look back on my childhood, I don't recall hearing my parents make derogatory remarks about other ethnic groups, nor do I recall any discussions about inequality, discrimination, or privilege. I suspect that my family's view was one that espoused "if people work hard enough, they can achieve, no matter what their skin color or cultural differences." Inadvertently, I was taught not to see my advantage as a White, middle-class person.

I carried this thinking with me into my early adulthood and college environment, where it manifested itself in a belief that almost everyone in the United States spoke or should speak English, that anyone could gain entry into college if he or she just tried hard enough, and that "discrimination" was just a word that "angry people of color" used to push their weight around. I was oblivious to the fact that having White skin, speaking standard American English, being able-bodied, and supporting a Christian belief system were all "unearned assets" (McIntosh, 2000) that afforded me entry into places and opportunities less available or not available to everyone. As I reflect, my worldview was not challenged in my college classes or other higher-education contexts.

COMING INTO CONTACT

After earning my masters degree, I began working for Upward Bound and Educational Talent Search programs. While employed in these programs, I provided services to students from different ethnic groups (Asian, Hispanic, African American, and Native American), and I worked alongside colleagues who represented these groups as well. This was the first time I had genuine and sustained contact with people whose skin color was different from mine. My obliviousness was challenged, and I started to realize how truly ignorant I was of the obstacles people of color face in achieving their goals. However, I still did not understand the significance of their home culture and consequent expectations. For instance, the Native American students in our Upward Bound program often requested leave from our summer session to participate in Pow Wows and other cultural events. When I became the director of the program, I honored the students' requests to be gone for a week or more; but, inside my head and heart, I questioned and disliked the disruption. I did not understand the meaning or the importance of Pow Wows or why our students had to miss school for such events. Sometimes, these students would leave for the week and then not want to come back to finish out the summer session. In response, I settled on the premise that the students were "less able" to adjust and were missing out on a good thing—six weeks on a university campus with good teachers and an awesome residential staff.

Elizabeth Minnich articulates the thinking in which I was grounded this way: ". . . whites are taught to think of their lives as morally neutral, normative, and average, and also ideal, so that when we work to benefit others, this is seen as work that will allow 'them' to be more like 'us' " (cited in McIntosh, 2000, p. 32). As the program director, I could have taken the opportunity to look at our program for ways to make it more culturally sensitive and welcoming. Instead, I wanted the students of color to fit into the program; that is, I wanted "them" to be more like "us." When my students of color talked about discrimination, oppression, and feelings of alienation—the consequences of systems based on privilege, *I didn't really see it or "get it"—the reality of their experiences.*

INTELLECTUALIZING

After 7 years of working with Upward Bound, I quit my job and attended graduate school to obtain a doctorate in counseling psychology. One of my fellow students was a gentleman who identifies himself as Chicano. He introduced me to multicultural literature in psychology and counseling. He shared his concerns about the inequality of mental-health services for people of color, and how people of color typically preferred to counsel with someone from their own culture. I found this perspective insulting and thought, "Aren't White counselors good enough for these people?" Intellectually, I was able to take in the information from the multicultural literature and the concerns about the inequality of mental-health services, but when his perspective and experience challenged my view of the "normative, average, or ideal," in which a White counselor might not be viewed as "good enough," I became disconcerted and defensive. I continued to listen to his stories of discrimination, gross misunderstanding, oppression, and profiling by Whites in authority, *but I didn't really hear him—once again, I didn't "get it."*

DEFLECTING COGNITIVE DISSONANCE

After I had completed my doctorate and had spent a year in the Midwest as a staff psychologist at a university counseling center, I received a faculty appointment at Colorado State University, where I developed a friendship with Val, my coeditor. Our friendship brought together many differences. Val is Black; I am White. She was born and raised in a city; I was born and raised on a farm. She experiences oppression and discrimination because of her skin color; I experience privilege (a term I use in retrospect) because of my skin color.

As I previously mentioned, I had been told stories by my students, colleagues, and friends of color without truly accepting the validity of their articulated experiences. Eventually, I was challenged to feed my intellectual hunger for understanding multicultural issues, and I accepted Val's invitation to attend a "Women of Color" conference.

Upon our arrival at the conference, I experienced the uncomfortable feeling of being one of a few White women in attendance. I began to wonder whether I had made a mistake in coming. I wasn't a woman of color, and I assumed others would wonder why I was there. I truly didn't think or feel I should be welcomed, and I wondered what I was going to face or be a target for.

As the sessions progressed, I became enlightened, but also dissonant. I became particularly irritated during one session when the women of color expressed anger and hurt toward White women. I felt like a target and wondered why I wasn't positively recognized for my presence, as a White woman, at the conference. Val encouraged me to listen and stay emotionally and psychologically present, even though I wanted to run away by mentally/emotionally disconnecting and focusing on other thoughts or feelings.

During that time and later, Val and I would have what I call "difficult dialogues." She wanted me to truly listen to the stories of oppression and discrimination, and I wanted to deflect the issues by claiming Whites are treated poorly, too. I didn't want to see my own privilege as a White person and the invisibility of others who represented minority cultures. *I just didn't really want to "get it."*

CRITICAL INCIDENT: "HOW CAN I HELP YOU?"

As our friendship and work relationship progressed, so did our level of dialogue. We would occasionally meet for lunch to discuss ideas relative to teaching our predominately White population of students about issues of diversity and privilege. When Val and I had ended one such business lunch at a nearby restaurant, we decided to check into the possibility of using that restaurant as a meeting place for future business activities that would include more of our colleagues. Val approached the receptionist, a White woman, to inquire about the cost and availability of the facility. The receptionist craned her neck to look around Val, and then asked me, "How can I help you?" As this scene played out before me, so did a flashback of the scenario I used to open this introduction.

In that instant, my privilege failed to blind me in a way that had previously kept me from "getting it." I saw how my White skin made me visible and others invisible. I saw why the Native American students I worked with in Upward Bound might not want to come back from a Pow Wow or Sun Dance ceremony to a summer school on a university campus that was insensitive to their cultural values. I saw why a person of color might want to work with a counselor of color. I saw how being recognized is an event that I experience and expect as natural, and how not being recognized is disrespectful, discriminatory, and oppressive. I saw how what I experience and expect in everyday life is an unearned privilege. I saw why I needed to be a believer—one who believes the stories of inequity shared by friends, students, and colleagues of color. Although I can't truly understand the experiences of people of color, the sum of my past experiences, united with critical incidents such as this, helps me to see that privilege exists and that I am one of its beneficiaries.

CREATING THIS BOOK

Following this eye-opening experience, I began to explore the literature on multicultural issues in psychology and counseling (for example, Helms & Cook, 1999; Pedersen, Draguns, Lonner, & Trimble, 2002; D. W. Sue & Sue, 2003), looking for evidence of what is needed to help privileged individuals "see it," "believe it," and most importantly "get it"—the discrimination and oppression others experience because we are potentially blind to our own points of privilege. This body of literature seemed to be missing the personal stories often so essential to understanding the concept of privilege, the impact of privilege on one's professional and personal interactions with others, the process of acknowledging one's own privilege, and the subsequent journey involved in changing one's beliefs and behaviors.

I discussed this gap in the literature with my coeditor, Val. She gave me literature from the teacher preparation field to read. We talked some more, and the idea that emerged was that we would ask professionals in the helping fields to share their personal stories about how they came to recognize their own privileged statuses, and how that recognition has changed them personally and professionally. We believe that students in training programs need to read about other professionals like themselves who have additionally come to acknowledge their privileged statuses associated with being White, male, heterosexual, able-bodied, Christian, and/or economically advantaged, and who have integrated this acknowledgement into their practice and/or teaching.

With this idea on paper and a book contract in hand, we sent out a call for papers, asking people to tell us about their journeys toward understanding their own privilege and the subsequent impact on their professional roles. We received numerous submissions covering a broad range of issues such as ableism, anti-Semitism, classism, heterosexism, racism, and sexism. Author after author shared stories of injustice, inequality, and privilege, in which they or their colleagues, friends, students, and partners experienced the "phenomenon of invisibility" or other ramifications of the aforementioned "isms." Their stories of personal and professional struggles and triumphs in recognizing and addressing issues of their own privilege and the prejudice and discrimination experienced by others provide opportunities for readers to explore these concepts from many perspectives—a necessary exercise, since we have observed in our classes that acknowledgment of privilege in one area (for example, racism) does not automatically transfer to recognition and understanding in other areas (for example, heterosexism, anti-Semitism).

As you, our readers, explore the topics in this book, we ask that you be open-minded and sensitive, for the sharing of these stories has not come without cost. Feelings of vulnerability, guilt, shame, embarrassment, and the like have all been part of the process of bringing this important topic into view in this way. In preparing this introductory chapter, I (Sharon) personally became aware of my vulnerability and feelings of shame about my own journey. My lack of understanding and sensitivity seems abhorrent. However, I also recognize the value of disclosure in furthering my journey and the journey of others. It is with this understanding and extreme appreciation that we wish to acknowledge and thank all of the authors for their honesty, their willingness to be vulnerable, and their valuable contributions to this book.

REFERENCES

Helms, J. E., & Cook, D. A. (1999). *Using race and culture in counseling and psychotherapy: Theory and process.* Boston: Allyn and Bacon.

McIntosh, P. (2000). White privilege and male privilege: A personal account of coming to see correspondences through work in women's studies. In A. Minas (Ed.), *Gender Basics: Feminist perspectives on women and men* (2nd ed., pp. 30–38). Belmont, CA: Wadsworth/Thomas Learning, Inc.

Pedersen, P. B., Draguns, J. G., Lonner, W. J., & Trimble, J. E. (2002). *Counseling across cultures* (5th ed.). Thousand Oaks, CA: Sage Publications.

Sue, D. W., & Sue, D. (2003). *Counseling the culturally diverse: Theory and practice* (4th ed.). New York: John Wiley & Sons.

Part I

Stories of Privilege

1

White Out

Privilege and Its Problems

HEIDI A. ZETZER

IDENTITY AND THE POLITICS OF LOCATION

I am an educated, employed, White, heterosexual, 40-something woman who is 5 feet, 7 inches tall and weighs 114 pounds. I go to church (occasionally). I have a husband and two sons, ages 10 and 13. I grew up in the '60s with an irreverent, hippie artist father and a sympathetic, conventional artist mother. I attended integrated public schools in Cleveland suburbs with lots of Christians and Jews. I lived in the midst of racist jokes and interracial relationships. Like many of my White contemporaries, I was raised to see myself as a "color-blind" individual living in a cultural mosaic.

I come from a flock of aversive racists (Dovidio, Gaertner, Kawakami, & Hodson, 2002). No one I knew would ever admit to racist thoughts or actions, notions of White superiority, or fear of "the other," but the subtext was often there. The explicit message was that we are all created equal and the Civil Rights movement was a good thing. The implicit message was that Whites just happen to be better than Blacks at certain things, and affirmative action is a questionable thing. Praise for Black achievements belied the expectation of none. Concerns for safety, housing prices, and miscegenation were characteristic of the private conversations that White families had with one another. White privilege was far outside anyone's consciousness, while fear of being called a racist was well inside it. The psychological discordance between the text and the subtext was very confusing. How could I be free of prejudice and filled with prejudicial thoughts? How could I be color-blind and react so viscerally to cultural differences? How could my Black friends and White friends be so similar and yet so different?

As a graduate student in counseling psychology in the mid-80s, I participated in a variety of cross-cultural counseling courses and diversity workshops offered by prominent psychology programs at the cutting edge of multiculturalism.

These experiences helped me comprehend the discord. They led to a tremendous growth in my intellectual understanding of cultural differences, but on a deeper level, I was left unchanged. In the language of the Multicultural Change Intervention Matrix (Pope, 1993 as cited by Reynolds, 1997), I experienced first-order, but not second-order, change. For individuals, first-order change is characterized by increased awareness, knowledge, or skills, whereas second-order change results in a paradigm shift. I entered graduate school as a naive "well-meaning White person" (WMWP) (Wolfe, 1995), and I exited as a knowledgeable one; but I still did not fully and deeply comprehend the impact of daily racism on people of color and the part that WMWP (like me) play in its perpetuation.

It was not until I became a university professor and joined a diverse team of multicultural counseling educators that my perceptions of the world and myself began to change. I started a journey that is endless and essential. I finally understand what my colleagues of color; lesbian, gay, or bisexual (LGB) students; working-class and Jewish friends; and large-bodied companions have been telling me: there are no breaks from the work of living in a multicultural community. Oppression is real, and seeking social justice for oneself and others is a difficult job. Once, while speaking to a colleague, I said that I was weary of the resistance I encountered while teaching a multicultural awareness course to graduate psychology students. She wanted to support me and offered, "Well, you won't have to deal with it when the quarter is over!" That might have been true if I were to have retreated into my privilege, but I have come to the conclusion that the comfort of privilege is not worth its price. The cost to oneself and one's friends is too great.

The purpose of this chapter is (a) to describe a critical incident in my multicultural development, an incident that highlights some of the relational and psychological costs of racism and white privilege and illustrates the value of dialogue as a constructive response to multicultural conflict; and (b) to introduce multicultural dialogue as a key ingredient to transformational learning—the kind that sinks into our bones and is remembered.

EDUCATOR AS STUDENT: WHITE RACIAL IDENTITY DEVELOPMENT AND TRANSFORMATIONAL LEARNING

Models of White racial identity development (WRID) (Carter, 1997; Helms, 1995; Rowe, Bennet, & Atkinson, 1994) provide educators with benchmarks for their students' growth. But what if I apply one of these models to myself? I agree with the basic premises of these models, which assume that "No child is born wanting to be racist!" (D. W. Sue & Sue, 2003, p. 254) and that there is no protection from breathing the "smog" of cultural racism (Tatum, 1997, p. 6). White people benefit from institutional and individual manifestations of racism, however indirectly or unintentionally, and this creates a dilemma for fair-minded White folks. How can I see myself as a just person when I willingly participate in a system that is inherently unfair? This dilemma has motivated my WRID.

If I apply D. W. Sue and Sue's (2003) five-stage process model of WRID to myself, I can track my evolution from the *conformity* phase in childhood, high school, and college; to the *dissonance* phase of graduate school; to the *resistance and immersion* phase of my early career; to now. Now, I see myself in the *introspective phase,* and, curiously, this phase describes perfectly my motivation for writing this chapter. I am in an existential crisis, disconnected, isolated, and confused. I am roiling around in a developmental eddy, asking, "What does it mean to be White [at my institution]? Who am I in relation to my whiteness [as a parent, educator, and administrator]?" And "Who am I as a racial/cultural being [who embraces principles of social justice]" (D. W. Sue & Sue, 2003, p. 257)?

Sometimes I feel like I am in a "White out"—lost in a blizzard of white privilege and unable to discern my next step. Personally, what I lack is contact with White folks who are expanding or questioning their worldviews. I often feel isolated and alone. I feel supported by my White, heterosexual, middle-class colleagues, but few are actively involved in moving themselves or the institution in the direction of multiculturalism. We do not connect with one another very easily. My insights into myself as a heterosexual White woman are often painful. I am aware that the further I go in my development, the less I cry for myself (feeling shame for my mistakes) and the more I cry for humanity (feeling sadness for the acts of violence or indifference that we intentionally or unintentionally perpetrate on one another).

I see how the tears of my wounded ego used to silence the voices of my colleagues of color. My colleagues took steps to relieve my hurt feelings by quieting their own frustration or disdain to take care of me. I have learned that I can listen to their accusations and their requests for accountability, and search for the ways that I contributed to their concerns. In the past, I would respond instantly and automatically. I gave myself only two choices. I could swallow their accusations whole or reject them outright. Now, I am getting better at allowing myself time to reflect on their words before leaping to a response.

What brought me to this place? Like Ponterotto (1998) and Kiselica (1998), I have matured as a multicultural being through relationships with colleagues. One of the greatest surges in my multicultural development can be attributed to my collaboration with three diverse colleagues: Juliet Betita (Pilipina American), Keith Mar (Chinese American), and Muriel Shockley (African American). (Naturally, we have multiple identities, but for the purpose of this narrative, our racial/cultural identities are the most salient.) We sat around my kitchen table with the intention of revising Antioch University's Multicultural Awareness course, but we serendipitously discovered that our reciprocal disclosures about oppression and privilege, of all types, were more powerful and more meaningful than the literature we planned to provide our students.

The topics of our meetings flowed spontaneously between course design and personal revelations about race, class, gender, and sexual orientation. We revealed our vulnerabilities gradually. Keith, Muriel, and Juliet described how they felt when someone made a racist comment, treated them differently because of their appearance, or ignored their racial identities. I disclosed my fear of difference, or of being seen as racist. We also identified and examined various sources of privilege. For example, Keith holds male privilege, Muriel has class privilege, Juliet possesses heterosexual privilege, and I have white privilege, just to name a few. The multiplicity of our identities became undeniable. Periodically we confronted each other with respect and compassion. We learned to tolerate the discomfort of our differences, which allowed us to gain valuable insight into each other's perspectives.

Over the course of two years, we transformed these focused conversations into a new approach to multicultural counselor training, which we call Multicultural Dialogue (MCD) (Betita, Mar, Shockley, & Zetzer, 2001; Zetzer, Shockley, Mar, & Betita, 2000). We define MCD as an authentic conversation about what it means to walk in the world as a member of a multicultural group. The purpose of MCD is for people to hear each other's stories and perspectives so that they can learn from each other and grow in ways that promote their racial/cultural identity development (RCID or WRID) (adapted from Swindler, 1983). We modified Swindler's 10 principles of interreligious dialogue (1983, p. 1) for use in our classrooms.[1] The principles are guideposts for students to use as they listen and respond to each other's experiences of and perspectives on oppression and privilege. For example, three of the principles call for students to allow each other to self-define, to abandon "hard-and-fast assumptions" about "the other," and to aim to experience the other's culture from "within." We have observed that MCD nurtures the presence of Rogers' (1957) core conditions in our classrooms and leads to broadened perspectives on oppression, privilege, and multiculturalism.

The notion of dialogue as an interpersonal enzyme is not new (Bohm, 1996; Isaacs, 1999; Patterson, Grenny, McMillan, & Switzler, 2000). Even its application to diversity training has been done before (W. G. Stephan & Stephan, 2001; Wilcox, 2000). But we did one thing very differently. Keith, Muriel, Juliet, and I started the course with a three-hour demonstration of MCD. This was an exciting teaching strategy for me. The four of us sat in a "fishbowl" with 60 students seated around us, and we provided them with our own version of *The Color of Fear* (Wah & Hunter, 1994). For example, during one of our dialogue demonstrations, I confessed that I felt guilty for being White. Muriel replied that she saw White guilt as an impediment to change, and that she wished I would just get over it and move myself to action. I felt relief at hearing this because I thought that I was *supposed* to feel guilty when confronted with my racism or white privilege. Muriel's comment made me realize that my guilt was paralyzing me. My shame prevented me from empathizing with people of color and stymied me from striving for social justice. After the demonstration, students were invited to ask questions and make comments.

The MCD demonstration was followed by instructor-facilitated dialogue throughout the remainder of the quarter. Our hope was that MCD would raise

---

[1] The author is indebted to Dr. Jim Malarkey, from The McGregor School of Antioch University, for introducing her to Swindler's principles of interreligious dialogue.

student consciousness. For me, however, the most powerful result has been my own transformation. Now I am absolutely certain that I will never be the same. I have a fuller understanding of my racial identity and privilege, and a renewed vision of myself as an agent of social change.

For me, social change depends on genuine participation. It means engaging in reciprocal self-disclosure as often as I can. It means sharing knowledge and experiences of culture, oppression, and privilege with colleagues, friends, lovers, family members, students, and clients. It means paying attention to race, gender, class, sexual orientation, ability, and other aspects of identity that are meaningful to us. It means wondering what my appearance says to the other person. It means asking for feedback and contemplating it before I respond. This kind of dialogue is both draining and exhilarating.

THE COST IS IN THE CRUX: A CRITICAL INCIDENT AND MULTICULTURAL DIALOGUE

My perspective on this critical incident has changed dramatically over time. Multicultural dialogue and personal reflection led me to three important insights. Each insight produced a "disorienting dilemma" (Mezirow, 1991) for me and challenged my ability to receive feedback that is incommensurate with my well-meaning White identity.

Several years ago, as part of a multisite faculty conference-design team, I was responsible for facilitating the opening session on leadership. The purpose of the session was to describe what motivates someone to serve as a leader. A participant mentioned moral indignation as a driving force. I thought this was a productive avenue for elaboration, so I invited more responses on this topic, but my inquiry was met with blank looks. My anxiety started to rise, and I feared that I had gotten off track. I felt I needed help. So in a room comprising mostly White people, I looked to an African American colleague, who was also on the design team, and asked her to talk about how anger motivates her work in the field of social justice. I hadn't known her for long, but I had already had several conversations with her about her passion for this work, and I thought that her comments might deepen the discourse. Her facial expression told me instantly that she was angry with me. She politely declined to speak. There was a long, awkward pause. I found myself thinking, "Please say something! Please help me out!" She looked away from me and didn't say anything more.

First insight

I was surprised by her reticence—baffled, really. What could I have done wrong? I was relieved when the large-group discussion ended and I could stop facilitating and start reflecting on my actions and her response. My realization of wrongdoing was sudden and distressing. I experienced that sinking, awful feeling associated with failing to grasp the situation until it's too late and wanting desperately to take it all back. My initial understanding of this critical incident was that I had failed to step outside of myself and consider the situation in which I was prompting my colleague to speak. It was unsafe. At the time, the atmosphere on her campus was rife with racial conflict, and my colleague was serving as the sole source of support for African American students. She was politically vulnerable. I knew this when I addressed her, but I lacked the sense to situate her in that context. I was blinded by my own needs and unconscious of the privilege afforded to me as a White woman in that setting. I was free to speak without someone attributing my attitudes to my race. I could be seen as an individual and not a representative of a racial/ethnic group. I could assume that my perspective would not be challenged because of my race/ethnicity. I arrived at the conference unhampered by a history of endless questions about my race or racial perspective that are part of being a "racial/ethnic minority" in the United States (Johnson, 2001; Kivel, 1996).

I felt tears in my eyes. My distress stemmed from my dismay over my own ineptitude and my fear of the impending confrontation. At a minimum, I had broken any sense of trust that might have existed between us. I had identified myself to her as a conscientious White person, and I had proven myself to be an unconscious privileged White person. I tried to talk to her right after the morning session, but she refused. She was visibly perturbed. Others asked me, "What happened? What's wrong?" None of the White people I talked to seemed to know what was awry.

We did not talk until later in the day. My colleague was furious with me. We sat in the presence of other team members and engaged in a dialogue about my actions and her response. The conversation was extremely difficult and extremely valuable. Both of us made explicit efforts to understand and articulate each other's perspectives. As we spoke, we saw the institution's role in building the context for what happened between us. The lack of faculty diversity and absence of support for African American students were two factors that made the campus climate stressful (at the time, the Multicultural Affairs Office was without personnel). I gained a fuller understanding of what I had done and the impact my white privilege had on someone I admired.

Second insight

I had been in these situations before and had resisted taking responsibility for the unintended impact of my behavior. I used to leap to my own defense. This time, I knew that it was vital for me to *reflect on my actions first*. This stance allowed me to hear some of what my colleague had to say. However, it was not until a full year later, after an e-mail exchange, that I gained some deeper insight into my behavior. My colleague wrote:

Heidi,

One of the elements that I think is very important when peeling back the onion (so to speak) as it relates to unlearning issues of oppression and privilege is the false sense of superiority that whites adopt/construct in their relationships with persons of color. I believe that is what you experienced with me, stay with me on this . . . the more you learn about how oppression operates, you learn that anger is a natural state in the unlearning process. However, liberation can be achieved through cognitive dissonance, which is also a natural stage that can be achieved in the unlearning oppression process. Oppression work is a journey, and the work feeds into the quality of our lives as human beings.

After first resisting and then contemplating this e-mail, I reached a deeper level of understanding. I came to realize that I had assumed too much. Not about her willingness to speak or what she would have to say. I assumed that I could *define her contribution*. I assumed that I was *entitled* to do that. This was more than a facilitator's mistake; this was a *White* facilitator's mistake, and, of course, it was my mistake. Certainly, I aim to avoid making the mistake again. In the past, I might have vowed to stop participating altogether—to avoid the risk and to stay away from multicultural situations in which conflict might occur. However, I will not change and grow unless I maintain my commitment to "difficult dialogues" (Sue, Bingham, Porche-Burke, & Vasquez, 1999). I understand that I am unfinished in my multicultural development, and, as a result, I am committed to increasing my multicultural competence (Sue, Arredondo, & McDavis, 1995). This requires participation in a multicultural community, which in turn necessitates that I recognize my fallibility, own it, learn from it, and remain open to another person's experiences of me. I also understand that I have a responsibility to behave differently next time.

Third insight

I recently requested feedback on this chapter from my colleague. I feel grateful to her for continuing to dialogue with me about historical events. My latest insight is the most painful one. I did not understand this until now, but it's clear that I ignored my colleague's right to confidentiality when I used my political location to elicit the disclosure of experiences and viewpoints, which she had shared *privately and in the context of the conference design team*. This is a disturbing realization for me and a perfect illustration of the way in which unexamined white privilege destroys trust in multicultural relationships. I had privileged my needs over her rights without even realizing it. This latent insight gives me an opportunity to behave differently in the future and to move in the direction of increased congruence between my actions and my identity as a WMWP.

ANALYSIS

The costs of racism and white privilege for people of color are evident on macro and micro levels (Neville, Worthington, & Spierman, 2001). On a macro level, there are tremendous structural-economic disparities in our society (D'Andrea & Daniels, 2001; D. W. Sue & Sue, 2003). The legacies of historical oppression are evident in modern-day inequities (Collins, 2000; Takaki, 1993) and have yet to be completely undone. On a micro level, there is increasing awareness and understanding of the physical and psychological impact of racism for people of color (R. Clark, Anderson, Clark, & Williams, 1999; Contrada et al., 2000; Lowe et al., 2000; Thompson & Neville, 1999).

The costs of racism and white privilege for White folks, however, are less obvious. On a macro level, there is an astonishing loss of productivity, which affects the quality of life for everyone (Neville et al., 2001). On a micro level, the costs include, but are not limited to, loss of connection to one's ancestors, condemnation for affiliating with "those people," discomfort with people of color, and witnessing or participating in oppressive practices (Kivel, 1996). Spanierman, Heppner, and Neville (2002, p. 3) identified three overlapping domains in which Whites may experience the costs of racism: The costs of racism to Whites may be cognitive (for example, distorted perceptions of reality, lack of knowledge of others, confusion regarding the coexistence of democracy and racial inequality), affective (for example, fear of others, anger, and guilt), or behavioral (for example, having relationships exclusively with other Whites, censoring oneself to avoid a perceived tension, being rejected by other Whites when challenging racism).

The varied dimensions of the costs of racism to Whites will be referred to collectively as psychosocial costs. Spanierman, Heppner, and Neville (2002) devised an instrument designed to measure these costs—the Psychosocial Costs of Racism to Whites Scale (PCRW). In my view, the costs associated with each of these domains converge at the crux of multicultural relationships.

One way that racism and white privilege affect multicultural relationships is through the periodic resurrection of racist double binds. According to Mahmoud (1998), racist double binds are perpetrated when a person with more power or privilege torments a less powerful person by conveying contradictory overt and covert messages that leave the respondent with no cost-free alternatives. If the respondent confronts the instigator of the double bind by identifying the contradictory messages, the instigator is likely to play the victim and accuse the respondent of being hostile, argumentative, or hypersensitive.

A typical example of this occurs when students of color are asked by their instructors to offer the Black/Latino/Indian/Asian person's perspective on a particular issue. The students risk appearing uncooperative or overly sensitive if they do not comply, but abiding by the request violates their integrity. The faculty person is using her or his position to define the student's contribution, and students of color must accept this definition or risk being silenced or censured for their resistance. Other double binds are expressed in White-proffered statements such as "I don't see you as Mexican/Indian/Black. You aren't like the rest of them." People of color are left with two choices: (a) deny one's own identity and be seen as good, or (b) own one's identity and be seen as bad.

I exercised my power and privilege in my attempt to define my colleague's contribution to the discussion on leadership. The *overt* message looked like an innocent invitation to speak, but the covert message was "Walk into this minefield because *I* need your help and *my* needs (or the needs of the organization) supercede yours." Granted, I did not consciously concoct this situation, but I did initiate the dilemma. My colleague had two poor choices: (a) comply with my request and disclose privately held observations and opinions, which would have the effect of reinforcing white privilege, or (b) resist my request, which entailed the risk of appearing uncooperative or overly sensitive.

Mahmoud (1998) argues that narcissism is behind the double bind, and I have to agree. I asked my colleague to speak because I was worried about embarrassing myself. Later, I could not accept my colleague's reaction to me because it would damage my well-meaning White identity. The risks to me both during and after this critical incident were strictly *personal*. I could either (a) take a close look at myself and feel empathic remorse for hurting someone, or (b) defend against this insight. The risk for my colleague was *personal and political*. She could decline to speak, or she could speak up. Both of these options were confounded with individual and institutional ramifications.

Oppression and privilege flow beneath the surface of multicultural relationships like an underground river. All parties are aware of it on one level or another. Every so often, the river rises and we have an opportunity to witness its impact and change its course. The critical incident I just described provided me with multiple revelations. I realized that I am likely to persist in putting my multicultural relationships at risk if I do not unpack my invisible backpack of privilege (McIntosh, 1989) and engage in antiracist actions. I also realized that it is getting harder to live in a state of incongruence. The dissonance between my well-meaning White identity and the impact of my behavior is like mental tinnitus. I am in a chronic state of discomfort.

Other White people in the United States are in a similar state. Winant refers to this as racial dualism (1997, p. 41). The Civil Rights movement and related reforms have

> . . . partially transformed white racial consciousness. Obviously they did not destroy the deep structures of white privilege, but they did make counterclaims on behalf of the racially excluded and subordinated. As a result white identities have been displaced and refigured: they are now contradictory, as well as confused and anxiety-ridden, to an unprecedented extent.

The incommensurability of racialism and democracy (Myrdal, 1962 [1944] as cited by Winant, 1997) creates cognitive dissonance and emotional distress for the WMWP.

As I have matured as a person, I have come to realize that I am dependent on the positive appraisals of people of color. Somehow, if I am deemed a "good White person," I can relax my vigilance and breathe a sigh of relief. This is faulty thinking. At my age, my self-regard stems primarily from my *self-appraisal* and not the appraisal of others. Even if I got preapproval as a "good White person," I would still make the mistakes that I do. I would still struggle with cultural delusions produced by privilege, and I would still unintentionally trample on the rights of my colleagues and friends. I cannot leap over my own development and arrive at a place where it's easy all the time. A White student in one of my classes expressed this wish eloquently: "I just want to *be*." I often find myself wishing for this kind of comfort; but I know, deep down, that I need to find my voice and work toward greater congruence between how I see myself as a WMWP and how I behave in the world. If I am lucky, then my colleagues will be patient with me when I blunder.

The critical incident I described illuminates "the recursive relationship between structural and ideological racism" (Neville et al., 2001, p. 260). My colleague and I work in a university system that is progressive and "well-meaning" but incomplete in its own multicultural organizational development (D. W. Sue et al., 1998). Social justice requires transformation of institutions as well as individuals. If privilege is what allows an individual or an organization to "just be," then this freedom is not earned, but instead owned as an entitlement.

CONCLUSION: ALLIES, ADVOCATES, AND ACTIVISTS

In the past, I used my counseling and facilitation skills to avoid authentic engagement with people of color. I was afraid of revealing a hidden bias, a stereotype, or a prejudice. I would ask open-ended questions and use politically correct terms to minimize the chance that I might say something offensive. I understand now that, rather than increasing my trustworthiness, I greatly reduced it by appearing fake. I expected people of color to reveal themselves to me, while I displayed little of myself.

I now realize that if I avoid in-depth, forthright dialogues about oppression and privilege, I lose the opportunity to form meaningful relationships with colleagues and students who are different from me. If I dampen the expression of my colleague's observations of oppressive attitudes or practices in my workplace, then everyone loses the opportunity to be understood or to engage in understanding. As an instructor and colleague, I have learned the value of trading privileged comfort for the reward of real dialogue across differences. I have learned that my students will be more courageous in their communication with each other if I participate as well as facilitate, if I model authenticity, if I self-correct, and if I repeatedly demonstrate that the development of multicultural counseling competence is a life-long process of deconstructing early learning and staying open to the experiences of others.

I find walking the talk and displaying my imperfections extremely challenging, but multicultural dialogue requires just that. Interpersonal multicultural conflicts are unavoidable and part of living in a pluralistic society. These critical incidents beg for a dialogic response. When I unintentionally say something that reveals a stereotype, prejudice, or privilege, I am suddenly faced with behavioral choices, nearly all of which coincide with the ways in which White folks in higher education tend to respond (D'Andrea & Daniels, 1999). I can aggressively defend myself (anger), passively retreat (generalized apathy), or distance myself from the discussion (intellectual detachment). My personal goal, however, is to grow more tolerant of my own discomfort and maintain a level of engagement that will lead to intrapersonal insight and interpersonal détente or resolution. I am deeply honored and sincerely grateful for the moments of multicultural immediacy that I have had with colleagues who are different from me. It is through these relationships that I have grown to recognize the cost of white privilege.

I am experiencing a painful and delightful merger of my real and ideal self. The process has involved letting go of unrealistic self-impressions (for example, I am without prejudice) and of accepting my imperfections (for example, the critical incident described here). My multicultural experiences remind me of the psychotherapeutic process of change (Highlen & Hill, 1984). I continuously cycle forward and back in a spiral of progress that brings me closer to my colleagues and my authentic self.

Speaking and behaving authentically is about finding one's voice. Feminist educators have said this for many years. An oppressive society divides us, silences us. It privileges a few and marginalizes many. Unity through diversity is a well-worn adage, but the theme has more than one meaning. During the past several years, I have experienced a unity of persons and a unity of *self* that is priceless.

Finding one's voice is a metaphor for integrating the disparate parts of oneself and the disparate parts of one's community. Finding one's voice is the first step in creating individual and institutional change. Ongoing dialogue is one way to build the alliances that are needed to transform people and systems and turn intention into action.

DISCUSSION QUESTIONS

1. In what ways are you oppressed? In what ways are you privileged?

2. One-half of the conference design team thought my actions were not worth condemning. The other half thought my behavior was reprehensible. What do you think?

3. Do you think that I am speaking from a place of "white guilt" and/or "political correctness"? How do you contrast these phenomena with ethical growth and development? Do you think that I was not "honest enough" in my interpretation of this critical incident, and that my perspective is still limited by my white privilege? How?

4. If you are a White person, how would you feel if someone asked you to talk about your anger regarding oppression and privilege in a room full of your friends or colleagues? Have you ever tried doing that? If yes, what happened? If no, why not?

5. Have you had similar experiences? How did you resolve them in your own mind? How did you resolve them interpersonally?

6. Have you ever been confronted by someone who experienced your actions as oppressive? In what ways did you respond defensively? In what ways did you respond openly and with a willingness to learn?

7. What does it mean to engage someone in multicultural dialogue? What are your barriers to multicultural dialogue? How can you overcome them?

8. Where are you in your racial/cultural or White racial identity development? How might your status in your own racial/cultural identity development or White racial identity development affect your perceptions of this narrative?

9. What have you learned about yourself by reading this narrative?

REFERENCES

Betita, J., Mar, K., Shockley, M., & Zetzer, H. (2001, November). *Challenging racism, privilege, & oppression: Building bridges through multicultural dialogue.* Workshop presented at The Multicultural Center, University of California, Santa Barbara.

Bohm, D. (1996). *On dialogue.* New York: Routledge.

Carter, R. T. (1997). Is white a race? Expressions of white racial identity. In M. Fine, L. Weis, L. C. Powell, & L. M. Wong (Eds.), *Off white: Readings on race, power, and society* (pp. 198–209). New York: Routledge.

Clark, R., Anderson, N. B., Clark, V. R., & Williams, D. R. (1999). Racism as a stressor for African Americans. *The American Psychologist, 54,* 805–816.

Collins, P. H. (2000). *Black feminist thought: Knowledge, consciousness, and the politics of empowerment* (2nd ed.). New York: Routledge.

Contrada, R. J., Ashmore, R. D., Gary, M. L., Coups, E., Egeth, J. D., Sewell, A., Ewell, K., Goyal, T. M., & Chasse, V. (2000). Ethnicity-related sources of stress and their effects on well-being. *Current Directions in Psychological Science, 9,* 136–139.

D'Andrea, M., & Daniels, J. (1999). Understanding the different psychological dispositions of white racism: A comprehensive model for counselor educators and practitioners. In M. S. Kiselica (Ed.), *Confronting prejudice and racism during multicultural training.* Alexandria, VA: American Counseling Association.

D'Andrea, M., & Daniels, J. (2001). Expanding our thinking about white racism: Facing the challenge of multicultural counseling in the 21st century. In J. G. Ponterotto, J. M. Casas, L. A. Suzuki, & C. M. Alexander (Eds.), *Handbook of multicultural counseling* (2nd ed., pp. 289–310). Thousand Oaks, CA: Sage.

Dovidio, J. F., Gaertner, S. L., Kawakami, K., & Hodson, G. (2002). Why can't we just get along? Interpersonal bias and interracial distrust. *Cultural Diversity & Ethnic Minority Psychology, 8,* 88–102.

Helms, J. E. (1995). An update of Helms's white and people of color racial identity models. In J. G. Ponterotto, J. M. Casas, L. A. Suzuki, & C. M. Alexander (Eds.), *Handbook of multicultural counseling* (pp. 181–191). Thousand Oaks, CA: Sage.

Highlen, P. S., & Hill, C. E. (1984). Factors affecting client change in individual counseling: Current status and theoretical speculation. In S. D. Brown & R. W. Lent (Eds.), *Handbook of counseling psychology,* 334–396. New York: Wiley.

Isaacs, W. (1999). *Dialogue and the art of thinking together: A pioneering approach to communicating in business and in life.* New York: Random House.

Johnson, A. G. (2001). *Privilege, power, and difference.* Boston: McGraw-Hill.

Kiselica, M. S. (1998). Preparing Anglos for the challenges and joys of multiculturalism. *The Counseling Psychologist, 26,* 5–21.

Kivel, P. (1996). *Uprooting racism: How white people can work for racial justice.* Gabriola Island, British Columbia: New Society Publishers.

Lowe, S. M., Chang, Y., Chapman, B., Dettinger, S., Henze, K., Latta, R., Mascher, J., Okubo, Y., & Park, J. (2000, August). *Hearing voices: Coping with racism among Asian Americans.* Paper presented as part of a symposium at the Annual Meeting of the American Psychological Association, San Francisco, CA.

Mahmoud, V. M. (1998). The double binds of racism. In M. McGoldrick (Ed.), *Re-visioning family therapy: Race, culture, and practice* (pp. 255–267). New York: Guilford Press.

McIntosh, P. (1989, July/August). White privilege: Unpacking the invisible knapsack. *Peace and Freedom,* 8–10.

Mezirow, J. (1991). *Transformative dimensions of adult learning.* San Francisco: Jossey-Bass.

Neville, H. A., Worthington, R. L., & Spanierman, L. B. (2001). Race, power, and multicultural counseling psychology. In J. G. Ponterotto, J. M. Casas, L. A. Suzuki, & C. M. Alexander (Eds.), *Handbook of multicultural counseling* (2nd ed., pp. 257–288). Thousand Oaks, CA: Sage.

Patterson, K., Grenny, J., McMillan, R., & Switzler, A. (2000). *Better than duct tape: Dialogue tools for getting results and getting along.* Plano, TX: Pritchett, Rummler-Brache.

Ponterotto, J. G. (1998). Charting a course for research in a multicultural counseling training program. *The Counseling Psychologist, 26,* 43–68.

Reynolds, A. L. (1997). Using the Multicultural Change Intervention Matrix (MCIM) as a multicultural counseling training model. In D. Pope-Davis & H. L. K. Coleman (Eds.), *Multicultural aspects of counseling series: Vol. 7. Multicultural counseling competencies: Assessment, education and training, and supervision* (pp. 209–226). Thousand Oaks, CA: Sage.

Rogers, C. R. (1957). The necessary and sufficient conditions of therapeutic personality change. *Journal of Consulting Psychology, 21,* 95–103.

Rowe, W., Bennett, S., & Atkinson, D. R. (1994). White racial identity models: A critique and alternative proposal. *The Counseling Psychologist, 22,* 120–146.

Spanierman, L. B., Heppner, M. J., & Neville, H. A. (2000, August). Psychosocial costs of racism to Whites scale: Measuring the construct. Poster presented at the Annual Convention of the American Psychological Association, Chicago, IL.

Stephan, W. G., & Stephan, C. W. (2001). *Improving intergroup relations.* Thousand Oaks, CA: Sage Publications.

Sue, D. W., Bingham, R., Porche-Burke, L., & Vasquez, M. (1999). The diversification of psychology: A multicultural revolution. *The American Psychologist, 54,* 1061–1069.

Sue, D. W., Carter, R. T., Casas, J. M., Fouad, N. A., Ivey, A. E., Jensen, M., LaFromboise, T., Manese, J. E., Ponterotto, J. G., & Vasquez-Nutall, E. (1998). *Multicultural counseling competencies: Individual & organizational development.* Thousand Oaks, CA: Sage Publications.

Sue, D. W., & Sue, D. (2003). *Counseling the culturally diverse: Theory to practice* (4th ed.). New York: Wiley.

Sue, S., Arredondo, P., & McDavis, R. (1995). Multicultural counseling competencies and standards: A call to the profession. In J. G. Ponterotto, J. M. Casas, L. A. Suzuki, & C. M. Alexander (Eds.), *Handbook of multicultural counseling* (pp. 624–643). Thousand Oaks, CA: Sage.

Swindler, L. (1983). The dialogue decalogue: Ground rules for interreligious, interideological dialogue. *The Journal of Ecumenical Studies, 20,* 1–4.

Takaki, R. (1993). *In a different mirror: A history of multicultural America.* Boston: Little, Brown & Co.

Tatum, B. (1997). *Why are all the black kids sitting together in the cafeteria? And other conversations about race.* New York: Basic Books.

Thompson, C. E., & Neville, H. A. (1999). Racism, mental health, and mental health practice. *The Counseling Psychologist, 27,* 155–223.

Wah, L. M. (Producer and Director), & Hunter, M. (Co-Producer). (1994). *The color of fear* [Videorecording]. Oakland, CA: Stir-Fry Productions.

Wilcox, D. (2000). *Deliberative dialogue: A different kind of talk, another way to act.* Paper presented at The Summit on Blacks in Higher Education, American Association for Higher Education Black Caucus, Savannah State University, Savannah, GA.

Winant, H. (1997). Behind blue eyes: Whiteness and contemporary U.S. racial politics. In M. Fine, L. Weis, L. C. Powell, & L. M. Wong (Eds.), *Off white: Readings on race, power, and society* (pp. 40–56). New York: Routledge.

Wolfe, N. (1995). The racism of well-meaning white people. In M. Golden & S. R. Shreve, *Skin deep: Black and white women write about race* (pp. 37–46). New York: Doubleday.

Zetzer, H. A., Shockley, M. E., Mar, K., & Betita, J. V. (2000, August). Dismantling resistance with self-disclosure: Dialogue as innovation in multicultural training. In J. N. Valdez (Chair), *Overcoming resistance, achieving transformation: Innovations in teaching multicultural counseling skills.* Symposium conducted at the Annual Meeting of the American Psychological Association, Washington, DC.

AUTHOR'S NOTE

Heidi A. Zetzer, Ph.D., Core Faculty, Graduate Psychology Program, Antioch University, Santa Barbara.

I would like to express my appreciation to Sharon Anderson and Valerie Middleton for their editorial comments. Special praise is due to Richard Whitney and Michael Loewy for their valuable feedback during the construction of this narrative. I feel especially grateful to Juliet Betita, Keith Mar, Muriel Shockley, A. J. Thoroughgood, and Jesse Valdez for their contributions to my multicultural development. Portions of this chapter were presented at the 109th Annual Convention of the American Psychological Association, San Francisco, California, August, 2001.

Correspondence concerning this chapter should be addressed to Heidi A. Zetzer, Antioch University, 801 Garden St., Ste. 101, Santa Barbara, CA, 93101. Electronic mail may be sent via Internet to *hzetzer@antiochsb.edu.*

2

Supposed to Know [

On Accepting Privilege

DEBORAH MEGIVERN

INTRODUCTION

During my studies as a doctoral student in social work and psychology, I volunteered to become a facilitator for a graduate-level multicultural dialogue class focused on dimensions of oppression, privilege, and diversity. At first, I justified taking on this extra work, because I would soon be teaching graduate students about multicultural and social justice-oriented approaches to mental-health practice and policy—a tremendous responsibility, considering I had witnessed mental-health providers who were ill-prepared to work with diverse clientele. My second justification for taking a minor leadership role in this class was more compelling and significant to me. I was having a great deal of trouble accepting a basic element of social-justice learning—the struggle to acknowledge my own privileges.

UNDERSTANDING AND EXPERIENCING
WHITE PRIVILEGE: DEBORAH'S STORY

Even after nearly eight years in a graduate social-work program—in an environment in which discussion of oppression and privilege occurred frequently—I still had trouble with the idea that I had personally benefited from many advantages. It was not that I cognitively denied my privileges, particularly those gleaned from being White. My challenge was the intersection of being White and growing up poor. I struggled with feeling privileged when I could not get over feeling deprived; I could easily make a direct connection between current miseries and life-long disadvantages. Educating others around me who just didn't get economic or class oppression drew my focus away from my white privilege.

ROOTS OF AN IDENTITY

Although I am a White, heterosexual woman, the identity most salient throughout my life was "poor trash"—a welfare child. Many life experiences reinforce the importance of this identity over the more privileged identities I enjoy. Both of my parents suffered from psychiatric illnesses. My mother received disability

, and my father was employed as a janitor, which meant minimal in-
Economic struggles within my family led to bouts of homelessness, daily
ance on the Salvation Army for meals, and dependence on charity from public and private sources. Lack of food and heat led child-protective services to
remove my siblings and me from my parents to be placed in foster care. We were
eventually returned to our parents, but the strain of family separation and
poverty led my parents to divorce shortly thereafter. My mother became a single parent to six children, while my father moved into a roach-infested, single-
room-occupancy hotel.

The neighborhood in which we were being raised was dangerous and di-
lapidated. Indeed, the rampant negative influences likely contributed signifi-
cantly to the fact that three of my younger siblings were mandated to services
within the juvenile justice system, and two of them became drug dependent.
Eventually, one of my brothers committed suicide. I will always be convinced
that poverty and our childhood life circumstances played the largest role in
his death.

My departure from this life of poverty at the age of 17 was the result of support from family and friends, an extensive series of governmental interventions
(ranging from Head Start to Project Upward Bound), and a natural inclination
toward academia. As I was driven off to college, I felt relieved to have escaped
that life of dispossession. Unfortunately, the feeling was short-lived, for it was
during college and graduate school that I discovered the seemingly permanent
effects of my economic history. My identity, the essence of who I am, had been
shaped by adapting to long-term poverty. The majority of my classmates came
from middle-class to upper-middle-class families. There were daily reminders
of our differences.

In political science and economics classes, my privileged college classmates
degraded welfare recipients. I was too frightened of social exclusion to speak
up. Instead, I silently sat in isolation, absorbing the significant social distance between us. Outside of class, many acquaintances were frustrated with my seeming unwillingness to spend more time with them in social activities and less time
at work. They did not understand that, for me, work was not a choice.

My full-time work schedule throughout college did not allow much time
for socializing. Whether I was serving food to other students at the school's cafeteria during the day or taking their orders at the popular local restaurant in the
evening, I would overhear college classmates complaining about reductions in
their allowances from $500 a month to $250. They did not have to pay their
college expenses, and they even got allowances. They did not need to work. I
fantasized about what that would be like. It was hard not to feel bitter as I got
behind in my own course work during heavy work weeks. Chronic fatigue also
made me prone to headaches, stomach pain, and colds.

The burden of poverty lingered tangibly as well, because each life step I
took continued to be plagued by economic hardship. During graduate school,
I found myself in the role of parent when I obtained custody of my two
youngest siblings—accumulating more than $125,000 in student-loan debt

while attempting to raise them on a graduate student's stipend and other meager employment. It was under these circumstances of relative deprivation that I studied oppression and privilege in my graduate classes and learned extensively about white privilege. Certainly, it felt to me as though my entire life had been defined by deprivation. If there were white privileges to be recognized, I could not see them. In my mind, what on earth good had it done to be White? It had not spared me hunger, frostbite, lice, poor medical care, ridicule, violence, or trauma. This feeling of deprivation was especially true in academia, because the vast majority of graduate students, including students of color, had spent their lives in material comfort and security.

THE EMBERS OF TRANSFORMATION

Eventually, I gained an intellectual, if not intuitive, understanding of privilege through my graduate program. Vowing to continue work on my own issues of privilege, I decided to become a cofacilitator with a well-regarded lead instructor, Dr. Michael Spencer. Dr. Spencer offers multicultural dialogue groups as a major means for learning about social justice, oppression, and privilege in his Contemporary Cultures in the United States class at the University of Michigan. I maintained the goal of focusing on my privileged identities, but I often felt ambivalent. On the one hand, I felt guilt and defensiveness at being blamed for my culpability in race oppression, as class members of color described their experiences. On the other hand, I felt envy and bitterness toward those individuals who had been economically privileged throughout their lives. I craved their basic privilege of getting fundamental needs met and the sense of security that elicited.

About midsemester, I was asked by Dr. Spencer to give a presentation on classism and poverty. He knew this was an area I knew a lot about. As I presented general information to the class, I shared specific details from my personal experiences to give fellow students a sense of how economic labeling and stigmatization make an impact. At one point, I showed the class a Child Protective Services document that declared *me* guilty of child neglect when I left two of my siblings in the house while I went to rescue another younger sibling being beaten by kids at the local park. I was 12 years old at the time. We discussed whether the "guilty" verdict would have occurred for a middle-class family under the same circumstances, and most class members agreed that it likely would not have.

The presentation stirred a mix of emotions in me. To share the lack of power, the deprivation, and the humiliation was empowering. Nonetheless, the stigma of poverty and child neglect, even though I was only 12 years old at the time, still stung. I felt I had performed a duty to other poor people by telling our story, but the cost was shame that took weeks to shake off.

At the end of the presentation, an African American graduate student I respected a great deal approached me. She told me honestly, "I feel bad for you;

but to be blunt, by the end of your talk, I was still thinking, 'So what? You're still White.' I guess I think that being White makes a big difference." Her words stung; her expression seemed defiant and accusatory. It felt as though my oppression was deniable, because I was White. The weight of race oppression was her burden. To me, it seemed as if she could not see my burden of class oppression or her own class privilege as long as her awareness stayed entirely within race oppression.

It dawned on me, eventually, that I was not going to be able to own my white privilege until I let go of enough of my own oppression to really listen and internalize the privilege. My classmate's comment was a precipitant to the gradual coherence and redirection of my conflicting thoughts and feelings. There we had been, both in pain from dealing with the ramifications of oppression, yet we had been at odds.

When I recalled that exchange later on, the importance of accepting my white privilege finally became clear to me on an emotional level. If I was unwilling to move beyond my oppression, how could I expect anyone else to do as much? This meant I was going to have to really attend to all the daily instances in which my race advantaged me. If I apply for an apartment, I know any rejection would be because I don't have enough credit. In my community, police officers chronically stop my neighbors for "Driving While Black," while I cruise by without significant worry of harassment. I did not have to question whether my race was a factor. I had personally witnessed millions of examples of white privilege as I grew up in a predominantly African American neighborhood; but I had not focused on these. As I became more willing to explore the totality of my life circumstances, I became more conscious of my privileged identity and not just my oppressed identity.

During this period of awakening and transformation, I was fortunate to have the guidance of authors such as June Jordan (2001), who taught me that people who are oppressed have to examine their privileges just as often as they grapple with their oppression. Jordan (2001), an African American woman, described an interaction with a White, female student who declared her (Jordan) to be "lucky" for having lived with oppression. From the student's perspective, dealing with oppression gave Jordan a cause or purpose to her life. Alternatively, this student felt she was "just a housewife and mother," and thus, a "nobody" (p. 39). Jordan used this experience to reflect on the ramifications of gender, race, and class oppression. In that exchange, she saw that this student did not see others' oppression as her own cause or her purpose. There was no unity between them as they struggled against gender and race oppression.

Later in her essay, Jordan (2001) writes about an African woman and an Irish woman joining in solidarity to solve a problem. "It was not who they both were but what they both know and what they were both preparing to do about what they know that was going to make them both free at last" (p. 44). This was the lesson. Without understanding my white privilege—privilege being the constant companion to oppression—I could not "know" or work against either class or race oppression. If I didn't fully know what others with whom I wanted solidarity experienced, we would be unable to be free of our respective oppressions together.

THE REPEATING PROCESS OF SELF-EXAMINATION: CONCLUSIONS AND LESSONS LEARNED

Examining one's own privileged status is a constant process. I have had to continually revisit my tasks as a member of oppressing groups. Freire (1970) called this repeated process of self-examination "critical consciousness." Specifically, I have to repeatedly remind myself that I cannot expect others to examine their economic privileges if I am not willing to work on owning my white privilege. I knew the vexation that came from waiting for others to accept their class advantages; that economically secure people took for granted their safe neighborhoods, regular meals, and designer clothes always seemed to make poverty worse.

So I planned to appreciate my white privilege, notice it, and then work to extend these privileges to others. For example, not long ago, I was riding on a city train. A beautiful African American child, about four years old, was smiling and talking to passengers. When this little girl and her mother exited the train, a White man with all of the markers of being from a lower-class background made a derogatory comment about the young girl's hair, which had been combed out to a full Afro. I winced to hear his insensitive and disparaging views. He was part of the system of White oppression, a blatant racist asserting cultural dominance based on skin privilege. Only a few moments later, an aging African American man trudged up the aisle of the train carrying a mop and a bucket. He looked weary, confined to cleaning up the mess made by other people on train cars.

This story is relevant in my transformation because my previous instincts would have been to overlook the obvious signs of race oppression. In the past, I would have mentally felt united with the poverty of the janitor, feeling connected to him by the fact that I had scrubbed my share of toilets, and because my father has been a janitor most of his life. I would not have focused on what I had in common with the lower-class White person, or how I personally benefited from systemic oppression based on race. However, this time, I understood in that moment the privilege of being White, and I reminded myself how my race had almost certainly played a beneficial role in my escape from poverty. How many people had just assumed, in part because I am White, that I was bright and easily educated? How often had my "merits" been recognized where they may have been overlooked if I had darker skin? In that moment, I recognized that I was exceptionally blessed to be riding to a sports event on the train, enjoying my free time, having the funds to pay for leisure, and possessing the capabilities to avoid doing the kind of work that would put that immutable wearied look on my face.

More and more, I recognize that I am fortunate to have had experiences with being disadvantaged. The circumstances of my life have allowed me to develop an empathy that has resulted in deeper interpersonal relationships with others. The weight of oppression has alerted me to the need to participate actively in efforts to change societal injustices. I have come to consider much of what is white privilege to be a set of basic rights all people should be entitled to. I am working, through social and political action, dialogue in the classes I teach, and constant reexamination of my self-awareness, to challenge the oppression–privilege dichotomy. There is a certain gift in feeling as if, just maybe, I might be a part of the solution.

DISCUSSION QUESTIONS

1. How does the complication of overlapping identities affect this author's struggle to identify her race privilege?

2. Describe in your own words the author's transformation in identity. Then, consider your own social identities and try to identify any transformative experiences related to oppression and privilege from your own life.

3. How might this author interact differently with a client from a different race now than before her self-exploration?

4. The author states that white privilege is mostly a set of basic rights that all people should be entitled to receive. First, give examples of white privilege that go beyond basic rights. How would White individuals relinquish an unearned privilege of this nature?

5. In what ways does this author demonstrate the importance of "critical consciousness" and continual self-reflection as a critical component of cultural competence for mental-health practice?

6. The author repeatedly describes feelings of marginalization related to her mixed identity of being both poor and White. She laments the lack of community, based on class, in higher education. In what ways might multicultural education transform colleges and universities into environments in which people collaborate across nontraditional social-identity groups?

7. How might a student from outside the United States view the dynamics of class and race in the United States after reading this author's story?

REFERENCES

Freire, P. (1970). *Pedagogy of the oppressed.* New York: Continuum.

Goodman, D. (1995). Difficult dialogues: Enhancing discussions about diversity. *College Teaching, 43*(2), 47–52.

Jordan, J. (2001). Report from the Bahamas. In M. Andersen & P. Hill Collins (Eds.), *Race, class, and gender: An anthology* (4th ed., pp. 35–44). Belmont, CA: Wadsworth Publishing.

McIntosh, P. (2001). White privilege and male privilege: A personal account of coming to see correspondences through work in women's studies (1988). In M. Andersen & P. Hill Collins (Eds.), *Race, class, and gender: An anthology* (4th ed., pp. 95–105). Belmont, CA: Wadsworth Publishing.

Miner, B. (2001). Taking multicultural, antiracist education seriously: An interview with Enid Lee. In M. Andersen & P. Hill Collins (Eds.), *Race, class, and gender: An anthology* (4th ed., pp. 556–562). Belmont, CA: Wadsworth Publishing.

Reed, B., Newman, P., Suarez, Z., & Lewis, E. (1997). Interpersonal practice beyond diversity and toward social justice: The importance of critical consciousness. In C. Garvin & B. Seabury (Eds.), *Interpersonal practice in social work: Promoting competence and social justice* (2nd ed., pp. 44–77). Boston: Allyn & Bacon.

Wade, J. C. (1993). Institutional racism: An analysis of the mental health system. *American Journal of Orthopsychiatry, 63*(4), 536–44.

3

White Male Privilege in the Context of My Life

RICH FURMAN

UNDERSTANDING AND EXPERIENCING WHITE PRIVILEGE: RICH'S STORY

I am White and male, but also Jewish. As a White male, I have often been presumed to possess certain positive attributes before I have exhibited them. That is, I am usually presumed competent, intelligent, and skillful based solely upon my physical type, manner of speech, and experiences that may or may not have occurred.

At times, thinking about my own white privilege is difficult. This is largely because, although I have white skin, in many ways I do not consider myself White, but Jewish. Non-Jews rarely understand what I mean by this without some explanation. All my life, it has been clear to me that I do not think or feel as the majority of White males do—I tend to be more emotional, more willing to engage in debate and conflict, and more animated. Many Jews experience a dual identity crisis by sometimes being able to pass as members of the dominant society while hiding a portion of their identity that is often celebrated in other venues. Both the ability and inability to hide one's identity makes one painfully aware of the costs and benefits of the ability to assimilate. The following stories illustrate this phenomenon.

STORY ONE

My days before I embarked upon my graduate-school experience were full of hope and awe. I imagined I was on the precipice of an epic adventure into a new, mystical, multicultural land where experiences of difference were cherished and commonalities were the foundation of mutual sharing. Perhaps such naiveté is commonplace among the soon-to-be-initiated. Regardless, my fantasy of finding a place in our United States where multiculturalism was a simple, easy-to-take-for-granted norm was soon to be discarded. It has been 12 years since my first day of graduate school yet I remember it as if it were yesterday.

The welcoming party was typical of such events: basic finger foods, short speeches from administrators, and second-year student leaders assigned to both inform and assure us anxious neophytes. What struck me as ironic, sad, and bizarre was how the students broke into small groupings based almost entirely upon ethnicity, gender, and race. Certainly, in a school with a social-work curriculum, people would be able to transcend traditional barriers. After about an hour, I decided to approach a group of African American women to say "hello." In my usual fearless and, in retrospect, painfully oblivious manner, I walked over to the group and said, "Hi, my name is Rich. I am shocked that we are all talking only to those of the same race or sex, so I thought I would try to desegregate the party." Two of the women smiled brightly and laughed. Another scolded me fiercely, "Segregation is what White men have done to us historically. I am *choosing* to talk to my sisters here. This is not segregation. Have a nice day."

At first, my reaction was utter shame. Clearly, not only had I committed a grave error, but also, in that moment, I felt responsible for hundreds of years of racism and oppression. In that moment, I was no better than a whip-cracking southern slaveholder. Because I had not worked through this issue previously, I was not able to simply apologize for my gaffe and rectify the situation. Instead, I had to endlessly ruminate about the incident, shifting blame onto the young woman, myself, or both of us.

STORY TWO

One year after graduate school, I obtained a position working as the clinical co-ordinator in a residential treatment program for adolescents with emotional disabilities. My responsibilities included developing treatment plans for the residents, providing therapy, and conducting family visits. I was also responsible for helping the line-level counselors implement the treatment plan and be "clinical" in their approach. All in all, I did a good job. It was curious though that I was in a supervisory position over much more experienced yet less educated workers, most of whom were African American. Being aware of my difference as the only White person in the building much of the time was not difficult; some of the children made me painfully aware. One day a child told me that I did not care about him because I was "just some [blank, blank] White guy who was there to keep Black people down." Not having worked through my white privilege, I responded defensively. I assured him that he was wrong, that I did care. Exasperated, he shrugged his shoulders and stomped off.

STORY THREE

As I originally was typing the previous stories, I was sitting in a café in a trendy area of Los Angeles. The café was full of people reading, studying, and talking. An African American man walked in with a backpack, similar to the one that was sitting at my table. He laid it down on a table next to a young White woman and took out books and paper to write, just as I had done several minutes earlier. As the young woman got up to use the bathroom, she asked *me* to watch her things.

Just a half hour before, however, she had left her things on the table unguarded as she used the bathroom. The only part of the scenario that was different now was the presence of the African American man about the same distance away from her as I was.

At the instant she asked me to watch her things, I became painfully aware of what had happened and wondered whether my African American counterpart was also conscious of the situation. I struggled with how to respond in the moment. After a split second had passed, in which all these things raced through my mind, I told the young woman that I would not be able to watch her things because I was just about to go to the bathroom myself. As soon as I said this, she organized her things, placed them into her bag, and walked to the bathroom with her bag in tow.

In the bathroom myself, I wondered whether there was something for me to do in this situation to challenge my white privilege. Was it enough merely to refuse to be party to such racism, or was something else required? Because I did not have a relationship with the woman, I decided to do nothing. I went back to my table and sat down, and I felt powerless and angry. I wished I could find the words to speak to the man about the situation, but how could I talk about such things with a stranger when I had problems doing so even with those with whom I was close?

FROM THEORY TO PRACTICE: REFLECTION ON WHITE PRIVILEGE

White male privilege has distinct costs. As the recipient of benefits bestowed upon me solely due to the color of my skin, I sometimes experience resentment from others that I find baffling and unfounded. When I don't understand the essence of my white privilege, I become reactive or shut down. My encounter with the group of African American women illustrates how white privilege, and my lack of understanding of the phenomenon, cut off communication. A proper analysis would have revealed that both our behaviors could in some way be understood as a natural byproduct of years of white privilege and its legacy of anger and resentment. I lost a valuable opportunity to learn from her experiences, and a valuable opportunity to relate to her as an equal by never speaking to her about the situation. In fact, I never spoke to her again. Feeling too conflicted and ashamed, I was unable to work through these difficult feelings.

In the second scenario, I again cut off communication by invalidating the feelings of the youth who told me in earnest what he was feeling. While he might have been wrong about me, he was expressing his real feelings about a society that devalues him, a society that considers it more likely that he will go to prison than to college. Had I validated his anger and expressed my desire to understand his experience, we might have been able to create a dialogue. I might have been a far more effective therapist to him personally had I worked through my own guilt and shame, which caused me to react defensively. Although in both instances I cut off communication, after the second experience, I had embarked on a higher level of ethno-relative development and was better able to reflect on how I might use my privileged status to validate and encourage this disenfranchised youth.

The more I work to understand my white privilege, the more I come to some kind of acceptance of it and continue to learn how I wish to deal with my privileges and paradoxes. When in this frame of mind, I am freer to choose my responses, as the following conclusion to the third story illustrates.

I became wrapped up in my contemplation about challenging the thinking of the woman who asked me to watch her things while she went to the rest-room. It took me awhile to become aware enough to try to understand how the African American man might be feeling if he was aware of the situation. Words such as *discounted, devalued,* and *dehumanized* scrolled across my con-sciousness.

I decided that although I would not bring up the situation directly, I would challenge the behavior that I had witnessed by attempting to make some kind of human connection with him. I excused myself for interrupting and asked him what he was reading. It was a book of poetry, one of my great passions, so we talked about writing and poetry. When the young woman re-turned from the bathroom, she reclaimed her seat between the two of us. In order not to be rude by talking around her, I asked my new acquaintance if I could join him. He was pleased to accept, and we continued our conversa-tion. Fifteen minutes later, the young woman gathered her things to leave. I bid her a nice day and smiled at her, holding eye contact for several seconds too long as she walked out the door. Did she understand what I was trying to say to her? I will never know, but I felt better for attempting to communicate with her on some level.

CONCLUSIONS AND LESSONS LEARNED

One of the most important things I have learned in regard to privilege and other issues pertaining to the -isms is that humility and self-forgiveness are essential. We must accept our histories and defects without focusing on debilitating guilt, shame, or anger. These limiting reactions are not positive teaching tools, and none of them serve to resolve situations in a healthy way. Instead, they tend to lead one to be defensive or to submerge the pain as a self-protection strategy.

It is also important to realize that working through white privilege is a process, not an event. I cannot say that I have fully come to grips with my white privilege. Sometimes I am blind and insensitive to others in ways that I see only upon reflection. Sometimes I am overly critical of myself and attribute insensi-tivity where none existed. Part of my struggle is to find balance and tolerance—that is, tolerance for others and for myself as well.

DISCUSSION QUESTIONS

1. What options can you think of for handling the stories discussed in this chapter?
2. What other options did the author have for resolving his conflicts?
3. What would you have done differently in the last story? Why?
4. What have been some of the benefits of white privilege to you or people you know?
5. What are some of the emotional consequences of white privilege for you and those you know?
6. Have you recognized your own privilege, whatever area it is in? If so, what is it?
7. What was the most important lesson you learned from the narrative?

REFERENCE

McIntosh, P. (2000). White privilege and male privilege: A personal account of coming to see correspondences through work in women's studies. In A. Minas (Ed.), *Gender basics: Feminist perspectives on women and men.* Belmont, CA: Wadsworth/Thomson Learning.

4

Understanding and Experiencing Class Privilege

COLLEEN LOOMIS

The social construction of social class in the United States is controversial (Fussell, 1992; Storck, 2002). Many people would agree that there is a middle class and an upper class (for example, Kennedy and Rockefeller families), but there is not a consensus about the class or classes beneath the middle class. In this arena, perhaps most well known is the "working class" made popular by essays written from adult children in academia who were raised in working–class families (see Dews & Law, 1995; Tokarczyk & Fay, 1993) and by popular media (for example, Hollywood films such as *Good Will Hunting*). One challenge I face in writing this chapter is how to categorize my childhood social class. I began with the label "lower class" and migrated to "working class" or "working poor." My life experiences are dissimilar from the Hollywood and academic versions of working class as well as those of a few friends and colleagues who self-identify as having "working-class roots" or having been raised as "poor White trash." My social, economic, and cultural context differed. In this chapter, rather than address my understanding of various classifications of social class, I focus on ways that these aspects of my life circumstances influence my understanding of class privilege through experience.

GROWING UP WITH MORE THAN A FEW AND LESS THAN MOST

My three brothers and I grew up in low-income circumstances in the United States. Shelter, clothing, and food were sometimes scarce during our early childhood. For example, our mother speaks about my not having shoes during a New York winter. Moving often to where my father had work or where extended family would help us, we lived in a variety of housing situations (a few without conventional plumbing). When I was seven years old, we settled for the next six years into a two-bedroom, 60-foot trailer—one of a few in the neighborhood—

located on a dirt road in a relatively rural area. I have fond memories of this neighborhood, such as swimming in a nearby lake and riding the bus to school because it was too far to walk. Social welfare assisted with the support of our family by providing food stamps, and a few kind neighbors supported us with offers of food, shoes, and hand-me-down clothes, before and after my father left. My memory of going with my mother to buy groceries and hearing derogatory remarks about us while we made our purchase with food stamps seems to mark the beginning of my awareness of social class differences at the individual level. (For the group level, see Storck, 2002).

The infiltration of middle-class families into our neighborhood brought with it more experiences with classism. A few years after we had settled in, wealthy individuals and property-development companies purchased land in our neighborhood and built homes for middle-class and upper-middle-class families. As more and more families moved into our neighborhood, the local swimming hole gave way to privately owned and commercially developed waterfront properties, and resource-rich public schools were built within walking distance.

By the time I went to high school, the neighborhood transformation was nearly complete, although a few homes with families living in poverty remained (protected by a "grandfather clause"). I attended high school with students whose families had much more material and educational wealth than I had ever seen. My mother and father had eleventh-grade and sixth-grade educations, respectively. Our family did not have opportunities to socialize across class boundaries, and we did not always have a working television, so my exposure to working- and middle-class culture was limited. However, economic class distinctions in the high school were apparent daily. The stigmatization began on Monday morning when I, along with about seven other students out of 500, had to stand in line to receive our free-lunch tickets for the week. During the week, peers excluded me from their friendship circles, and teachers excluded me from certain preparations for higher education. Speaking generally from my experience, middle-class families socialized their children to spend time with similar others, and teachers tended to help those students whose families were preparing them for college. The way I talked (for example, "We was goin' to the store and. . .") and where I lived (in a trailer on a dirt road) excluded me from many social and college-preparation activities. Parents, teachers, and guidance counselors did not advise me to take college-prep courses or to pursue other resources that would prepare me for higher education, although I was an honor student from primary through secondary school. Instead, they (my parents, teachers, and guidance counselors) focused on what they viewed as my basic needs, such as food, safety, and completing high school (they knew that my two older brothers had dropped out and were, as we say, "in trouble with the law"). During that time, researchers reported a strong direct effect of social class on university access, regardless of race and gender (Lang, 1985; Thomas, Alexander, & Eckland, 1977).

I graduated from high school after completing my third year of studies. At 17 and not "culturally" prepared for college (for example, I had not taken the SAT, and I did not understand the process of seeking college admission), I enrolled in basic courses at a community college. To support myself, I worked full time operating a check-sorting machine at a bank from midnight to 8:00 A.M.

Through meeting other employees who had been called in to fix problems, I learned about and was interested in becoming a computer programmer. My interest was mostly in the money and the hours—programmers were well paid, worked "eight to five," and were on call occasionally. But the only viable option to career development while supporting myself was to join the military, or so it seemed at the time. I reasoned that in the U.S. military service food and shelter would be provided; I would have work, income, and physical exercise (that is, I would not have to pay member fees to go to a gym); and I could get a college education (at the time, TV advertisements often highlighted that joining the military was a way to get a college degree as well as to "see the world"). After visiting a recruiter and scoring well on exams, I was selected and encouraged to choose between the Navy and the Air Force. I wrote my employment letter of resignation and met with my supervisor.

After discussing with my supervisor my reasons for wanting to quit and join the military service, he suggested he tear up my resignation letter and create a position for me as a computer-programmer trainee. I agreed. I continued to work at the same place, transferred to the day shift, and sporadically attended community colleges part time. One year later, I moved to a city two hours away to live with a partner and obtained a computer-programmer job at another bank. I enrolled in a two-year college and completed an associate's degree in liberal arts six years after graduating from high school.

FORAY INTO MIDDLE CLASS

Several relocations and relationships later, I was living in a different state working as a computer programmer for a computer hardware manufacturer. I applied for positions as a programmer in the oil and gas industry but was not hired because I did not have a four-year university degree. My partner at the time respected my intellect in spite of my not having a degree, and encouraged me to become my own boss. He taught me the basics of starting a business. With only $500 capital, which I used to incorporate, I founded a computer consulting company and subcontracted myself to a major oil company. In this case, as a business owner, I did not need a pedigree. After a few months, when I was no longer living paycheck to paycheck but was one paycheck ahead of my bills, I used my income to hire another employee. Repeating this method of building the business, within five years my company had 12 employees. During the first three years of being the janitor, bookkeeper, employee working on client sites, and president of my company, I focused on garnering material symbols of middle-class culture, such as driving nice cars, wearing a designer wardrobe, dining out, buying music, and traveling. But I did not simultaneously pursue further education.

Although I had obtained, but not secured, many middle-class markings, I felt a deep emptiness inside whenever someone asked me where I went to university. When I told them I did not have a degree, my coworkers at client sites and my employees paid me (seeming) compliments such as "Wow! You started and run your own business without having a degree?" It was expected that my not being university educated meant that I was somehow less capable. In a more prestigious social circle, I dined with other entrepreneurs and adults who had trust funds and raised money for worthy causes. I had never heard of a trust fund before moving in the oil and gas social circle. I dated within this group of friends and at least twice men broke off their relationships with me very soon after they learned that I was not "born with a silver spoon in my mouth." A kind friend explained this point to me because it was the first time I remember hearing that expression, and I did not know what it meant. Other men were wiser, so to speak, and flirted, learned my background, and did not pursue me further. One potential suitor told his sister that it was okay for me to be a friend of the family, and perhaps even charitable of them to be kind to me, but that he would never date me, given my family background. I began to realize how my past socioeconomic standing limited my intimate life as well as my educational, professional, and social life. Again, I felt a need to hide my background to be included or to participate more fully in my current, seeming, peer groups, which I've since learned is common among us folks with a history of lesser economic means (Granfield, 1991). Consequently, I simultaneously enjoyed the status of being a successful entrepreneur without a four-year degree and suffered the stigma of not being formally educated nor having a middle-class or better family background.

I wanted a degree to remove stigma, but I also wanted it so I could participate in conversations about university life and for its intrinsic qualities. I longed for a traditional university experience (for example, living on campus, attending classes, reading, spending endless hours in the library, and, importantly, not having to work), which I had heard about in retrospective accounts within my social circle of the time. I realized that a traditional experience was not possible given my accidents of life history—in this case, age and circumstances—(for more information on how contexts shape choices, see Sloan, 1996), so I continued working full time and enrolled in a four-year university to complete a bachelor's degree. Sixteen years after graduating from high school, I graduated with a four-year university degree with a major in psychology and a minor in computer science, having decided that a computer-related degree would not change my income potential as a business owner. It was during those final two years of undergraduate work that I learned enough about the system of higher education (for example, student loans, mentoring, and letters of recommendation) to dream about and to pursue the dream of living a scholar's life.

SIMULTANEOUSLY OPPRESSED AND OPPRESSOR

Backing up a bit, beginning in high school, I became aware of class markers and began hiding my inherited class and pursuing middle-class symbols such as speaking Standard English (see also Dews & Law, 1995), wearing classic clothes, and obtaining a formal education (Granfield, 1991). I operated mostly under the model of assimilation (Berry, Poortinga, Segall, & Dasen, 1992)—that is, the more one looks and acts like a person from the middle class, the more access one gains to the middle class.

Occasionally, throughout the years, folks questioned me in ways that seemed like tests of my authenticity as a "middle-class" person. However, the question that most frightened me was the one listed on several graduate-school applications: Please describe your background and discuss any adversity you have had to overcome. I panicked, but was cognizant enough to seek advice from an uncommon mentor, Tod S. Sloan, who helped me to see the connection between my personal experiences of oppression and my professional interest in using psychology for liberation. He also provided some of the socialization for higher education (for example, criteria for selecting graduate programs, strengthening an application) and helped me to tell my personal story in a way that would be acceptable to the academic audience. In graduate school applications, I made what I recall as my first, nonapologetic public disclosure of the circumstances of my childhood. I explained how those experiences contributed to the development of my sensitivity to the issues reflected in my interest in community psychology, a discipline dedicated to "liberating oppressed peoples."

Later, through graduate study and my postdoctoral fellowship, mentors gave me varying and sometimes conflicting advice on this issue of class disclosure. (I wondered to myself whether they would give the same advice to my colleagues about race, ethnicity, or sexual orientation.) I began to realize that my questions about if, when, how, to whom, and why to disclose my class background would continually surface, and that the consequences of that disclosure would often be unclear. I also noted that my middle-class peers do not carry this burden. A few scenarios illustrate this point.

During my third year of graduate studies, I worked on a research project, conducting a process evaluation of a local, community-based career and learning resource center. One objective of the center was to facilitate women's work and movement from unemployment and underemployment to living-wage jobs (Loomis et al., in press). My childhood experiences, my passionate concern and respect for the hardships of poverty, my care surrounding issues of women's poverty, and an opportunity to grow professionally all had attracted me to the research project.

Our research team leader built a diverse team of women who differed by ethnicity, race, age, religious background, educational background, sexual orientation, and years of study. Obviously, not all these categories are visible, so information about members' identification with one or more groups was not necessarily common knowledge. One afternoon, the team leader talked about her recent recruitment of another research team member, noting how this new member was similar to an existing member because both had attended prestigious, private high schools that developed intellectual prowess. My jealousy of those who enjoyed the benefits of parochial education and the subsequent favoritism that often followed them into higher education surfaced. In spite of, or perhaps because of, previously being oppressed by the act of "classism favoritism" based on educational privileges, I oppressed another woman on the team on similar grounds by criticizing her writing abilities and implying that she had not overcome her "working-class language skills." Retrospectively, I see how my access to at least some language instruction on Standard English, as well as my independent study of middleclassness, provided me a level of privilege. Naively, I simultaneously was the oppressed and the privileged oppressor.

On another occasion, while we were discussing research-interview transcripts, one team member made a pejorative, stereotypical remark something like "that's the way poor people think." I was incensed although unaware of the depth of my anger until I analyzed my desire to get back at her because she was one of "them"—the middle- or upper-middle-class oppressors. First, I felt personally affronted, because in my mind I often identify with being a poor person—or, more accurately, one who lives in poor circumstances. Second, I thought I was the "classism police" and that a comment like that was cause for citation. I was determined to raise class consciousness among my colleagues at all costs, even at the cost of outing myself as a product of poverty. I said something like "Oh really?" and asked further questions, in an effort to reveal others' underlying assumptions (for example, "Poor women have children as a way of generating income," and "Poor women are not smart enough to know. . . ."). From this exchange and other similar ones, I was dubbed the "class expert" in particular and the "diversity expert" in general. I proudly wore the badge and enjoyed respect from team members for what seemed like the first time. I felt as though I was finally the one with the privileged knowledge. It is only in retrospect that I see the conundrum of my being "the class expert." My placement in a position as an expert on classism was an act of classism. That is, team members tended to defer to me because of my class background. My voice became privileged. This dynamic is a problem because the diversity and voices of "outgroups" is lost when one person appoints another as the voice of those who are Black, gay or lesbian, women, or poor.

To further complicate the class issues on the research team, each of us wrote a brief biography that provided our individual and collective standpoint as researchers. Through personal reflection and graduate education, I came to value the subjective aspects of the research process that included self-disclosure of researchers' standpoints (Reay, 1996). In my personal experience of this process, however, I became aware that asking someone for her or his standpoint might sometimes be a classist act. The form of the request (for example, orally, in writing, in confidence, or anonymously) for this type of information is another way that standpoint determination is classist. Thus, the thought of submitting my biography to all my colleagues—particularly those who marginalized me because of my class—was not a welcome thought. Even though they had some idea of my roots, I did not want to explicitly describe my background in this particular context with all the individuals on the team. Not without self-incrimination, I spoke up and asked that one person collect our biographies and write the method section describing the researchers in a way that our identities would remain somewhat anonymous, at least to our reading audience.

CONCLUSIONS AND LEARNINGS

This narrative highlights some of the unintentional consequences of classism and provides insight into professional and personal struggles and triumphs I encountered from such experiences. The early acts of oppression related to my socioeconomic circumstances were often subtle and largely unnoticed by me. As I progressed from childhood to adulthood, these indicators became more obvious and hurtful. By adulthood, I had learned to hide some of my class markers to avoid being a subject of oppression (similar to Carolyn Leste Law, in Dews & Law, 1995). Instances of class oppression often go unnoticed by me until someone else points out these transgressions. My own lack of awareness of personal acts of classism is in part a residual effect, or artifact, of class socialization within the poverty class. We are socialized to believe that we are not oppressed by others. It also reflects my present position as more a part of the middle-class culture.

Biases in my thinking contribute to professional and personal behaviors that perpetuate classism. Working through the process of developing personal and professional identities that acknowledge the issues associated with my past, and present access to resources is a continuous exercise. A central issue in this process is asking and answering the question, "What are the consequences of showing my class?" This question is multifaceted in that it brings to the surface other questions, such as, "Should I, a seemingly middle-class professional with roots in poverty, disclose my socioeconomic background?" and, "If so, to whom, when, how, and under what circumstances do I disclose?"

Like a few others fortunate to experience some degree of social mobility, I face both oppression and privilege. Oppression, in its most obvious form, most often occurred at times when I did not hide or could not hide my class background. Alternatively, privileges came most often when others perceived me as a middle-class person, perhaps because I consciously, or unconsciously, presented myself as middle class, or the interactions provided incomplete class clues. There were times when I received the unearned privileges associated with being, or presenting, middle class, and times when I was oppressed because of acts of classism in which I was designated or self-ordained as the oracle of a particular socioeconomic class. Privilege and oppression coexist.

Recently, I decided that one of my biggest professional challenges is the personal struggle of constantly evaluating and reevaluating the circumstances under which to include or exclude my class experiences—including contributing to this edited book. Paradoxically, I believe that my greatest triumph is that I continue to struggle with these issues. In conclusion, I suggest that professionals carefully consider the context and the consequences of disclosing, or asking another to disclose, one's class background (see also Hoyt, 1999). It is often difficult to assess the effects of disclosure. But simultaneously, we have a responsibility to challenge and confront classism by having or not having information about an individual's socioeconomic class status and by using or not using that information to appropriately circumvent its perpetuation.

DISCUSSION QUESTIONS

1. In what ways are your childhood circumstances similar to and different from the author's?

2. Contrast the author's report of material and educational resources to your own understanding of "working-class" resources.

3. To broaden the classism framework, consider ways social categories interact. For example, reflect on what you learned about the author. What is her ethnicity? What is her sexual orientation? Is she faced with disabilities? Which if any of these characteristics did you assume? Were you right?

4. Thinking specifically about the lack of preparation for higher education, how might the author's experiences have differed if she were Asian?

5. The author writes that she often identifies as a person living in poor circumstances, even though she no longer does. How does identifying with "the poor" affect professional interactions?

6. How did the author approach consciousness raising about social class? How do you do it? What are some other strategies that might be helpful?

7. Consider the roles of oppressed and oppressor. The author tells us about being oppressed in her personal life, particularly as a child and young woman, and being both oppressed and the oppressor in her professional life. How might she avoid oppressing others (for example, should she not disclose personal experiences)?

REFERENCES

Berry, J. W., Poortinga, Y. H., Segall, M. H., & Dasen, P. R. (1992). *Cross-cultural psychology: Research and applications.* Cambridge: Cambridge University Press.

Dews, C. L. B. & Law, C. L. (Eds.). (1995). *This fine place so far away from home: Voices of academics from the working class.* Philadelphia: Temple University Press.

Fussell, P. (1992). *Class: A guide through the American status system.* New York: Simon & Schuster.

Granfield, R. (1991). Making it by faking it: Working-class students in an elite academic environment, *Journal of Contemporary Ethnography Special Issue:* *Stigma and Social Interaction, 20*(3), 331–351.

Hoyt, S. K. (1999). Mentoring with class: Connections between social class and developmental relationships in the academy. In A. J. Murrell and F. J. Crosby (Eds), *Mentoring dilemmas: Developmental relationships within multicultural organizations* (pp. 189–210). Mahwah, NJ: Lawrence Erlbaum Associates, Publishers.

Lang, D. (1985). Stratification and professional education within the academic hierarchy. *Journal of Research & Development in Education, 19*(1), 10–20.

Loomis, C., Brodsky, A. E., Arteaga, S., Benhorin, R., Rogers-Senuta, K., Marx, C., & McLaughlin, P. (in press). What works in adult educational and employment training? Case study of a community-based program for women. *Journal of Community Practice.*

Reay, D. (1996). Dealing with difficult differences: Reflexivity and social class in feminist research. *Feminism & Psychology, 6*(3), 443–456.

Sloan, T. S. (1996). *Life Choices: Understanding Dilemmas and Decisions.* Boulder, CO: Westview Press.

Storck (2002). 'Reality' or 'illusion'?: Five things of interest about social class as a large group. *Group Analysis, 35*(3), 351–366.

Thomas, G. E., Alexander, K. L., & Eckland, B. K. (1977). *Access to higher education: How important are race, sex, social class and academic credentials for college access?* Baltimore, MD: Johns Hopkins University Center for Social Organization of Schools.

Tokarczyk, M. M. & Fay, E. A. (Eds.). (1993). *Working-class women in the academy: Laborers in the knowledge factory.* Amherst, MA: University of Massachusetts Press.

AUTHOR'S NOTE

I thank my family for the wealth of experiences that enriched my life, in spite of and because of our circumstances. I acknowledge that my debt to Tod S. Sloan for his ongoing contribution to our dialogue on oppression cannot be repaid, but I am grateful. Also, I thank Keith Humphreys and Tod Sloan for their feedback on early drafts of this chapter. Support for preparation comes from the Department of Veterans Affairs Office of Academic Affairs and Health Services Research and Development Service.

5

Deprivations and Privileges
We All Have

MA. TERESA TUASON

INTRODUCTION

I was born and raised in Baguio, a small city in the northern island group of the Philippines. I am one of six children. My parents came from poor families and became teachers, a profession that does not pay well. We all lived in a one-bedroom apartment. We had no cars and no medical insurance, and subsequently, we rarely went to the doctor when we had an ailment. Before my parents could afford the apartment we rented, we stayed in my maternal grandparents' shack with my mother's four other siblings. We ran to the neighbor's house when there were typhoons or strong winds for fear the shack and we would be blown away.

I knew we were poor; it was evident by what we ate in school (that is, our lunch box from home almost always contained a serving of rice, one small piece of meat or fish, or a few pieces of vegetables; or, on more difficult days, just rice with soy sauce or used oil for flavor), what clothes we wore, what toys we could not have, and occasionally by the fact that I was hungry on the days when we could not afford three decent meals a day. And although poverty was a common experience for those around us, I had always felt that we were poorer. We were six children to feed, and we had to share and divide everything into six portions, including one chocolate bar. I knew we were poorer because my mother would do anything to augment the family income, including selling foodstuffs and dry goods to her co-teachers. As children, we had also sold candies to our classmates to save up for a much-needed pair of shoes. Unlike other families, my parents could not afford a maid to help in the house or take care of us. So even at an early age, we were cooking, hand washing and ironing our school uniforms, washing the dishes, and fetching water. I also know that we never traveled to another place, and we never had family vacations.

Although my parents did not bring home much money as teachers, their profession helped us to become educated. For our elementary education, the religious congregation that ran and owned the university at which my parents taught schooled all six of us. Because of this, we had obtained our elementary education for free. For high school and college, some of us obtained scholarships because we excelled in school. My parents paid for tuition fees for the rest of us with money directly deducted from their salaries. I knew from my mother's and father's paychecks that most of what they earned went to schooling us. My parents had prioritized education before food and clothing expenses.

UNDERSTANDING AND EXPERIENCING
CLASS PRIVILEGE

As a result of obtaining a variety of scholarships, I earned a Bachelor of Science degree in psychology and a Master of Arts degree in child and family psychology from the same Catholic university in Quezon City. After having earned my bachelor's degree and while doing my master's program in the evenings, I taught third-grade boys for three years as my income-generating job. Then, after I obtained my degree, the psychology department asked me to teach undergraduate and graduate courses. During weekends and several hours in the week when I was not teaching, I practiced psychotherapy. In the Philippines, because of a lack of instructor resources, master's degree holders were given a lot of responsibility. Because there is no licensing body and no ethical and professional standards to practice by, master's degree holders practiced therapy mostly because there was much demand for this. I was informally supervised in my psychotherapy practice only because I sought it. In addition to studying and working full time, I financially supported a sibling through college.

After finishing my master's degree and practicing psychotherapy for four years, I decided to apply to Ph.D. programs in the field of counseling psychology. I applied to counseling and clinical psychology programs in the United States and in Europe. This was hard to do from far away because the mail took much longer, and all the application fees and test requirements—for example, Graduate Record Examination (GRE), Test of English as a Foreign Language (TOEFL), and Test of Spoken English (TSE)—were expensive. I also applied for several scholarships knowing that if I did not obtain one, I would never have a chance to pursue my Ph.D. in a different country. I was disappointed and very angry when I did not get a scholarship and a program acceptance on the first try, but I applied once more, thinking that the wisdom of timing could be on my side the second time around. I was rewarded with an opportunity to pursue my dream, and I finished my Ph.D. in counseling psychology at the State University of New York at Albany.

Coincidentally, Albany provided me with my first experience of feeling and being different. In Albany, and at the University of Utah where I had completed a predoctoral internship and postdoctoral fellowship, people around me did not look like me, and I realized that everyone around me reminded me of how different I was.

After two years in Utah, I went back home to the Philippines, hoping and expecting to bring back and share what I had learned in the United States. Unfortunately, my culture's high-power distance (that is, perceived inequality in a hierarchy between a less powerful individual and a more powerful individual [Hofstede, 2001]), traditionalism, and hierarchy did not allow me to fulfill my dream of applying what I had learned. For example, I was told by the Psychology Department chairperson in the Philippines not to teach the course any differently from how it had been taught during the past 20 years. The chairperson reprimanded me for incorporating what I had learned in the United States and wanted me to teach as if I had never gone to study at the doctoral level. Additionally, the economic and political crises in the Philippines could not offer me a starting point for a professional life. Even with good intentions, advanced educational degrees, and hard work, I was not able to afford myself a decent life in the Philippines. So I moved back to the United States, and I secured a counseling-center job in Illinois.

DESCRIPTION OF CRITICAL INCIDENT
THAT INCREASED AWARENESS
OF RACE PRIVILEGE

Having now lived in the United States for about 5½ years, my experiences with issues of diversity relative to race and socioeconomic status has increased. It is here that I have experienced what it means to be treated as different, as Asian, or as someone of color. When I think of this experience, it is definitely a mixed blessing, because although it is my experience that I am treated differently because of my color, it is also here that I experience being empowered to work, to teach, to do clinical work, and to be a psychologist. I am not only working and doing what I love best, I am also, at the same time, earning and giving my family and myself a chance of a better life. Back home in the Philippines, I could work as a psychologist and a professor until I died, and I still could not afford to buy myself a car, build a house, or educate my children. Here in the United States, with the occasional reminders that I am away from home, the opportunities make it a place to dream, to work, and to feel justified for working.

My most painful struggles with prejudice and discrimination have been precipitated by strangers, making me feel both hurt and unsafe. Most incidents have been based on reactions to my physical appearance as Filipino—that is, my having straight, black hair; small eyes; darker skin; and small build (at 5 feet 1 inch in height). For example, about six months ago, I was walking home when a car containing three young, White teenagers passed. They were repeatedly shouting, "Go away! You are not supposed to be here! You are not supposed to be here! Go away! You don't belong here!" I was hearing this in my head, all 20 minutes of my way home. I was so afraid they would come back and hurt me physically.

I was scared and pained, and I was thinking, if only they would give me a chance to talk, to speak, I would let them know why I am here and let them know how hard life is where I am from. I also wanted to explain myself and tell them how I have likened being Asian in the United States to being in the middle of two worlds, not quite belonging to either world, but being in the middle. I am never here nor there. It was difficult to leave my family, especially my ailing parents, and it was difficult to leave my friends, especially those who I learned so much from and who are so endeared to me like family. If only I could tell those teenagers that I am here now in hope of a better life. What I would hope for in such a conversation is that they would gain an understanding of the helplessness in my situation and the power and privilege in theirs. I also would hope they would see that I am not any different from their own grandparents,

parents, or ancestors who may have come here to the United States for economic opportunities and freedom.

On a different occasion, I was at an intersection waiting for the stoplight to change in my favor, when five White teenagers occupying the car beside me shouted at me and spoke to me in what seemed to be an imitation of the Chinese language.

When I tell friends and colleagues about instances such as these, I typically get responses of disbelief, an apology for the actions of the offenders, or remarks that ignore the pain and minimize the source. However, the more subtle discrimination I experience from colleagues, and the insensitive comments about socioeconomic status are still the most hurtful and the hardest to deal with.

With the aforementioned experiences of overt racial discrimination, I pretend not to hear, I pretend not to look, I pretend to be unaffected. I process these within myself, and then I try to forget. With colleagues, I wish to let them know what it means and feels like to be poor, what it means when deprivation is experienced over and over, and what they can do to be sensitive to these issues.

Although I no longer feel poor, working with clients who are poor and listening to colleagues' comments recycle these issues for me. At work, for instance, a colleague came back from vacation and mentioned how her back was aching. The colleague candidly commented on how she and her family slept in third-world beds, and drove third-world cars on third-world roads. I did not immediately realize how much this statement hurt me—not until this colleague apologized to me, knowing that I was born and grew up in a third-world country, the Philippines, and still consider it my home.

I also feel hurt when other people complain about what they are deprived of here, when I know and have experienced deprivation in other parts of the world. For example, a colleague talks about the amount of money her family spent buying a horse, and another talks about the amount of money she spent buying work suits. These are all comments about their reality and are not meant to be hurtful. I, however, cannot help but compare these amounts of money to the amount of money my parents need for medical care, and to the amount of money I need to send home.

In another instance, a colleague asked me what she could do for a client who had no place to stay. I immediately told her of the city's homeless shelter, where it was located and what it was like, and I asked if she knew whether the client had eaten or even had something *to* eat. My colleague admitted that she did not know this and had not thought to ask the client. My heart sank at the lack of awareness. It would not have taken much to ask these questions, especially if the client had already admitted financial strife.

On yet another occasion, I presented a client case to my colleagues. As I talked about the client's cultural context, family-of-origin issues, poverty, difficulty trusting another, and struggle being in college, my colleagues agreed about how resilient this client was and how therapy had benefited her. But then someone blurted out that, although this client might be helped in therapy, the client "would be killed anyway" when she went back to her neighborhood. I was appalled at the bias and the insensitivity. My colleague was clearly coming from her own fear and judgment about the culture. I was hurt when I heard this, because this culture and this neighborhood is what my client regards as home. I told myself, it is because of people's ignorance and statements like these that my client would never tell anyone, even a friend, where home is.

CONCLUSIONS AND LEARNINGS

What I am conveying is the same point that cultural scholars have reiterated: that it is important to be aware of one's own cultural background so one can be sensitive to and realize, understand, and accept the similarities and differences in culture (D. W. Sue & Sue, 2003; Brislin & Cushner, 1996; Gudykunst, 1994; Landis & Bhagat, 1996; Sue et al., 1998), and even to celebrate and appreciate these differences and their beauty.

We cannot end discrimination unless we realize privilege. In many instances, the help of those privileged individuals will be required to lessen the acts of discrimination experienced by those who are oppressed. It is a danger to ignore culture (Pedersen, 1994) and a danger to ignore the privileges we all have. We all are influenced by our culture, because we all grew up in a form of a family, a community, and a society. We all are still experiencing everyday events that shape us and that constantly hone our culture. As much as deprivations and disadvantages are part of our culture, so are our privilege and our histories. Intrapsychically and within culture groups, healing comes from an understanding of pain, and also an acknowledgment of privilege in other areas of life—understanding and acknowledgment that eventually will envelope the hurt. Personally, this meant that I recognize that I am privileged in other areas such as having attained an education, having the drive to pursue my dreams and the resilience that pulled me through, having the respect of friends and a wealth of friends. In essence, for the oppressed, movement comes from allowing the hurt and pained side to heal, and consequently feeling empowered by embracing the privileged and deprived aspects of the culture. Additionally, among groups and within the human race, healing also comes from the privileged people's acknowledgment of the status, power, and identity that dictate other people's lives. For instance, in my life, what I acknowledge as a catalyst to this understanding is having learned from a close friend that rich people can be good people, too. I then experienced and felt liberated from my anger when at least one person from the oppressive culture made a deliberate choice not to oppress. In essence, it is for the privileged to realize how they can advocate lessening oppression and share empowerment and privilege with others.

I have found counseling sessions—individual, group, or both—to be safe places for one to talk about hurts and deprivations, and about privilege. It is when we talk about the prevailing inequalities, the historical beginnings and status, and our cultural identities that we begin to feel safe to move beyond oppression and recognize what power we have in changing. It is when we acknowledge power that has been bestowed on us by our roles, the color of our skin, and the accident of our births and families that we extend ourselves and are able to understand somebody else's oppression. Then, we own our responsibility to end the oppression and advocate for equity, respect, and justice. The safe places to which we entrust these vulnerabilities and these movements are deep connections, such as friendships, families, and therapeutic relationships.

CASE SCENARIO APPLICATION

The counselor is from a poor and Filipino background, and the client is depressed, middle class, and Caucasian, with German heritage. The therapeutic relationship is good, and there is apparent connection. However, there is a stuckness in the process that is clearly due to differences that remain undiscussed. In the sessions, assumptions and expectations about each other's backgrounds are heightened and cause a lot of tension. Yet, to make things easy for the two of them, the client and counselor go along, pretending that these things are not there. The counselor decides to bring this up, and both talk about what they were used to and what their families' biases have been, of one from another culture and one from another socioeconomic status (SES). This discussion ultimately became the pivotal point in therapy (that is, when the client realized the blessings and privilege she had, and when she found her direction in terms of what she wanted to do in her life). It turned out that the client's deprivation of dreams (lack of direction and drive) was the counselor's privilege (having had to leave the Philippines to strive for a better life), and the counselor's financial deprivation helped the client see her own resources that she previously took for granted.

DISCUSSION QUESTIONS

1. What do you know about Filipino and German cultures?
2. If you were the counselor in the case scenario, what would you have done to facilitate talking about the differences that mattered in therapy?
3. When and how do you know that race, SES, and other forms of diversity are at play in the counseling relationship, such as the one in the case scenario?
4. What would it be like if the situation were different—the counselor is middle class and Caucasian with German heritage, and the client is poor and Filipino?
5. How are we oppressed to be poor? To be rich? To be White? To be of color?
6. What are the privileges, deprivations, and assumptions or expectations when one is poor? Rich? Of color? White?
7. When I am prejudiced and give hurtful remarks to another, do I hurt myself too? When I am biased, how do I lose a part of my humanity?

8. Who are the people in our lives who have opened our eyes to oppression? Who are those who have enabled us to look at our prejudices and act with more knowledge and empathy? Who are the people in our lives who have taught us to react otherwise, and who expose us more to our humanity?

9. Do we have friends we care for who are of color? Who are Asian? Latino? African American? Poor? Rich? How do we talk about these differences?

10. How do you think it is to live constantly proving oneself, earning respect and understanding, because one is poor and of color?

REFERENCES

Brislin, R. W., & Cushner, K. (1996). *Intercultural interaction. A practical guide* (2nd ed.). Thousand Oaks, CA: Sage.

Gudykunst, W. B. (1994). *Bridging differences: Effective intergroup communication* (2nd ed.). Thousand Oaks, CA: Sage.

Hofstede, G. (2001). *Culture's consequences* (2nd ed.). Thousand Oaks, CA: Sage Publications.

Landis, D., & Bhagat, R. S. (Eds.). (1996). *Handbook of intercultural training* (2nd ed.). Thousand Oaks, CA: Sage Publications.

Pedersen, P. (1994). *A handbook for developing multicultural awareness.* American Counseling Association, VA.

Philippine Statistical Yearbook, 2000. Annual per capita poverty thresholds and incidences of population by region. National Statistics Coordination Board.

Pollard, K. M., & O'Hare, W. P. (1999). America's racial and ethnic minorities. *Population Bulletin, 54*(3), 1–48.

Sue, D. W. (2001). Multidimensional facets of cultural competence. *The Counseling Psychologist, 29*(6), 790–821.

Sue, D. W., Carter, R., Casas, J., Fouad, N., Ivey, A., Jensen, M., et al. (1998). *Multicultural competencies: Individual and organizational development.* Beverly Hills, CA: Sage.

Sue, D. W., & Sue, D. (2003). *Counseling the culturally diverse. Theory and practice.* New York: John Wiley & Sons.

6

Seeing Through Another Lens

KAYING LO

I am a Hmong woman born in Thailand and raised in the United States. My family came to America as refugees when I was three years old. I am bilingual in Hmong and English. I have a master's degree in marriage and family therapy and practice in a nonprofit mental health organization. It is my hope to continue my education after a few more years of doing therapy. Ultimately, I would like to open a private practice and teach. As a woman of color and the daughter of refugee Hmong parents, I am continuously balancing the demands of my culture with mainstream expectations.

UNDERSTANDING AND EXPERIENCING PRIVILEGE: CRITICAL INCIDENTS

I was invited to a birthday party for a close acquaintance of a friend, Susan. (Pseudonyms have been used to protect the privacy of all individuals involved.) When I agreed to attend, my assumption was that this would be a typical college party with loud music, drinking, smoking, and socializing. However, when I arrived with my partner, I was shocked to find that almost everyone had a disability and was in a wheelchair. The only people without physical disabilities at this party were Susan, my partner, and me. Due to my limited experiences with people with disabilities, it had never occurred to me that they could hold the same type of parties as everyone else.

When my partner and I first entered the party, I felt awkward in trying to maneuver through all the people in wheelchairs to find a place to sit. As Susan introduced us to everyone, I became consciously aware that I had inappropriate ideas about what was acceptable behavior for interacting with people who have disabilities. I kept reminding myself not to stare or say anything that might be perceived as offensive regarding individuals with disabilities and noticeable physical differences. My fixation with acting appropriately may have come across as rude because I did not make much eye contact with the people to whom I was being introduced.

Tim, a man who was a quadriplegic, was sitting next to me. He called a friend over to help him light a cigarette and hold it in his mouth. Their interaction was natural, but I found I felt protective of Tim. Inside, I ignorantly thought *your body is under physical strain already, and smoking will only make it harder.* This was the same thought I had when everyone started drinking.

It was difficult for me to view the people at the party as physically capable or healthy because of their disabilities. I became aware that I felt overly protective of them. For example, when Tammy wanted to go to the bathroom and had to manipulate her wheelchair down a small, cluttered hallway, I was worried that she might have a hard time. I had a compelling desire to get up and help her. When I saw that she creatively maneuvered her way to the bathroom, I felt foolish for not having enough faith in her capabilities to deal with such a minuscule task, a task that she undoubtedly dealt with daily.

During the course of the evening, everyone had consumed large quantities of alcohol, and Tom wanted to impress all of us. He gracefully leaped out of his wheelchair to the center of the room, where he did a handstand. His performance was astonishing, and it shocked me. Despite his flawless efforts, I kept thinking that maybe someone should have assisted him in case he could not do it. I am ashamed to say this thought stemmed from my foolish assumption that a person with disabilities is completely dependent and helpless without his or her wheelchair.

Strauss and Quinn stated that some specific schemas (for example, "how women should act," "how people with mental retardation should be treated," "what behavior is appropriate in the workplace") affect what to notice and how to act. These schemata provide the broad themes around which a person's own actions are organized and the actions of others are judged (as cited in Pengra, 2000). Seeing others through these schemata then guides the analyses of and responses to situations and other people. For example, a schema about certain physical characteristics identifies some people as less valued. Therefore, it is probable that those characteristics will be noticed. In my ignorance, I failed to recognize at the party that the wheelchair is only a tool, and it does not define the person who uses it. Just like everyone else, people with disabilities are whole individuals, with or without their wheelchairs.

At one point during the evening of the party, I had a conversation with Tara, who informed me of her personal struggles with being labeled "disabled." She stated that many people do not treat her as a valued individual, instead seeming to focus only on her disability. In Tara's process of coming to understand her position as a woman with a disability, she told me that she has acknowledged and coped with stereotypes, not allowing society's misconceptions to affect her self-esteem and personal worth. One of Tara's fears was being a burden to others simply because she uses a wheelchair. Like most people, she also expressed wanting to be loved, accepted, and valued.

After my conversation with Tara, I gained a new understanding of how issues of privilege and oppression are comparable for people with disabilities and people of color. Yet, I also understand how these issues are not the same, and how they should not be compared. In addition, I gained an understanding of how my dominant culture status (able-bodied) automatically puts me in the category of privileged. In my role as a member of the privileged group, I inadvertently participated in stereotypical thinking and behavior. My experience at this party shows me that although I might be sensitive to discriminatory or oppressive issues that affect me as a woman of color, I am often unaware of similar issues that plague others.

In another situation in which I recognize my privilege, I was invited to a holiday dinner with many of the same individuals who attended the aforementioned party. When we arrived at the restaurant, Todd, the coordinator of the event, went to inform the host about the number of people in our party. The host was conversing with Todd about accommodations when I walked over to inquire about the waiting time. Immediately after I walked over, the host shifted his attention and questions from Todd, who was in a wheelchair, to me. The host attempted to set up arrangements with me, overlooking Todd, even though he was in front of me and had been dealing with the situation. Shortly after I noticed this, I indicated that I was only a guest and that Todd could answer his questions more accurately.

In my life, I have experienced both privilege and oppression. The holiday dinner scenario put me in a position of privilege in relation to Todd. The host presumed that I had knowledge and authority over our dinner plans because I did not have a visible disability. I did not earn the position of privilege; rather, it was offered to me regardless of its validity. In my interactions involving people with disabilities, I have experienced unearned power and advantage, and I have seen what being in a privileged position is like. I did not have to demand or work for respect; rather, it was simply given to me because I did not have a physical disability.

In contrasting situations, my partner and I have gone to restaurants where he was given respect and authority because he is a Caucasian male and I am a woman of color. These discriminatory acts, whether conscious or unconscious, send messages of incompetence, dishonor, and irresponsibility regardless of merit and provoke in me feelings of anger and discouragement. I imagine that Todd, Tara, and others experience similar emotions when they are overlooked, disregarded, or patronized.

CONCLUSIONS AND LEARNINGS

To understand the consequences of labeling, in comparing interracial relationships to those between able-bodied people and those with disabilities, Liachowitz (1988) discussed Gordon Allport's classic study of prejudice. Several writers have used the concept of "stigma" to explain responses, both to racial and physical differences. There are clear similarities between biased responses to people with disabilities and to people of color. First, most people who diverge from either racial or physical norms share the problem of evoking unpredictable, but unusually negative, responses from the majority populations. Second, whether based on biological ascription or social attribution, minority groups often face a common personal and political dilemma. Third, members of both groups are often forced to meet their need for belonging, and their need for personal and political recognition, by establishing or joining groups composed "of their own kind." Many nonmainstream members want the same treatment afforded those who meet culturally accepted norms; but they think they may need, and they often construct their lives, to rely on the extraordinary treatment that society gives to an abnormal group.

Upon reflection, I realize that the party scenario helped me to begin my process of examining how I stereotype others because I associate myself with being able-bodied. The restaurant scenario increased my sensitivity in recognizing my own privilege. My recognition of how Todd was treated by the restaurant host was largely the result of my own experiences of being treated in a similar manner.

Although I am somewhat embarrassed and angered by these experiences, I am also very grateful for them. These experiences gave me the opportunity to gain insight into myself and refute my assumptions about the potential of people with disabilities. However, I did come to realize that one of my initial assumptions was true: It was indeed a typical college party, complete with loud music, drinking, smoking, and socializing.

DISCUSSION QUESTIONS

1. What physical characteristics and/or social conditions influence the distribution of privilege in America?

2. How is individual privilege defined? What does it mean to have privilege?

3. Can someone gain or lose privilege in our society?

4. Can you list at least one situation in which you were automatically given privilege over someone else? Were you aware of your privileged status? If so, did you address the situation?

5. What can one do to become more aware or sensitive to the experiences of how privilege affects different groups of people?

6. You are at the grocery checkout lane and you witness a situation in which a non-English speaking person is struggling to find the appropriate amount for payment. The cashier repeats this person's total a few times as the person continues to count out dollar bills. The line is moderately busy, and you are next. You are unable to speak the same language as the non-English-speaking person. Would you interfere with this situation? If so, what would you say? What issues of privilege are happening here?

REFERENCES

Liachowitz, C. (1988). *Disability as a social construct*. Philadelphia: University of Pennsylvania Press.

Pengra, L. M. (2000). *Your values, my values*. Baltimore, MD: Paul H. Brooks Publishing Co., Inc.

7

Dirty Secrets
and Unholy Unions

Disability-Based Oppression and Privilege

PAUL E. PRIESTER

UNDERSTANDING
AND EXPERIENCING PRIVILEGE

I am a 40-year-old, European American, nonphysically disabled, heterosexual male. My awareness of privilege associated with being nondisabled developed through a friendship with Eric. I met Eric, a fellow counselor, when I was working at a community-based substance-abuse treatment center. Eric has a spinal cord injury as a result of a tractor accident when he was a child. Due to this injury, Eric uses a wheelchair for transportation. I had, up to the point at which I met Eric, viewed such individuals as "wheelchair bound"; however, Eric educated me that this view itself is offensive and pejorative. He views his wheelchair as a source of freedom and mobility, not as a deficit. For example, he says that most people are highly dependent on their automobiles for transportation, yet we do not refer to them as "automobile bound."

Before my discussions with Eric, I had never really analyzed the language our society uses to describe individuals with disabilities. Eric offered me some of his favorite examples—the terms *invalid* or *cripple*—to demonstrate the negative connotations imbedded in our language. These phrases suggest that an individual who uses a wheelchair for transportation purposes is somehow an invalid person, or deformed (as *cripple* would suggest). Later in my rehabilitation counseling education, I would learn that these are excellent examples of the ways in which our society participates in the process of the "deification of normality" (DeLoach & Greer, 1981). That is, a standard is established based on nondisabled norms, and then any individual who does not "rise" to that standard is seen as deficient, incapable, pathetic, and in need of assistance.

INCREASED AWARENESS OF PRIVILEGE

As I became closer friends with Eric, we began to socialize together outside of work. As a former restaurant worker, I have strong preferences about my choice of restaurants, which resulted in a pattern in our dining. Typically, I would suggest a restaurant, and then Eric would ask, "Is it accessible?" I would ponder the question for awhile and then say, "Yes." When we arrived at the restaurant, we would find obstacles, such as three steps leading to the front door. While there were only three steps, these steps rendered the establishment off limits to a person in a wheelchair. At first, I did not understand Eric's anger and refusal to eat at any of these businesses—until he expressed the sentiment that, in his view, having those three steps was equivalent to having a sign hanging outside that said, "African Americans are not allowed to eat here." Eric felt that he was being excluded in a similar way.

Accessibility issues also affected Eric in his role as a talented billiards player, successful in professional tournaments. Eric often participated in tournaments that were not wheelchair accessible. The accommodation for accessibility that these businesses offered was having two or three bulky bouncers lift and carry Eric up the stairs. Eric found this "accommodation" to be offensive in that it maintains the myth of helplessness and perpetuates dependence on others for participation in daily activities. By spending time with Eric, I have become more aware of how I benefit from the privilege bestowed upon me as a man without a physical disability.

One way in which I personally struggle with my awareness of privilege is that I accept the benefits without questioning the need for change. Each time I enter a restaurant with three stairs before the front door, I am made aware that I am entering a space that is explicitly excluding my friend Eric. This is an uncomfortable awareness, yet I do nothing to challenge the restaurant owner to make changes. The analogy that comes closest to portraying the way I feel is when someone tells me a very salacious and inappropriately intimate piece of information about a third person. Afterward, each time I am in the presence of that third person, I am keenly aware of the information and highly uncomfortable that it was disclosed to me—it is the "dirty secret." My privileged access to a location actively denied to individuals with disabilities is my "dirty secret."

I will admit that, at this point, I do not have the energy or enough sense of social justice to demand change in the physical environment to make it accessible to individuals with disabilities. I am presently at a stage at which I continue to learn to challenge my own internal attitudinal barriers. For example, I realize that it is OK for me to feel grateful for my own physical health, but not to do so by thinking, "It could be worse, I could be in a wheelchair." To do this is to prop up my sense of self-worth by standing on the backs of individuals with disabilities. For an empirical example of this same process, see Fein and Spencer (1997). I sometimes feel overwhelmed with knowing that I am at a stage at which my energies are spent changing just my own privileged mindset when there is often a greater need for intervention in the surrounding physical world.

Another incident that brought my relative privilege to awareness was when Eric and his fiancée who were childhood sweethearts decided to get married. They were both Roman Catholics and began the process of arranging for a wedding within the Church. The priest who was guiding them through this process inquired of Eric specifics relating to his spinal cord injury (that is, at what vertebrae level the trauma had occurred). Later, when they met to complete paperwork, the priest informed them that he was not going to allow the marriage process to proceed within the Church. He went on to explain that the sole purpose of marriage was for procreation, and that he had contacted medical professionals and determined that whether Eric would be able to sire offspring was uncertain, given his spinal-cord injury. This pronouncement caused a fury of outrage from Eric, his fiancé, and their families, but the priest refused to reconsider. They were forced to marry "outside of the Church," which is highly stigmatizing to traditional Roman Catholics.

I had spent considerable time pondering the heterosexual privilege that I have to marry the person of my choice. I think often about how it would be to be gay or lesbian and have this right denied by our society. But I had never thought that this privilege to marry the person of my choice could also be denied to Catholic individuals with disabilities. Many heterosexual and nondisabled individuals take this privilege for granted. Indeed, one of the notions that we hold sacrosanct is that we are free to choose whom we will marry. This incident brought to my attention the injustice that exists in our society regarding this privilege.

CONCLUSIONS AND LESSONS UNLEARNED

Much noise has been made by counseling educators to include issues of disability in multicultural counseling training. A recent content analysis estimated that only 28 percent of multicultural counseling course syllabi explicitly address disability as a content area (Priester, 2001). If this consciousness raising is not occurring in the majority of formal multicultural classes, the counseling trainee is compelled to explore these issues independently.

So how can individuals learn about these issues on their own? My suggestion is to explore and challenge your internalized negative stereotypes and then intentionally cultivate personal relationships with individuals with disabilities. It is my opinion that only in the context of an ongoing personal relationship can we learn about how the world is for other people. Similarly, it has been only through my personal, intimate relationships with people of color that I have also come to an awareness of the extent and pervasiveness of racism in our society. Through my relationship with Eric, my eyes were opened to the reality that our society is set up to specifically exclude and devalue individuals with disabilities. The flipside of this awareness is that the world in which I live has specifically been arranged so that I, as a nondisabled individual, am included, invited, and valued at the expense of individuals who are different from me.

I have learned this reality in professional areas of my life, as well. When I first discovered that I was going to be working as a therapist for adolescent sex offenders with developmental disabilities, I had considerable trepidation. The "sex offender" label is not what concerned me because I had been working with similar adolescent clients. Rather, the "developmental disability" label is what caused me to question the job assignment. I thought that it would be terribly boring to do clinical work with individuals with mild mental retardation. My assumption was that a high level of intellect in my clients was required to do effective psychotherapy, and that such a process with adolescents with mild retardation would be tedious and unrewarding. In this situation, I was basing the value that I held of an individual upon his or her relative intelligence.

Our society makes this same value judgment in many subtle and explicit ways. An example of an explicit devaluing of an individual is the use of in-vitro amniocentesis tests. Amniocentesis is a procedure in which embryonic fluid is assessed for evidence of chromosomal disorders. The results of this test can suggest whether or not a fetus is likely to have Down syndrome. When my wife was pregnant with our first child, her physician offered this test to us. The physician's suggestion was that if the fetus has Down syndrome, we may want to reconsider having the baby and chose to abort the pregnancy. Hypothetically, for each one of us, in the absence of results suggesting the presence of Down syndrome, the decision was made that fetal development was allowed to proceed and we were allowed to grow and live. This is a concrete, explicit example of nondisability privilege.

I was not even aware that I harbored a similar, albeit subtler, form of the same oppressive attitudes related to relative worth based on intellectual ability until after I developed relationships with these aforementioned clients with mild mental retardation. These individuals soon became my favorite group with which to work. I got past my personal barriers and realized these were loving, wonderful kids who deserved respect, and who had much to offer in a relationship. In that clinical situation, I believe that I changed more than my clients as I "unlearned" the lessons I had been taught in our society about individuals with developmental disabilities. For me, this process of unlearning starts with my identification of, and then challenging, the negative stereotypes that I hold of individuals with disabilities. If I am lucky, the unlearning process can continue in a personal relationship with an individual who happens to have a disability.

The unlearning process will continue indefinitely as I come to awareness of new ways in which I benefit from unearned privilege. My journey started with awareness of White privilege. Then, I discovered the privilege from which I benefit by not having a physical disability. I have also learned about the subtle ways in which I oppress individuals with developmental disabilities by devaluing them based on their intellectual abilities. And then when I had children, I discovered subtle ways in which I benefit from gender-based privilege (that is, not "hearing" the baby crying because I know my wife will take care of the problem, or similarly not "smelling" the dirty diaper). Where will my unlearning process take me next? I am starting to explore ways in which I depersonalize individuals based on their social class. For example, when a busboy clears my table at a restaurant, am I appreciating this individual as a complete human being with a family and dreams? Or am I viewing him in a role: as a servant?

I experienced this class-based invisibility once in my life. During graduate school, I worked as a waiter to support my family and my studies—at one point at an upscale, private dining club. One night, I worked at a private reception there. I was walking through a room when a wealthy, middle-aged woman in full gown started gesturing at me. As I approached her, she pointed to dirty cocktail glasses on a nearby table and loudly overenunciated, *"Por favor"* (indicating that she would like me to clear the glasses). I should note that at this dining club

I was the only White waiter. My colleagues were all Latino or Filipino. My ethnic background is Irish and German. In this situation, I was invisible to her. She did not see me as an individual, but in a role, as a servant. Because she was used to interacting with Latino servants, she had responded in her stereotypic manner. In the same way, I fail to see the woman checking out my groceries or the janitor in my building. An important component of class-based privilege is having the power to decide who is visible and who is playing a depersonalized role. For my unlearning process to continue, I need to be open to the process, challenge myself, and seek out relationships with individuals who differ from me.

DISCUSSION QUESTIONS

1. You or your partner is pregnant. The doctor tells you the results of your amniocentesis test. Your baby will have Down syndrome. What do you do? If you choose to terminate the pregnancy, why? What does this say about the relative value that is placed on infants based on their intelligence potential? Is this an example of the consequences of deifying normalcy?

2. You are entering a nightclub and see a sign posted that says, "No African Americans Allowed in This Establishment." What do you do?

3. You are entering a nightclub with three high steps outside the door. What do you do? Discuss the similarities and differences in your response to questions 2 and 3.

4. In what ways are you "broken"? Is it OK to be "broken"?

5. How would you feel if your faith community did not allow you to get married to the person that you love? Does this disability-based oppression remind you of any other characteristics that faith communities or states might use to deny someone the ability to marry the person they love? Do you think gays or lesbians should be allowed to marry? What about individuals with mental retardation? How about people with inheritable conditions?

6. Can you think of any ways in which you feel good about yourself by standing on the backs of persons with disabilities?

REFERENCES

DeLoach, C., & Greer, B. G. (1981). *Adjustment to severe physical disability.* New York: McGraw-Hill.

Fein, S., & Spencer, S. J. (1997). Prejudice as self-image maintenance: Affirming the self through derogating others. *Journal of Personality and Social Psychology, 73,* 31–44.

Priester, P. E. (2001, August). An overview of current cross-cultural counseling training practices. In P. E. Priester (Chair). Current practices and innovative approaches to multicultural counseling training. Symposium conducted at American Psychological Association, San Francisco, CA.

8

Increasing Awareness of Heterosexism and Homophobia

A Personal and Professional Exploration

ALLISON L. CASHWELL

CRITICAL INCIDENTS THAT INCREASED AWARENESS OF PRIVILEGE

With the exception of my gender, I typify the dominant culture of the United States. I am an English, Irish, Scottish American female, pale white with freckles and red hair. Additionally, I am (relatively) young, Christian, able-bodied, of middle-class socioeconomic status (or at least I was before I went to graduate school!), and, most importantly in this context, heterosexual.

While attending graduate school, I became friends with Linda, a European American, lesbian classmate, my first such close relationship with a woman with a different sexual orientation from my own. As our relationship progressed, I also came to know her partner, Polly, and their young son.

In November, 1998, the city in which we lived would vote on Human Rights Ordinance Number 22, which, if passed, would legally prohibit discrimination against citizens based on their sexual orientation. While the original Human Rights Ordinance, including sexual orientation as a basis for discrimination, had been unanimously approved by the City Council on March 3, 1998, constituents of our city successfully petitioned to separate sexual orientation from other forms of discrimination (for example, race, color, creed, gender). Thus, failure to pass Ordinance 22 would make it possible for citizens to continue to legally discriminate against citizens on the basis of their sexual orientation. Hoping to educate others about this important vote, Polly and I decided we would distribute literature door-to-door, encouraging the citizens of our city to vote to approve Human Rights Ordinance Number 22.

It was during this time that Matthew Shepard, a gay, European American male, was brutally beaten and murdered in Wyoming by two males because of his sexual orientation. He died on October 12, 1998. While attending a memorial ceremony that night surrounded by my friends, allies, and members of the gay, lesbian, bisexual, and transgendered (GLBT) community, I heard sadness, outrage, disbelief, and fear expressed at the fact that something this horrible could happen in the late twentieth century. I will never forget that night, listening to the speeches of faculty, staff, and students, marching *en masse* through town following the memorial service. I was crying, and, for the first time in my life, feeling afraid for the lives my friends, Linda and Polly, and for the lives of GLBT Americans everywhere.

After this experience, Polly and I were strengthened in our resolve to convince voters to pass Ordinance 22. We spoke to many, left literature for others, made phone calls, and knocked on many doors. Sadly, despite the public awareness of homophobia and the highly publicized murder of Matthew Shepard, Ordinance 22 did not pass. Linda and Polly told me they feared for their safety now more than ever before and intended to move away from our city when Linda completed her studies. And that is just what they did.

HOMOPHOBIA

Merriam Webster's Collegiate Dictionary (1996) defines *homophobia* as an "irrational fear of, aversion to, or discrimination against homosexuality or homosexuals" (p. 556). Because GLBT individuals face discrimination in the United States, many are forced to decide whether they will "come out" or not "pass" as heterosexual. Fonken (1996) states that "the process of coming out [is] rarely a one time event" (p. 19). Deciding whether to not pass as heterosexual or to come out could be viewed as the primary issue members of the GLBT co-culture face. Decisions about who to come out to and on what occasions was a constant topic with my lesbian friends and their gay male friends. Linda was out to her peers at school; however, Polly, although she desperately wanted to, had not come out at work, for fear that she would (and could, legally) be fired if she revealed her sexual orientation.

HETEROSEXISM

The concept of *heterosexism* is not defined in *Merriam Webster's Collegiate Dictionary*. Neisen (1990) defines heterosexism as "the continued promotion by the major institutions of society of a heterosexual lifestyle while simultaneously subordinating any other lifestyle" (p. 25). This idea of heterosexual privilege is subtle, and less evident than overt homophobia, to many heterosexuals. Before befriending Linda and Polly, I myself was unaware of the privileges afforded me in this society because I am "straight." When I questioned them about how to increase awareness of heterosexism in our culture, Linda and Polly (and other members of the GLBT community) suggested two cognitive-behavioral changes: (1) use inclusive language—for example, *partner* in lieu of *wife/hus-*

band or *boyfriend/girlfriend,* and (2) do not assume that all new people are straight. I took these suggestions to heart and began to use them, personally as well as professionally.

PROFESSIONAL CONTEXT

I am a Licensed Professional Counselor, a Certified Addictions Counselor, and an Approved Domestic Violence Offender Treatment Provider for the state of Colorado. Since 1998, I have worked predominantly with nonvoluntary clientele, people who are adjudicated through some form of public institution (for example, university disciplinary boards, city and county courts, drugs courts, social services) and are subsequently mandated to attend various types of counseling for educational purposes. The majority of my clients view these requirements not as education but rather as punishment.

Homophobia and heterosexism are two issues I am required by law to address in my work with male, court-ordered, domestic-violence offenders. In working with mostly White, able-bodied, heterosexual offenders, I am met with constant resistance when I present these issues in counseling. To decrease my frustration and increase empathy for my clients, it is helpful for me to recall my own journey toward awareness of heterosexism. Additionally, I use the Key model, created by Scott and Robinson (2001). Based on Helms' (1990) White Racial Identity Development model, the Key model describes five types of males who typify the dominant culture. Type I, Noncontact type, operates on a "fairness principle," which implies that White men want to continue the status quo and are not aware of the need for legal steps to correct discrimination in its myriad forms. Type II, Claustrophobic type, tends to blame members of nondominant cultures (for example, women, people of color, homosexuals) for preventing them from realizing "the American dream." Type III, Conscious Identity type, experiences dissonance between existing belief systems and reality. The Empirical type, Type IV, "recognizes that his privileged existence—earned through no effort of his own—is at the expense of" others who do not belong to the dominant culture (p. 420). Type V, the Optimal type, functions with an awareness of privilege and discrimination, and understands "that survival is assured not by oppressing others but by living peacefully and harmoniously with self and others" (p. 420).

Most of my clients fit squarely into Types I and II of this model. To encourage them to move toward the Conscious Identity type (and beyond) regarding the issues of homophobia and heterosexism, I am reminded of my friends' suggestions for increasing awareness around these issues. I am vigilant in my use of the words "partner" and "significant other" in describing relationships with intimates, and I tell all my court ordered clientele the story of my journey to increased awareness of heterosexism and homophobia vis-à-vis Linda, Polly, and Matthew Shepard.

CONCLUSION

It is my hope that readers of this chapter will come to appreciate personal and professional opportunities and challenges to increasing awareness of heterosexism and homophobia in our society. Using tools such as inclusive language, self-disclosure of personal experiences, identity development models, unconditional positive regard, education around preconceptions and stereotypes, and, most importantly, client empathy, those of us in the helping professions can influence the lives of many who might otherwise never have the opportunity to expand their understanding and acceptance of members of the GLBT community and other nondominant cultures of the United States of America.

DISCUSSION QUESTIONS

1. How do your personal experiences of privilege influence your work in the helping professions?

2. If you typify the dominant culture, discuss which type within the Key model best suits your awareness at this time. If you are a member of a nondominant co-culture, describe your experience of coexisting with the dominant culture of the United States.

3. How does your personal philosophy or theoretical orientation affect your clients' intercultural communication, understanding, and acceptance?

4. Make a list of tools you can use to increase your clients' awareness of heterosexism and homophobia.

5. Identify any critical incidents in your life that led to the increased awareness of privilege in your culture.

6. Discuss how privilege oftentimes unintentionally excludes members of nondominant cultures, and describe techniques those in the helping professions can use to increase awareness of privilege in clients and coworkers.

7. How does the use of inclusive language (for example, *partner* instead of *spouse* or *boyfriend/girlfriend*) affect your communication in the helping professions? Do you strive to use such language?

CASE SCENARIO

You are a counselor performing group therapy with heterosexual male, court-ordered, domestic-violence offenders. A client reveals to you during his initial interview that, although he offended against a female, he has recently discovered that he is gay. You explain to him that groups are gender and sexual-orientation specific, and that you must refer him to another agency because your agency does not have any gay male groups going at this time. Your client insists that he be allowed to attend the straight male group. Do you allow him to join the group? Why or why not?

REFERENCES

Fonken, L. E. (1996). *A phenomenological study of lesbian faculty experience in institutions of higher education.* Unpublished doctoral dissertation, Colorado State University, Fort Collins, CO.

Helms, J. E. (1990). *Black and white racial identity theory.* Westport, CT: Praeger Press.

Merriam Webster's collegiate dictionary (10th ed.). (1996). Springfield, MA: Merriam-Webster.

Neisen, J. H. (1990). Heterosexism: Redefining homophobia for the 1990's. *Journal of Gay and Lesbian Psychotherapy 1*(3), 21–25.

Scott, D. A., & Robinson, T. L. (2001). White male identity development: The Key model. *Journal of Counseling and Development 79*(3), 415–421.

9

Reflections on Heterosexual Privilege

S. CHERICE SOMMER, SUZANNE M. WEATHERMAN, AND DEBORAH L. COX

Heterosexual privilege is accompanied by an assumption of normalcy such that individuals do not realize they have it unless they give it up, either because they can no longer live the lie that they are heterosexual when they are not, or that they decide to become an advocate against heterosexism. People with heterosexual privilege are not presumed to have a sexual identity; they are simply considered normal. People without heterosexual privilege are reduced to only their sexual orientation and all the false stereotypes that go with it (Allen, 1995).

This discussion highlights the personal experiences of two White, lesbian counselors in training and their contemplations of heterosexism and privilege as graduate students in a counselor education program. They reflect upon themselves as both privileged and silenced in relation to their student peers and their community at large. The discussion also incorporates the thoughts of one counselor educator who tells about her own relationship to the issue of heterosexism.

CHERICE: FIRST AUTHOR

I am a European American woman, living in a conservative, Christian, predominantly White, Midwestern environment as a lesbian, and as a partner to an African American woman. When we are together we often experience heterosexist prejudice, while my partner also experiences racism. Separately, we more often experience prejudice through others' unknowing comments and behaviors associated with the assumption of heterosexuality. Assumptions enforce oppression.

CHERICE: "COUNSELOR IN TRAINING"

In one of my classes, a professor related a story of a female client who came to him seeking help. Included in the story was her sexual orientation as a lesbian. She warned the professor throughout the course of therapy never to try to change her in this regard—she was happy with this part of herself, and it was none of his business. Some years later, the client sent a letter to the professor, thanking him for his help. As a final statement, the professor laughed and told the class that the client ended up marrying a man and having children, despite her many warnings to him to steer clear of her sexuality. The class laughed along with him.

After I presented a paper, for a different class, on counseling with gay, lesbian, bi-sexual, and transgender clients, the professor acknowledged the information as both correct and valuable for other students to know. His final statement to the class was that he had never counseled anyone in a situation in which sexual orientation or gender identification was the main issue—and that although it was good to keep these issues in mind, he warned us against putting too much emphasis on the subjects once we were practicing in the field.

After "coming out" in one other class, I was taken aside by a woman who told me she was also a lesbian, but she felt it more appropriate to assess a situation more carefully and consider whether to come out was really important or necessary. She remained silent on the subject throughout the semester and never addressed me on a personal level again.

I was fortunate in yet another class of seven students to be one of two "out" lesbians. On numerous occasions, discussions would turn to our experiences, thoughts, and feelings as lesbian women on various subjects. Once the conversation became "too gay," discomfort and disconnection showed on the faces of other students. I always felt as if we were pushing the envelope of acceptance, overstepping our boundaries when this happened. A silence would come over the group, and eventually someone would change the subject.

CHERICE: REFLECTIONS

As I contemplate the profound issue of heterosexism, my mind wanders to the numerous moments as a graduate student when I felt my emotions range from uncomfortable to angry. I knew I would face challenges, but I never realized they would be ones of such a personal nature. I have felt the very essence of who I am becoming both drawn under a magnifying glass and shoved under the bed . . . people quietly resisting my experience, my reality; people silently wishing I were not quite so honest about myself. Although I am given verbal permission to express myself and to feel accepted by my classmates and professors, I rarely feel comfortable. I am being encouraged on one hand to speak and reveal myself, and then silenced and pushed back into the sameness of the crowd on the other hand. I am acknowledged, but not visible. I am tolerated and accepted, but not nurtured and encouraged.

Alone, each of these experiences seems small and meaningless. No one realized the impact of her or his statements. The threads of heterosexism seemed almost invisible at the time. And yet I vividly recall each incident, and more . . . far too many stories to tell.

Many times, I question my experiences. Is that how it really happened?
A constant questioning, evaluating, and sifting of my life story.
The push to identify and fit in with my dominant culture counterparts—
subtle yet overwhelming.

My words represent many other stories, stories that will never be heard, or possibly never even expressed. In this respect, I am validated in my frustration and know that to share such pain is meaningful. If I am not the only one, my voice surely does count. But what if I were the only one? Would it still count? As counselors, doesn't each story we hear become a vehicle by which to connect to individual experiences?

SUZANNE: "I AM"

Because it was expected, I grew up heterosexual in a heterosexual world. I had boyfriends at the expense of my relationship with my girlfriends. I had boyfriends at the expense of my relationship with my sister and my parents. I had boyfriends at the expense of my relationship with my community. I had boyfriends at the expense of my relationship with myself. I was thankful that I was pretty enough to be attractive to the boys because having a boyfriend added interest and value to my identity and allowed me to be accepted as a proper young girl in the 50s and 60s.

It is well established that in this country, as we grow up, the idea of heterosexual, romantic love is promoted and advocated through most experience: fairy tales, religious myths, books, television, movies, advertising, news broadcasts, magazines, music, theatre. Most of us learn from our families, our churches, our schools, our legal systems, our government, and our peers the unpleasant and sometimes intolerable consequences of being different from the heterosexual ideal.

As a young girl, I learned that if I didn't get married and have children, I would not be fulfilled as a woman. I was taught the conflicted message that I must be sexy but also virginal to "catch" a man. My parents stressed the importance of getting an education and even a profession, but their implication was to do these things before I ultimately settled down, got married, and had children.

SUZANNE: "COUNSELOR IN TRAINING"

Toward the end of my master's degree program in counseling, I read Adrienne Rich's (1982) *Compulsory Heterosexuality and Lesbian Experience*. I became interested in Rich's theory that the social requirement to be heterosexual keeps all women dependent on men by denying them the choice to explore and determine the meaning and place of sexuality in their lives. This theory informed my own research on a relatively new construct called heterosexism. After getting my degree, I wondered why I had not heard of heterosexism until I was 48 years old—a full 18 years after I identified as lesbian.

SUZANNE: NAMING THE PRACTICE

"Until we name the practice, give conceptual definition and form to it, illustrate its life over time and in space, those who are its most obvious victims will also not be able to name it or define their experience" (Barry, 1979, p. 100). Heterosexism is usually defined in ways that imply only lesbian, gay, bisexual, transgender, and queer (LGBTQ) individuals experience its negative effects (Fassinger, 1991; MacGillivray, 2000; Neisen, 1990; and Stewart, 1999). My experience of heterosexism compels me to use a much broader and far more inclusive definition: the ideological system that denies, denigrates, and stigmatizes any nonheterosexual form of behavior, identity, relationship, or community (Herek, 1990).

As a result of heterosexism (using this broader definition of it), all relationships except those based on sex between a man and woman, not just LGBTQ relationships, are valued less and often stigmatized by society. Such stigmatization undermines an individual's relationship with anyone and anything other than a romantically based relationship with a person of the other gender. This denigration includes relationships with our friends and acquaintances, with our parents and siblings, with our children, with our higher power(s) of choice, with the earth, and with ourselves.

SUZANNE: REVISITED

I now consider my role models to be brilliant radical feminists such as Adrienne Rich, bell hooks, Mary Daly, Carter Heyward, and Sarah Lucia Hoagland. These women profoundly suggest that the heterosexual worldview be set aside and that time be taken to consider a view that is not based on limiting, dualistic, hierarchical tenets that oppress women and force both genders to carry out that oppression to their detriment. Such role models entreat us to consider the idea that heterosexual norms are not necessarily normal and inevitable but perhaps unnatural and fraught with emotional and social problems.

What these radical feminists suggest is risky and takes courage. The risk is that of losing privilege. The more "out" I become, the more "vocal feminist advocate" I become, and the more prejudice I experience. But even with the stigma of being a feminist lesbian, I'm still pretty high on the social, hierarchal ladder . . . a White, able-bodied American who is well educated and financially secure, and who enjoys family acceptance. Admitting that I use these privileges as convenient excuses to escape and deny what is going on around me is the very thing that humbles me and allows me to see others' oppressions and, maybe more importantly, allows me to put my own oppression in perspective.

If you are a heterosexual or pass as heterosexual, the privilege you enjoy will be hard to surrender. I know this because even though I am a lesbian, when I teach and counsel, I remind myself constantly not to act according to the heterosexual norms that are a part of me: to limit my advice, narrow my vision, and take the accepted path. I push myself to challenge my students' and clients' thoughts about heterosexuality because, until we all do this, no individual or group can truly be free.

DEBORAH, "THE INSTRUCTOR":
REFLECTIONS

As a White, heterosexual, middle-class woman, I enjoy many privileges that accompany my statuses in society. I live in two different worlds—the world of dominance, definition, and access that is mine whether I endorse it or not, and the world of ever-increasing discomfort about the roles I'm asked to invalidate or define as "other" by my participation in a patriarchal culture.

In my work as counseling psychologist and counselor educator, I serve a primarily White/European and Christian graduate student body, one that tends to resist contact with "the other," particularly when that other is thought to represent ideas that conflict with dominant religious values. I teach a course on diversity issues, giving a great deal of attention to the topics of gender and sexual orientation.

I believe it's important for me to help dominant-culture students learn about their heterosexual identities (Worthington, Savoy, Dillon, & Vernaglia, 2002) and grapple with the biases they've learned so that they can meet their clients with respect and nurturance. However, I often hear the question, "Why must we spend so much time [typically three weeks of a semester] dealing with gay issues?" Recently, a student wrote in a reflection paper that she was offended and outraged that I would ask the class to attend a youth meeting at our local GLBTQ community center. Remarks such as "I think we need to focus more on ethnic groups than on gays and lesbians," or "Being gay is a choice, not something a person is born with—so it's not a real culture," toughen my resolve to keep heterosexism in the forefront despite the often angry reactions I encounter among students.

My feelings and responsibilities regarding heterosexism come also from my history. I grew up in a small southern town very rooted in fundamentalist Christian traditions. There were no openly gay or lesbian couples in our community, but we did have a disproportionate number of suicides—many of which I later came to realize were related to the pervasive heterosexism and impossibility of being for individuals who found themselves attracted to people of the same sex. For these people, the life choices were slim: Either live a lie, reject an enormous part of who you are, or accept the surety of denunciation from family, loved ones, church, and, in this context, God.

As a young woman witnessing these people's deaths, I had the privilege of considering them "other," "troubled," or "unfortunate," even though I did not know the details of their emotional lives. Now I understand that their despair was in a way connected with my own developmental crises because we all faced the imperative to marry and fit into those narrow roles accepted by our community. In this social sphere, the possibilities for self-expression and fulfillment were constricted for everyone, including me, because the marriage imperative formed the center of our relational world. Every rule and norm related in some way to the urgency for marriage. Roles for women and men were clearly marked out; for those unlucky souls who happened to appear too feminine to be real boys/men or too masculine to be proper girls/women, blatant social and emotional costs included social ostracism and religious condemnation.

As an illustration, I think of voices. People's voices were expected to fall within a limited range of volume and pitch, given their gender. In particular, women whose voices sounded deeper or whose speech sounded blunter, less apologetic, tended to be viewed with suspicion, labeled "mannish," or simply left out of mainstream social life. Whether or not a person was primarily heterosexual, to have a non-normative style, sound, or personality rendered her or him an icon for that which had been defined undesirable by the dominant, naming class.

Not until much later, when I was in graduate school and building friendships with people who were openly gay, lesbian, bisexual, and transgendered, did I become aware of my sexual privilege and embark on the discovery of a positive, integrated heterosexual identity. My first encounters with people who were openly gay or lesbian made me squirm with anxiety and disapproval. Talking openly about these feelings with my mentors and new friends gave me the opportunity to become familiar with myself as oppressor—and to begin incorporating a new worldview that could accommodate sexual diversity and, in fact, come to celebrate it.

Sometimes I reflect upon the angst I now experience as students criticize my emphasis on heterosexism, and I ruminate over their concerns and begin to question my motivations for teaching the way I do. Then I realize that the same uncomfortable resistance I'm getting can be magnified hundreds of times to approximate a sense of what GLBT individuals face in communities like these every day.

For counselor trainees to sharpen their empathic skills, I think they must learn to celebrate the sexual/relational differences among individuals. To do this, they probably need to first deal honestly with sexual privilege. If they are heterosexual, they must come to see themselves as oppressors because of their participation in defining what will be included in—and what will be excluded from—the circle of acceptability.

So for me to teach about heterosexism requires that I not only encourage dialogue between my students and those who differ from them in sexual orientation, but that I also relinquish certain privileges as a member of a dominant, defining class. By questioning the marriage imperative and asking others to do the same, I open myself to their criticism and their pain, the pain of letting go of ingrained notions about what is and what should be. By making my classroom language more inclusive (for example, "relationship status"), I shed the protective cloak that endorses heterosexual privilege by defining the norm. By expanding our class discussions of sexuality to include a broader, more complex, and more fluid view of people's relational patterns over a lifetime, I invite people to wonder whether I am ever or was ever attracted to women. What do I give up in this process? Perhaps the false respect of heterosexual people that often comes from assuming we're all insiders, members of a system that calls us superior.

CONCLUSION

Instructors and students are challenged to hear the voices being educated, particularly when those voices represent "the other," and to resist heterosexism in their classrooms and mentoring relationships by promoting honest dialogue. To prepare for this kind of activism, educators may benefit from taking inventory of their unearned sexual privileges and considering which of these they might be willing to forfeit to help their students and communities grow. As examples, instructors can (1) evaluate the ways in which they present themselves to their students (for example, as "married" versus "partnered"); (2) assess the case examples they use for elements of heterosexism and make changes where needed; and (3) suggest and include texts written by and about GLBT individuals. Activities such as these, although they may appear to be simple, can have a profound and lasting effect on the way a course is received by both GLBT and heterosexual students, through challenging common notions of what is normal and providing new frameworks for understanding sexual difference.

The real acceptance of unique experience, as a valuable and necessary part of student education, informs our training and contextualizes the world in which we work. The visible nurturance of diversity within any program shows its trainees how to accept the worldviews of others, even when those views are very different from the trainees' own.

DISCUSSION QUESTIONS

1. What are the threads of heterosexism in this counselor training program? In other types of programs?

2. What impact does heterosexism have in the lives of heterosexual students? What impact do assumptions of heterosexuality have on GLBT students?

3. What social, emotional, and/or professional impact results from relinquishing heterosexual privilege for students? For educators?

4. In what ways could you give up heterosexual privilege? What kind of impact could that have on your teaching, counseling, learning, or social advocacy?

5. Carter Heyward (1989) suggests, "Our sexuality is our desire to participate in making love, making justice in the world; our drive toward one another; our movement in love; our expression of our sense of being bonded together in life and death" (p. 295). If sexuality is more than romantic bonding but encompasses nonsexual relationships with friends,

family, community, and world, how can we best encourage our clients and students to seek the more complex meanings of their own sexuality?

6. Try constructing scenarios of interactions between friends of different sexualities and genders. How does heterosexism change the nature of the friendships? How do a nongay and a gay male show affection in a friendship? A lesbian and a nongay male? Two lesbians? Does the intimacy level change? What are the expectations between two nongay women friends versus a nongay woman and man friendship? What about other relationships?

REFERENCES

Allen, K. R. (1995). Opening the classroom closet: Sexual orientation and self-disclosure. *Family Relations, 44*(2), 136–141.

Barry, K. (1979). *Female sexual slavery.* Englewood Cliffs, NJ: Prentice-Hall, Inc., 100.

Fassinger, R. E. (1991). The hidden minority: Issues and challenges in working with lesbian women and gay men. *Counseling Psychologist, 19,* 157–176.

Herek, G. M. (1990). The context of anti-gay violence: Notes on cultural and psychological heterosexism. *Journal of Interpersonal Violence, 5,* 316–333.

Heyward, C. (1989). Sexuality, love, and justice. In J. Plaskow & C. Christ (Eds.). *Weaving the Visions.* San Francisco, CA: Harper, 293–301.

MacGillivray, I. K. (2000). Education equity for gay, lesbian, bisexual, transgendered, and queer/questioning students. *Education and Urban Society, 32*(3), 303–324.

Neisen, J. (1990). Heterosexism or homophobia? *Out/Look, 3*(2), 36.

Rich, A. (1982). *Compulsory heterosexuality and lesbian existence.* Denver, CO: Antelope Press.

Stewart, C. (1999). *Sexually stigmatized communities.* Thousand Oaks, CA: Sage Productions, 221.

Worthington, R. L., Savoy, H. B., Dillon, F. R., & Vernaglia, E. R. (2002). Heterosexual identity development: A multidimensional model of individual and social identity. *The Counseling Psychologist, 30*(4), 496–531.

10

"Men Can't Be Raped"

The Challenge of Sexism in Counseling

HEATHER TREPAL

DESCRIPTION OF CRITICAL INCIDENT

On the college campus where I work, we have an annual rape-prevention program for all first-year students. A peer theatre troupe performs skits related to different rape scenarios (for example, date rape, drug-facilitated rape, female victim-male perpetrator, male victim-female perpetrator), which are followed by a question-and-answer session with the students. During one of these sessions, several of the students, both male and female, strongly argued that a scene in which a male was the victim and a female was the perpetrator was unrealistic. When asked to defend their positions, one student replied, "Everyone knows that men can't be raped."

It has been suggested that gender is a social construction (Mintz & O'Neil, 1990; Thompson, 1995). How we come to view men and women, and how we participate in dialogues about those views, is how others come to construct their ideas of gender. It has also been suggested that gender socialization and sex-role rules have an impact on the issue of rape for both men and women (Pino & Meier, 1999). Statements such as "Men can't be raped" are formed by a social construction of gender that includes specific and limiting sex-role expectations for both men and women. Statements such as "Men can't be raped" are also part of a social construction of gender that has an impact on male survivors' experiences of rape and the meaning that is made from those experiences. Different aspects of gender socialization may impact a person's experience and personal interpretation of rape and healing. For example:

As a woman, I am generally accepted if . . .

- I express my anger, fear, or hurt (to a friend or a counselor). In both the college counseling center where I now work and in the rape crisis center, we see far more female clients than male clients, particularly clients with issues involving rape and sexual assault.

- I hear stories about rape that have happened to members of my own sex, in which women are the victims and men are the perpetrators (Groth & Burgess, 1980). For example, television movies about rape frequently involve some variation of the female/victim–male/perpetrator situation.

- I comment on the attractiveness of a member of my own sex and show affection for her without being tormented (Pollack, 1998). Men are often criticized for showing affection for a same-sex friend while women are socially conditioned to show affection to their female friends.

- I enjoy both the physical and emotional components of sex. Haines (1999) states that although many messages about sex are incongruent, women—particularly women survivors—are encouraged to break the myths and restrictions about sexuality.

As a man, I am generally accepted if . . .

- I do not express a variety of emotions, seek help, or tell others (such as a friend or counselor) when I am hurting (Lew, 1988; Pollack, 1998; Thompson, 1995). As a colleague of mine said, "Anger is the default emotion for men—the only emotion they are socially allowed to convey." Another colleague told me that once, when he was doing a presentation on counseling services, men in the group told him that "counseling was for the weak," and that they were afraid that someone might find out if they went to the campus counseling center. For a man to seek help can take a lot of courage.

- I do not hear stories about rape in which members of my own sex are the victim and not the perpetrator (Groth & Burgess, 1980). For example, sexual-assault presenters inform audiences typically that, although men are also victims/survivors, they will use the pronoun "she" for the sake of ease. By doing so, presenters not only reinforce masculine-sexist stereotypes (for example, men as perpetrators) but also disqualify the experiences of the male survivors in the audience.

- I avoid things that could be associated with femininity. Pollack (1998) has stated that a code exists for boys, part of which dictates that expressing feelings or emotions and behaviors that could be associated with femininity is "taboo" (p. 24). This situation connects with the point above: Expressing emotions (for example, sadness) and the behaviors associated with these emotions (for example, crying) is socially acceptable for women and not for men.

- I have "fear or hatred" toward non-heterosexuals. Pollack (1998) states that this attitude comes from a combination of gender socialization and misunderstanding about sexuality in general. Many male survivors question the effect of rape on their sexuality (Lew, 1988).

- I enjoy non-relational sex. Lew (1988) alluded to the fact that men are expected to enjoy sex without the constraints of emotional involvement and to be the aggressors in sexual situations. Sexual healing can be a component of healing from rape. Ideas about sexuality can hinder or help that process.

Many of the issues for male survivors of rape are invisible. Society suggests to men that they (a) be reluctant to seek help, (b) restrict their emotions, (c) engage in competition and aggressive behavior, among other things, and (d) accept gender-specific roles (Thompson, 1995).

REFLECTIONS

Although this is difficult to admit, in the past, I inwardly and unconsciously believed that "men can't be raped." Whenever I worked with a male survivor as a client, I looked for a sign to show that he somehow wanted the sexual activity and that he was not raped. I had unwittingly become part of the problem by somehow convincing myself that men always wanted sex, no matter the circumstances of the encounter. If a male client didn't show any emotion or didn't cry when discussing his sexual assault, I had to fight off the thought that he must have enjoyed the sex! Given a display of rage, I might have assumed that somehow the male was less responsible for the assault. By believing that my male clients were any more responsible for their rapes and sexual assaults than my female clients, I was truly practicing sexism.

MAKING CHANGES

To overcome my struggles with sexism, I decided to start with self-monitoring. I realized that I did not know a lot about men's issues, so I studied the literature on men and sexual assault. I learned that men do not report rape for many different reasons. Some buy into myths such as (a) all men who get raped are gay, (b) men don't get raped—they are the strong ones, and (c) women cannot rape men—rape is a sexually motivated crime (Lew, 1988). In addition to buying into the myths, men are taught by society that they will be made fun of if they report rape (for example, teasing by male peers, "Hey, *I'd* like to get *raped* by a woman").

Pino and Meier (1999) state that men are far less likely to report a rape or sexual assault when it calls into question their male identity. This has implications for both heterosexual and homosexual men. For example, both heterosexual and homosexual men might begin to question their sexual orientation. While heterosexual men might wonder why they didn't fight back, homosexual men might wonder whether they were being punished for their sexual orientation.

Sue and Sue (1999) have stated that the culturally skilled counselor should be (a) aware of his or her own cultural heritage; (b) aware of value differences; (c) aware of biases and values, and the effects they might have on others of a different culture; (d) comfortable with differences; (e) sensitive to circumstances and able to refer clients to counselors of their choice; (f) aware of and acknowledge beliefs, atti-tudes, and feelings that are prejudiced (for example, sexist, racist, anti-Semitic, homophobic, ageist); and (g) be engaged in the ongoing process of change. Counselors have a tendency to define gender roles narrowly (for example, crying as weakness for males, anger as pathology for females). By first addressing oneself and examining one's own beliefs, values, assumptions, and biases, and then addressing differences in these perspectives between oneself and one's client in therapy sessions, a counselor is able to work effectively within the *constraints* of a gendered socialization.

In addition, as counselors, by addressing our own beliefs as well as those of our clients, we hope to create space for our clients, both male and female, to develop broader conceptions of masculinity. We, as counselors, can challenge socially and historically constructed views of masculinity and teach our clients to do the same.

CONCLUSION

My male clients have also taught me a lot. For instance, working in a "feminist" organization, I felt free to decorate my office as I chose—with pictures, quotes, and items representing all things feminine and empowering to women. Quite a few men clients informed me that this was not only unsettling to them, but also irresponsible. By decorating with feminine gender objects, I was possibly negating their experiences and was not providing empowering models for my male clients. They also suggested incorporating male-centered contexts into our program literature (for example, brochures, advertising) and using non-sexist language.

By examining my attitudes and beliefs about men, and by working with men, I was able to begin to have a dialogue with myself about my work. I concluded that I needed to actively seek out training on men's issues. And this meant all kinds of men (disabled; gay/bi/transidentified; men of various racial, ethnic, and religious backgrounds) and their issues. In addition to training, I needed to take it upon myself to read about men's issues. I started to write about my work so that I could share ideas and educate others.

DISCUSSION QUESTIONS

I had the privilege of attending a conference presentation about working with male survivors. I am borrowing the following activity, "Attitudes toward working with men," from the presenter, Thomas Neill, MSW, LISW (2001) of the Cleveland Rape Crisis Center.

Close your eyes and think of the following questions:

1. How do you feel about talking to men about their history of sexual assault? Comfortable? Uncomfortable? Indifferent? Really uncomfortable?

2. How comfortable are you discussing sexuality issues with men? Are you comfortable asking men about their sex lives, sexual orientation, and

sexual and reproductive health, including use of correct or slang terminology based on the language they use?

3. What comes up for you when a male client expresses strong emotion (for example, anger, rage, sadness)? Do you feel you are less likely to challenge a male client, or possibly likely to try to pacify him, to keep him from "going there"?

4. Does talking to male survivors ever make you revert to thinking about the men in your own life—your father, brothers, partners, friends? Do such discussions make you fear for the safety of other men you know?

5. Are you afraid that seeing men vulnerable and fragile will shatter some of your own societal myths that you uphold for certain men in your life? ("My husband is the rock of the family and I can't imagine him dealing with anything like that.")

6. Do you ever think it must be more difficult physiologically, or physically, for men to be raped than it is for women? Does it seem impossible for men to be raped by women? Does any part of you think that it is easier for a guy if a woman rapes him than if a man does?

7. Why does the notion of a 30-year-old man having sex with a 15-year-old girl nauseate people, while the idea of a 15-year-old boy having sex with a 30-year-old woman is easier to tolerate? Are you one of those people? Do you honestly feel that a 15-year-old girl's experience is more traumatic?

8. When do men push your emotional buttons—both in real life and in direct service work?

9. Do you feel that you are competent to work with male survivors because you are skilled working with female survivors? Do you feel as though gender makes no difference—a survivor is a survivor?

10. What does your staff look like? Are there any men on your staff? Do you actively recruit men as you would any other demographic to ensure a diverse team and promote choice among whom clients can work with?

11. Do you feel that men are equally capable of working with female clients? With female survivors?

12. Do you "own" your biases, assumptions, values, and beliefs around men and discuss them with your supervisor so those biases do not interfere with your work?

Carefully think about and reflect on your answers to the preceding questions. Pay attention to which ones struck a chord with you. Where are your growing edges? Where is the work that you need to do to keep your gender lens from interfering with your valuable clinical work?

REFERENCES

David, D., & Brannon, R. (Eds.). (1976). *The forty-nine percent majority: The male sex role.* Reading, MA: Addison-Wesley.

Erikson, B. M. (1996). Ethical considerations when feminist family therapists treat men. *Journal of Family Psychotherapy, 7*(2), 1–19.

Groth, N. A., & Burgess, A. W. (1980). Male rape: Offenders and victims. *American Journal of Psychiatry, 137,* 806–810.

Haines, S. (1999). *The survivor's guide to sex: How to have an empowered sex life after child sexual abuse.* San Francisco, CA: Cleis Press Inc.

Lew, M. (1988). *Victims no longer.* New York: Harper-Collins Publishers Inc.

Mintz, L. B., & O'Neil, J. M. (1990). Gender roles, sex, and the process of psychotherapy: Many questions and few answers. *Journal of Counseling and Development, 68,* 381–387.

Neill, Thomas (2001, October). Treating male survivors of sexual assault. Paper presented at the meeting of the Ohio Coalition on Sexual Assault, Columbus, Ohio.

Pino, N. W., & Meier, R. F. (1999). Gender differences in rape reporting. *Sex Roles, 40*(11/12), 979–990.

Pollack, W. (1998). *Real boys: Rescuing our sons from the myths of boyhood.* New York: Henry Holt and Company, Inc.

Stevenson, M. R., & Medler, B. R. (1995). Is homophobia a weapon of sexism? *The Journal of Men's Studies, 4*(1), 1–8.

Sue, D. W., & Sue, D. (1999). *Counseling the culturally different: Theory and practice* (3rd ed.). New York: John Wiley & Sons.

Thompson, N. (1995). Men and anti-sexism. *British Journal of Social Work, 25,* 459–475.

11

Exploring Male Privilege

Journey of Two White Middle-Class Men

DAVID H. WHITCOMB AND JAMES A. CUMMINGS

INTRODUCTION[1]

The highly educated, White, middle-class male of the 21st century is in a lofty but precarious position in our society. Wealth, power, and privilege have accrued to men of European ancestry ever since our "Founding Fathers" established the principles of a new form of government that was to be more egalitarian than any other in Western civilization. All of the U.S. presidents have been White men, and all of the massive American fortunes, until very recently, have been acquired by White businessmen, who have generally benefited greatly from the labors of women, children, and people of color. Some of these men have risen through the ranks without the benefit of formal education or an economically stable family. But the more typical pattern is for power and prestige to be passed down from father to son in our patriarchal society, with formal education serving as a rite of passage for maintaining a family's economic security. In the late 20th century, however, societal forces such as the women's movement and affirmative action started to shift power, in some instances, away from White, middle-class men. For example, in the case of gender, fewer women stayed at home to raise the children, and some even broke through the "glass ceiling" and became corporate executives. With a divorce rate of nearly 50 percent in the United States, many men who are awarded limited or no custody of their children lash out at the legal system and scapegoat women for being required to pay child support but having limited access to their children. With regard to race, many White men have witnessed an increasing proportion of persons of color in occupations that historically were occupied nearly exclusively by White men. They have blamed reverse discrimination for rates of unemployment among White men that are higher than at any time since the Great Depression. On two fronts, gender and race, many White men feel threatened and react with anger in a backlash against feminism and affirmative action.

Perhaps not surprisingly, the reaction of many White men to perceived loss of power may be disproportionate to actual losses of privilege. In fact, it is very

---

[1] Authors' Note: We would like to thank Denise Twohey, Ed.D., and Cyd Goodman McCray, M.A., for their inspiration and for their contributions to an earlier version of this chapter.

common for White men not to recognize their own privilege until it is either pointed out to them, by women or persons of color, or eroded by the empowerment of these traditionally oppressed groups. Although the loss of power may be felt most strongly in the working class (Weis, 1993), it is also experienced by White men in the middle and upper-middle classes. In this chapter, two White, middle-class men with advanced degrees will look at the changing face of male privilege, using experiences from their own lives, including a particular graduate-level course. They will also refer to feminist perspectives (Gergen, 2001; Miller, 1986; Pipher, 1994) and insights from the newer field of the psychology of men and masculinity (Levant, 1995; Pollack, 2000; Pollack & Levant, 1998).

PROFESSIONAL AND PERSONAL CONTEXTS OF UNDERSTANDING PRIVILEGE

We first explored gender issues together when the first author, David, was co-teaching a gender course in which the second author, Jim, was a student. We are both White, middle-class men who grew up in privileged surroundings, but differences in our professional and personal backgrounds influence our experiences with and outlook on male privilege. We discuss these similarities and differences throughout the chapter as we present our experiences with male privilege and reflect on research and theory that speak to our experience.

David's background

I am a 42-year-old man who was raised in a small, upper-middle-class commuter town with other White Anglo-Saxon Protestants (WASPs). Since age 17, I have worked in human services. My earlier career positions included work with clients who had developmental disabilities, work that focuses on welfare-to-work concerns, and work with youth residing in shelters and/or hospitalized in psychiatric settings. My post-master's experience includes work in university and substance-abuse counseling centers, a cancer institute, and a hospital emergency room. I am currently in my sixth year as a tenure-track assistant professor and director of a master's degree program in counseling. My clinical focus includes preventing HIV, counseling persons living with HIV/AIDS, and addressing coming out/adjustment issues with gay, lesbian, and bisexual persons.

At 18, I came out to my family as bisexual and settled into a gay identity upon entering my first long-term relationship a few years later. I am currently single and live in a rural region where GLBT people often find it difficult both to build a community and to be accepted by others who are not gay.

Jim's background

I am a 32-year-old White, heterosexual male of German and Northern Irish decent. I was born and raised in a rural Minnesota community and had a Roman Catholic, middle-class upbringing. I come from a traditional two-parent household and am the youngest of six children.

My higher educational training has been in the area of education. In 1993, I completed my undergraduate work with degrees in history and secondary education. After graduation I substitute taught, hoping to find a full-time teaching job. Between substitute-teaching assignments, I worked as a nurse's assistant at my father's care center for developmentally disabled folks. In 1995, I left teaching to pursue full-time work in sales until deciding in 2000 to resume my education by pursuing a graduate degree in school counseling, I combined my full-time studies with work as an adult-education instructor and a high-school tutor. I graduated in 2003, and I am currently employed as a school counselor in a rural school district.

I am married and have three preschool-aged children, including a newborn. One or two days per week I stay home with the children while my wife goes to work as a store-side manager for a major discount retailer. My wife began working for her current employer about the same time I decided to pursue my graduate degree. Prior to that, she was a stay-at-home mom.

We arrived at our current division of labor through a process that started a few years ago when I was selling insurance. Because we had only enough income for the basics, my wife decided to take a few evening shifts at the discount retailer. Soon after, she was recruited for a management mentorship program. She asked me whether I would be all right with staying home with the kids so that I could quit my job, which I hated. In other words, she would become the breadwinner of the family. Because this arrangement was a way out of the job, I said, "That sounds perfect." But I soon discovered that it didn't sound so perfect to some of my male relatives. The looks on their faces when I told them spoke volumes and seemed to suggest, "You're going to be the housewife?" My wife's family, in contrast, accepted the changes well.

After a couple months, though, I started to have second thoughts related to my feelings about gender roles. I felt that I should be the one out there bringing home the bacon and my wife should be at home with the kids. We were new to the area, and with no local friends, I started to get depressed and wanted to move back home. Spending your days with the kids isn't supposed to be depressing, but sometimes for me it was. My wife and I started talking about my going back to school. I did, and there was more balance in my life.

I feel fortunate that my wife is so open to nontraditional gender roles in the family. The flexibility offers us more freedom than the traditional system of male dominance and privilege.

SEEING WHITE MALE PRIVILEGE
FROM THE OUTSIDE

Sometimes we cannot recognize our own privilege (McIntosh, 1992) until we see it through a shared experience with another who does not share in that privilege. In the following stories we each describe a significant life event. These critical events increased our awareness of male privilege in our lives.

David's story

One evening my perception of privilege changed forever, despite the fact that the precipitating event seemed minor at the time. That evening I was with a friend I will call Rebecca, whom I met as a child at summer camp. Although we had lost touch for many years, a camp reunion a few years earlier had renewed our childhood friendship. Rebecca is from a prosperous Jewish family, grew up in a nearby suburb, and started a successful career after completing an MBA. During one of my brief visits in her home city, we went to a stylish midtown restaurant for dinner. It was crowded, but a young, attractive hostess quickly found a table for us. I thought nothing of it. So I was surprised when, soon after we were seated, Rebecca commented that she would not have been offered a table as quickly had she not been with a "blond man."

My initial reaction to Rebecca's comment was disbelief. My experience of being seated quickly at a fashionable restaurant was one I had come to expect, and I had never thought that any other well-dressed person elsewhere in the United States in the 1990s would be treated any differently. My immediate thoughts were that my interaction with the hostess, which lasted only a few seconds, was civilized, sophisticated, and entirely normal; it was unsettling for a trusted friend to view it any other way. I suppressed these thoughts and feelings, however, by politely validating Rebecca's experience of being commonly overlooked by hostesses due to her gender and ethnicity, and by quickly changing the topic to more familiar ground not related to perceptions of privilege and oppression. Only later, and gradually, did I start to deconstruct the experience and enrich my understanding of White male privilege.

I had known since childhood that, as an able-bodied, upper-middle-class WASP, I was a member of the dominant cultural group. I had been told repeatedly by my parents and others how "lucky" I was, but I had never before considered how the many interactions that make up my ordinary day could so often be facilitated by being, and perhaps more importantly, looking like, an upper-middle-class male WASP. There was no way to prove that we were seated at the restaurant more quickly because of the hostess's perception of my physical characteristics. I had to trust Rebecca's perception that the treatment she often receives as a woman who appears Jewish is of lower quality than that I am accustomed to receiving. My interactions with Rebecca over the years consistently demonstrated her pride in her cultural heritage and the accomplishments of her family. Her disclosure that she believes she is often marginalized by others' reaction to her gender and religion changed my perception of her self-concept and how she regards my cultural and gender status. In turn, my new perspective on our differences created an opportunity for me to explore my own privileged status.

Although this experience with Rebecca opened my eyes to my privilege as a White male, it was not the first nor the last such experience. And this experience is not unique to me. Other White males also experience privilege. McIntosh (1992) was one of the first feminist writers to discuss extensively the intersection of white privilege and male privilege. She lists dozens of examples of ways in which individuals benefit, often unknowingly, from their privilege. Similarly, Goodman (2001) describes many aspects of privilege that those who possess the privilege take for granted. Although sometimes we discover our own privilege from chance experiences such as the one I have described, we can help our students and others we work with in this learning process.

Jim's story

From 1996 to 1999, I worked as a salesman for an automobile dealership in central Minnesota. Three women were employed at the dealership—a secretary, a bookkeeper, and a part-time finance and insurance consultant. The rest of us—salesmen, managers, service representatives, mechanics, and car washers—were all White men.

As a member of the sales team, I witnessed sexism and sexual harassment on a number of fronts, but mainly in the accounting office and on the sales floor. For example, in the office where our bookkeeper and secretary worked, sexual banter was exchanged freely on a daily basis. The comments revolved around sexual acts, male and female genitalia, or the recent sexual conquests of certain male staff members. I remember a lot of nervous laughter, and the general feeling among most of us was "If the wrong person heard what we were talking about, we'd be sued!" Though the women in the accounting office seemed surprised and shocked by some of the statements, they contributed to these conversations at times. They would make vulgar comments, too, in the spirit of the moment, talking crudely about sex, for example. I don't think they felt good about it, but we didn't talk about that. There seemed to be pressure for them to be OK with the comments, to give the guys a break just for acting like guys.

The women, as far I know, were never pressured into "hooking up" with the male employees who engaged in this type of behavior, but the atmosphere nevertheless remained uncomfortable for me and some of the women. An older secretary, for example, would sit with her head down, shaking it in disgust when such talk occurred. Another woman in the financial area would sometimes walk away when the talk started. They didn't know how I felt about it because I bluffed pretty well about being just like the other guys.

At the time, what was happening seemed like fun and games. After all, the women did not vocally object to any of the comments or gestures made by the men. I can see why they didn't object. In fact, I now believe that their participation in the sexual talk represented self-protection. After all, my boss always liked to have nice-looking women working in the office and felt that they could be replaced at a minute's notice. Deep down, I knew these women were being harassed, but I thought my job would have been in jeopardy had I reported it. In the car business, for the most part, if someone has bad chemistry with the group, he becomes subtly ostracized and made to feel so uncomfortable that he doesn't want to work there anymore. As a man, I had the privilege of not being the target of the harassment, and with my educational background, I had the privilege of entering another field in which harassment would be less likely to occur.

The first class I enrolled in as a master's degree student was Psychology of Women, Gender, and Development. At the same time, I saw myself as an open-minded person when it came to human relations. During my undergraduate experience, I had worked and studied with people from diverse cultural backgrounds who possessed far differing beliefs and values from my own. Looking back, I learned much by having some of these students as my friends. On the other hand, I felt a lot of fear and apprehension when I thought about attending and participating in this course. Because of my religious and politically conservative upbringing, I was worried that my sense of masculinity and my belief system about men and women would be challenged by my instructors and classmates. That made me uncomfortable, because I wanted to stay true to myself. Many thoughts entered my mind: "Am I going to say something that's going to offend somebody or get me kicked out?" "What are my brothers going to say if I tell them that I'm taking this course?" "Am I going to become a feminist or a liberal?" (This was the scariest thought of all.)

I decided to go into the class with an open mind, prepared to explore a variety of ideas. As a result, I enjoyed a surprise and had my eyes opened! The surprise was that many of my beliefs and attitudes toward women, men, and gender roles (such as the value of boys and men being able to express their emotions, and that of criticizing the media for exploitation of women's physical appearance) concurred with the beliefs of many of those in the feminist movement! My eyes were opened to the cultural contexts and conversations that are toxic to women and girls (Pipher, 1994). The readings and class discussions also helped me to realize that the women I worked with at the car dealership participated in the sexual banter as a means of protecting their jobs and perhaps their "friendships" in a toxic environment. I started to understand my position of power and privilege as a male, and the responsibility I hold to address conversations and contexts that demean and objectify women. The two books that made the biggest impression on me were *Masculinity Reconstructed* by Ronald Levant (1995), and *Reviving Ophelia* by Mary Pipher (1994). As I absorbed the messages offered by the authors, the worries I had going into the course dissipated. The course helped me, coming from a background of privilege, understand the struggle of those trying to gain a voice in a White, male-dominated society.

Despite my great relief at learning so much about gender roles and male privilege in a course I entered with so much apprehension, I continue to struggle with some of the content presented. For example, when reading and discussing *Silencing the Self: Women and Depression* (Jack, 1991), the focus on the women's relationships with men was solely on the negative actions by the men and negative reactions of the women. No one else seemed to be questioning, as I was, what responsibility women should take in bad relationships. Similarly, when we discussed the news story of a woman who killed all of her children during an episode of psychotic post-partum depression, I sat there seething, but I stifled my reactions when classmates assigned the responsibility to the husband rather than the wife who committed the crimes. I silenced myself rather than go out on a limb and risk being attacked. On another occasion, however, I did assert my opinions supporting the value of certain actions considered chivalric (such as saving the women and children first on the *Titanic*). I disagreed with a classmate concerning his views that gender stereotypical compliments made to parents of a baby girl were inappropriate. In these instances, I found more allies among classmates than I had expected, yet at other times I felt certain that my conservative views would not be well received. I was relieved not to have the opportunity to defend my position on abortion because the topic was never discussed.

CONTINUED AWARENESS
OF MALE PRIVILEGE

David's challenge

Recently, in co-teaching a gender course with a senior female colleague, the intersection of privilege and minority status challenged me. A few years earlier, this colleague had experienced a life-threatening illness that resulted in disability and a reduction in her teaching load. I felt honored to be invited to co-teach a course she had taught for years, and I was excited about the perspectives I could offer as a gay man who had studied gender issues. At the same time, I was aware of my authoritative tendencies and the fact that, since the onset of her disability, I talk more than she does. I wanted to fit into *her* course and gently mold it into *our* course. In a gender course, I believed that for me, an outspoken man, to upset the harmony of a traditionally woman-led curriculum would be disastrous role modeling. I shared my concerns with my colleague as we prepared for the class, and I mentioned them during our second class meeting. I hoped my self-disclosure in class demonstrated cross-gender sensitivity and teamwork. I felt the constant challenge of when to speak up and when to hold back. Marks (1995), another male professor who teaches a course on gender, shares his struggles of trying to teach on the topic without overpowering the female voices present.

Overall, I was pleased with our collaboration, though at times I wondered whether I was starting to pontificate on issues when my colleague and students became silent. Whenever I became aware of this dynamic, I would quickly conclude what I was saying, though I now wish I had asked for feedback on my use of power during mini-lectures. Students seemed to accept my self-disclosure about not wanting to overpower the female voices, but it is difficult to know for sure.

Jim's challenge

As I prepared to write this chapter, I read an article that examined issues of gender and social class among the Good Old Boys (Farr, 1988) and reflected on how this concept relates to my own experience. I've heard such phrases as "Good Old Boys" and "Old Boys' Club" several times in my life. The first time was when I was a paraprofessional in an educational setting. A middle-aged, divorced, White female staff member used the term to identify a group of older men who all worked for the school system. She described this "club" as "a bunch of old guys that get together to play basketball and then go out for drinks." According to her, what made it a Good Old Boys Club was that they, or the "club," had a long history of subtly but systematically excluding outsiders, especially women. Beneath this seemingly harmless surface, however, were harmful dynamics recognized by some of the women employees. Because some of the group members held positions of power, some women felt that the male employees (some of whom were club members) were held to lower standards of performance in the school system.

My second exposure to the phrase was when I was a counseling trainee; it came up in reference to the district leadership. Two of the female school counselors oftentimes spoke bitterly about the men who were in charge of district policy. One of the counselors claimed that her ideas were ignored at a recent district-wide meeting. When I asked her why she thought she wasn't being heard, she replied, "That's easy—he's a man!"

My most recent experience with this phrase relates to my wife. As a store-side executive for a large discount-retail chain, she and her female team members often discuss the negative presence of what they call "The Boys' Club." This group consists of the male store manager and several male executives at the same rank as my wife. These men share a camaraderie like the group mentioned previously, meeting outside the work setting for sports activities, dinner, and drinks. Occasionally, the female executives are asked to join in these activities, but they are usually excluded. The male executives are viewed by the female employees as "butt kissers" who are held to a lower standard of performance, are often praised for deeds done by others, and often receive opportunities for recognition and advancement not offered to the women executives. Although I had heard all of these stories before I read Farr's article on male-dominance bonding, they didn't come together in my mind as living examples of male privilege in my community until I read her critique of the Good Old Boys' Club. In sum, the article enlightened me to the fact that the "good ol' boys" phenomenon is something that is actually being studied as a destructive component of male privilege. At the time, I thought the female educators were male bashing. After hearing about my wife's experiences at her job and reading the Farr (1988) article, I began to understand where these women were coming from. If their experience was similar to my wife's at her job, I can understand why they would feel a sense of injustice at being excluded by the privileged men's group. I wouldn't go so far as to say they were oppressed, but I know I shouldn't have judged them so harshly at the time.

REFLECTIONS

Jim reflects

Despite my preconceptions that I would be inducted into radically different political thinking, the Psychology of Women, Gender, and Development course was the perfect springboard for me as I entered my master's program; it inspired me to learn more. As far as where I sit on the political spectrum is concerned, the course did not affect me that much. I've always considered, and will probably forever consider, myself a fiscal conservative and a social moderate. One thing the course taught me was that women should have the same opportunities as men when it comes to exploring, discovering, and developing interests and talents. It also made me realize just how much privilege I had as a boy growing up in my house, and how much of that privilege I took for granted. By taking the course, I feel better prepared to work with young people who are trying to cope with the damaging effects of our girl-hurting culture.

As a school counselor, I feel I now have some of the necessary tools for helping girls rediscover and nurture their authentic selves. I also want the boys I work with to understand that being a real man means treating people with respect and appreciating their differences. I also think the course has given me the needed skills for working with the parents and teachers of these children. When the emotional well-being of girls and boys is under attack, parents and teachers must learn how to recognize that truth. When I first wrote about my experience taking this course, I concluded that I would encourage teachers and parents to read such books as *Reviving Ophelia* and *Real Boys' Voices.* In my first two months on the job, I already have done so. I see that the boys I work with are suffering from the gender straitjacket Pollack (1998) describes, and I have recommended his book to them. In response to my recommendation to read Pipher's (1994) book, one mother told me: "This book is helping me see things that I didn't notice before about our society—a lot of this stuff is really scary!" It seems the book had a great impact on both her and her daughter. I recall feeling the same way as I read *Reviving Ophelia.*

In learning about male privilege, I offer the following advice for students taking a course focusing on the issue:

> It is important to be flexible, to consider and respect other viewpoints; but you don't have to abandon everything you believe in. If you have a rigid attitude, you won't learn anything about male privilege or gender roles. I also think it's important not to judge people unless you really know what their experience has been—to walk a mile in their moccasins, as Native American wisdom teaches us. I recommend that you look at a class like this as an opportunity for self-growth, and an opportunity to learn more about yourself, your family, and the people you live, work, and study with.

When I went home, I tried to inform others a little bit about what I had learned in class. Doing so didn't get me anywhere with my family of origin. I tried to tell them that their old ways aren't working in today's society. I imagine I sounded too uppity or preachy in my approach. So I think we need to be careful how we tell people what we've learned and how we think we've grown as a result of what we've learned, because it's tough to change people. Some people are more resistant to new ideas than others, and some will be turned off with what you have to say. This happens with men and women alike. Of course, many men don't want to change, but I have found that some women, even in my own family, also like gender roles just the way they are. If men end up having an advantage in society, that's all right with them as long as they are being comfortably provided for. If their husbands happen to control family decisions and the family's money, that's fine with them. It's not that way in the family I'm raising now, however, and learning about male privilege and alternatives to traditional gender roles has helped me come to new understandings with my wife and has influenced my early work as a school counselor.

David observes

During the process of writing this chapter, I became more aware of how male privilege shaped my upbringing and continues to affect my daily experience. I understand better how heterosexual privilege diminishes, but does not eliminate, my experience of male privilege. Having reflected upon these issues and delved into the literature more, I feel better prepared in my clinical practice and all my teaching, but particularly in courses focusing on diversity issues, to self-disclose about my experiences with male privilege, and to encourage others to take risks to discover issues of privilege in their own lives. In particular, I now appreciate that openness and readiness to change are key aspects in coming to terms with one's own privilege. Whereas sometimes individuals have a sudden transformative experience leading to a cognitive paradigm shift, change is more often gradual and incremental. Forcing concepts foreign to one's worldview is likely to alienate a student and possibly encourage a retreat into a developmentally earlier, more traditional, construction of power dynamics.

I now recognize that part of my privilege is having a career that allows time to study these issues. My understanding of male privilege is enriched by my relationships with women who point out my blind spots and inspire me to study gender issues in greater depth. Similarly, my experience as a gay man gives me enough of an outsider's perspective to enhance my understanding of male privilege; I draw upon that experience to guide my academic inquiry into the intersections of different kinds of privilege, and I attempt to pass along my insights. As an educator and therapist, I must be patient with those who have not been given the opportunity for such study. Typically, their beliefs will not suddenly transform, but I can help to open new horizons by challenging my students and clients at a level that allows them to feel somewhat grounded in a familiar worldview. I must also accept that the degree to which they come to understand male privilege as a powerful societal force will vary greatly from person to person. Some will start to conceptualize gender in ways that are new to them, whereas others will represent the feminist backlash (Faludi, 1991), viewing the idea of male privilege as a myth created by a feminist fringe movement.

My co-author Jim's learning experience implies a constant challenge that what is learned in class may be easily unlearned because students have important connections with others outside of class who hold steadfastly to traditional views. I also note that learning about male privilege does not stop even when one has started to teach about it—in fact, many new aspects come to light, as noted throughout this paper and summarized later.

In teaching about male privilege, I recommend that the instructor initially step back from advanced theoretical considerations of gender and try to understand the life experience of students who may be quite content with a patriarchal society they have not questioned to any extent. How could you help these students understand the privileged status of males in our society without eliciting defensive reactions that would last throughout the semester? What would be a good first step for your students to take to increase their awareness of gender inequality? What readings would you select to meet them at their level of understanding and advance that understanding at an appropriate pace?

Considering my experience as a junior faculty member who was asked to co-teach a course by the senior faculty member who had developed the course years earlier, I suggest that teachers consider the following questions when preparing to discuss male privilege in a classroom in which diversity in gender, race/ethnicity, sexual orientation, and ability/disability are represented:

1. In preparing for and co-teaching this course, to what extent would you blend or distinguish various "isms" that could arise in this situation, such as sexism, racism, heterosexism, and ableism?

2. How would you deal with male privilege in your interactions with your co-teacher and students, both in the classroom and in meetings and correspondence outside the classroom?

3. In trying to help students understand issues of male privilege in their future work as counselors, how would you decide what to self-disclose about your past experience and your experience teaching this class?

In working with male privilege with our clients, we believe it is important to understand who is benefiting and who is suffering from gender inequalities in their family, work, and social settings. For example, if your male client is directly benefiting from male privilege at work, and he entered a marriage assuming that male privilege would continue to be the norm, he may not understand his wife's increasing resistance to his dominance as her own feminist identity expands. Helping your client understand how he ultimately suffers from a gender hierarchy that initially benefited him may help him explore avenues for valuing his wife in new ways, thereby enhancing his marriage. In working with children, it may be helpful to ask what boys and men do well, ask the same about girls and women, and challenge any perceptions of gender inequality that arise. Any hints that the children believe that opportunities are not available to them because of their gender should be addressed with the children, their teachers, and their parents, even if some or all of these groups do not seem receptive to the issue.

Classroom instruction can be modified and extracurricular activities offered so that male privilege does not restrict opportunities for girls and boys.

CONCLUSION

In summary, these are some insights we have gained about male privilege: Often, male privilege is invisible to men but very visible to women; sexual harassment in the workplace is perpetuated when men who may not participate in it don't take a stand against it; and an outside perspective, specifically from women, was needed for us to recognize aspects of privilege we had taken for granted. Male privilege shares much in common with white privilege and heterosexual privilege, so much can be gained by discussing these issues in tandem.

Introducing the concept of male privilege to a man can engender denial even when suggested by a trusted friend, and defensiveness when presented by authors who sharply challenge mainstream views. Accepting one's privilege as a White man in today's society forces one to face the possibility of giving up unearned status that one has nevertheless felt entitled to by birthright. Such a possibility is often seen as threatening, so it must be handled carefully, acknowledging the important role that men and boys will still have in a more gender-equitable society.

DISCUSSION QUESTIONS

1. How do you open people up to the idea of male privilege without turning them off?
2. What thoughts are running through your mind as you prepare to enter this possible "unknown" of male privilege?
3. How would you describe female roles?
4. How would you describe male roles?
5. If someone brings up the topic of male privilege and wants to know what you think, what would you say?

Consistent with the previous discussion questions, we recommend that practitioners consider the following questions when preparing to work with their clients regarding male privilege:

1. How aware is your client of how male privilege is affecting him or her in various life roles?
2. How receptive is your client likely to be to a challenge of his or her beliefs about gender?
3. How will you deal with client resistance to changing his or her perceptions about male privilege?
4. What readings or exercises could you introduce that would meet your client's readiness for exploration and change?

REFERENCES

Anderson, K. J., & Accomando, C. (2002). 'Real' boys? Manufacturing and erasing privilege in popular books on raising boys. *Feminism & Psychology, 12,* 491–516.

Badgett, M. V. L. (1995). The wage effects of sexual orientation discrimination. *Industrial and Labor Relations Review, 48,* 726–739.

Badgett, M. V. L. (1998). *Income inflation: The myth of affluence among gay, lesbian, and bisexual Americans.* New York: Author and the Policy Institute of the National Gay and Lesbian Task Force (NGLTF).

Carlton Parsons, E. (2001). Using power and caring to mediate White male privilege, equality, and equity in an urban elementary classroom: Implications for teacher preparation, *The Urban Review, 33,* 321–338.

Faludi, S. (1991). *Backlash: The undeclared war against American women.* New York: Doubleday.

Farr, K. A. (1988). Dominance bonding through the Good Old Boys Sociability group. *Sex Roles, 18,* 259–277.

Gergen, M. (2001). *Feminist reconstructions in psychology: Narrative, gender, and performance.* Thousand Oaks, CA: Sage.

Goodman, D. J. (2001). *Promoting diversity and social justice: Educating people from privileged groups.* Thousand Oaks, CA: Sage Publications.

Jack, D. C. (1991). *Silencing the self: Women and depression.* Cambridge, MA: Harvard University Press.

Levant, R. F. (with Kopecky, G.) (1995). *Masculinity reconstructed: Changing the rules of manhood.* New York: Dutton/Plume.

Marks, S. R. (1995). The art of professing and holding back in a course on gender. *Family Relations, 44,* 142–148.

McIntosh, P. (1992). White Privilege and male privilege: A personal account of coming to see correspondences through work in women's studies. In M. L. Anderson & P. H. Collins (Eds.), *Race, class, and gender: An anthology* (pp. 70–81). Belmont, CA: Wadsworth.

Miller, J. B. (1986). *Toward a new psychology of women* (2nd ed.). Boston: Beacon Press.

Mooney, T. F. (1998). Cognitive behavior therapy for men. In W. S. Pollack & R. F. Levant (Eds.), *New psychotherapy for men* (pp. 57–82). New York: Wiley.

Pilkington, N. W., & Cantor, J. M. (1996). Perceptions of heterosexual bias in professional psychology programs: A survey of graduate students. *Professional Psychology: Research and Practice, 27,* 604–612.

Pipher, M. (1994). *Reviving Ophelia.* New York: Ballantine Books.

Pollack, W. S. (1998). *Real boys: Rescuing our sons from the myths of boyhood.* New York: Henry Holt and Company.

Pollack, W. S. (2000). *Real boys' voices.* New York: Random House.

Pollack, W. S., & Levant, R. F. (Eds.). (1998). *New psychotherapy for men.* New York: Wiley.

Sherrill, K. (1991, August). Half empty: Gay power and gay powerlessness in American politics. Paper presented at the annual meeting of the American Political Science Association, Washington, DC.

Sherrill, K. (1996). The political power of lesbians, gays, and bisexuals. *PS: Political Science and Politics, 29,* 469–473.

Vaid, U. (1995). *Virtual equality: The mainstreaming of gay & lesbian liberation.* New York: Anchor Books.

Weis, L. (1993). White male working-class youth: An exploration of relative privilege and loss. In L. Weis & M. Fine (Eds.), *Beyond silenced voices: Class, race, and gender in United States schools* (pp. 237–258). Albany, NY: State University of New York Press.

12

How I Got My Wings

CAROL L. LANGER

GROWING UP FEMALE IN THE 1950S: CAROL'S STORY

I was born and raised on a farm. At age 5, I had the task of gathering eggs; my brother, at 13 years old, was already driving a tractor, helping in the fields, and doing chores such as milking the cows, feeding the pigs, and taking care of the horses. At age 7, I was allowed to cook for the wheat harvest and hay crews. I cooked the one meal I knew how to cook: pork and beans with ground beef in them, canned peas, bread and butter, and a "scratch" German chocolate cake. My other chores included cleaning house, doing the laundry, helping with meal preparations, and babysitting for three neighbor children who were only slightly younger than I. I recall wishing that I could drive a tractor, milk the cows, and take care of the horses, because I'd much rather have been outside than inside. However, my father refused to teach me how to drive a tractor, saying, "That's man's work."

In 1967, when I graduated from high school, my career options were secretary, nurse, or teacher. I wanted to go to college and eventually become a doctor, but my mother threw me out of the house when I refused to go to secretarial school. I turned to some distant relatives who had set aside $500 for my college education, but they limited my options by refusing to allow me access to the money without their approval of my major. Becoming a doctor was not one of the options. Five hundred dollars would have paid for a year of my college in 1967. In fact, I graduated in 1971 with a four-year degree and owed only $900 in student loans. My father persuaded my mother to allow me to return home, so, by default, I chose teaching as my occupation. He didn't agree with my mother's actions, but he did agree with and reinforce my career options. His reasoning was that "if the children become sick, you can be with them; and you'll have all summer to spend with them."

I think my father was the kindest, most compassionate person I've ever met. He was a sensitive male who was attempting to live up to the standards of Jessie Bernard's (1981) "The Good Provider." I believe he measured his self-worth by his ability to house, feed, and clothe his family. He was a tenant farmer, and the day came when the crops failed. My mother had to get a job outside the home for our needs to be met. I think my father felt emasculated by this because my mother became the primary breadwinner, and, as a result, she made most of the decisions that would have been either joint decisions or his alone to make. Sexism through stringent sex roles had forced my father into a role that didn't fit him and that had great personal cost for him. It also made me more vulnerable because he no longer protected me as he once had.

It is only with the benefit of hindsight that I can recognize the impact that being born a female has had on my life. My marital status, career choice, and many life experiences are directly related to being female. Also directly related is my contemporary concern for professional recognition, future financial stability, and health issues, including the type and kind of medical care I can receive. Although I cannot address all of these issues in the space allowed, I will talk about sexism and how sexism relates to financial stability, professional recognition, and personal safety.

Sexism has affected me in profound ways. The irony is that I have not always been able to recognize the unequal treatment as sexism. Because I am a product of the society in which I was raised, this non-recognition was very much a part of the problem. For so much of my life, I just accepted things as a matter of course. There are some things, however, that one cannot simply ignore. The first story that follows is a revelation of what I would call the cocoon phase of my development, the second is the larva stage, and the third is the full-fledged butterfly phase.

MY METAMORPHOSIS IN PERSPECTIVE

The cocoon stage: waiting for life to happen

As a junior in college majoring in education, I met, fell in love with, and married David Langer. I was supposed to get married; that's just what one did—at least that's the message I received from society, my parents, and my peers. All of my friends were getting married, and although I was attracted to David, I didn't make a conscious decision to get married based on what I really wanted. I married because it seemed to be what I was supposed to do. Part of my reason for getting married was related to the wedding event itself: the white dress, the veil, the honeymoon. Romance was sold in Modern Bride, and I was definitely in the market for romance. I wanted to be like the brides I saw on the magazine cover, even though I don't think my husband was at all fascinated with looking like a groom. I was 19 years old.

Within our first year of marriage, I gave birth to our first child. Having children was never a conscious choice for me. One simply had children if one was married. It was a matter of course during the 1960s. I wasn't a hippie, so I received the message that I was to be responsible, get married, settle down, have a family, and be a productive member of society. People sometimes cringe when I say I never made a conscious choice to have children. They automatically assume that I wouldn't have had them if I'd had a choice. On the contrary, I just would like to have known that I actually had a choice. In the era in which I was raised, if one was married, one had children or people would whisper, "There must be something wrong with her." Sometimes the gossiper would go so far as to say, "I wonder if the problem is with him or with her?" If I hadn't married, I would have been called an old maid or a spinster. If I hadn't followed the wedding ceremony with a baby shower or two, I would have been labeled self-ish or barren. That's the way the world worked in that place at that time. I was 20, a senior in college, and the mother of a 4-week-old baby boy.

Within the next five years, we had two more sons. David was light years ahead of his generation of males in terms of male roles and behaviors that were acceptable in the 1970s. Males in the 1970s were supposed to be the primary wage earner, were not supposed to show emotions other than anger, and most definitely did not help with child care or housework, at least until the child was of school age. I'm reminded of the television classics *Ozzie and Harriet* and *Leave It to Beaver* when I describe the marital and parental relationships we developed. David did change diapers and rotate feedings, but he didn't do laundry or housework. I'm positive he did his own laundry prior to our marriage. I re-member the time he asked me to do his laundry for him; this was a huge event in my mind and indicated the depth of our commitment. Ironing his shirts was initially a labor of love. After our marriage, when he no longer did any laundry or his own ironing, the warm glow of ironing with affection wore off. During our nearly 10 years of marriage, I began to understand more about his behav-ior. He wanted what he perceived to be a traditional marriage, including sex-based division of labor. Conversely, I wanted a marriage based on who had the skills to do what needed to be done. This disparate perception of marriage never became a bone of contention, however. His job required him to travel a great deal from the time our oldest son was six, so I did everything for the home, in-cluding changing the oil in the vehicles, mowing and fertilizing the lawn, paint-ing and cleaning the gutters, and dealing with all the financial issues of the household. This was good practice for what was to follow—my more androg-ynous role was required for our survival.

From 1971 to 1973, when both of us were teaching high school, I was mak-ing $6,400 a year in part-time employment. I am not aware of comparable male salaries, but I am aware that the perception was that the male was the primary breadwinner and the female income was considered fluff—disposable income. The full-time salary scale for someone in my position was $12,000 annually. Teachers' income was based on their number of hours of education beyond the bachelor's degree and their years of teaching experience. On the surface, this sounds equitable. However, if one was expected to do child care and manage all household responsibilities, taking additional college credit courses was more difficult and had to be reserved for summer; and then child care was needed be-cause the children were out of school. These factors alone made additional hours prohibitive for women with such responsibilities. Additionally, most male faculty could subsidize their annual income by coaching, an avenue not open to most females. In fact, most of the women who were teaching in the school where I taught from 1971 to 1973 were elementary teachers. Most of the sec-ondary teachers and all of the administrators and board members were male.

In 1976, to increase our opportunities, we moved from the rural area where both of us were teaching to a mid-size Nebraska city of nearly 25,000 residents. This is when David assumed the position that required extensive travel.

That same year, I, a college-educated, professionally attired, and articulate professional, interviewed for a position as a bookkeeper. The questions I was asked included "How many days do you miss a month for, well, you know?" "Do you plan to have more children?" "What kind of birth control are you using?" As I sat there, trying to answer these questions, I became increasingly frustrated and uncomfortable. On the one hand, I needed the job to help support my family because we had underestimated our increased cost of living in the new area, so in that sense I felt vulnerable and trapped. On the other hand, I felt the questions were none of his business. I felt humiliated and objectified, and I was intensely angry thinking that if my husband had been the one having the interview, those questions would never have been asked. I felt violated. I don't even remember being asked about my qualifications for the position. The only comment I remember that might be related to my competence was something to the effect of, "Well, the college degree you have at least lets me know you can learn." I left that interview prior to its conclusion, thinking I wouldn't work for this man if he did offer me the job, and I called the state's Department of Labor. I was told that there was "nothing they could do" because it was "my word against his." It seemed to me that things were just that way, and I did not know how to further pursue the issue.

I was soon hired as a secretary-receptionist for a family-planning clinic. My husband was traveling, and child care was frequently an issue. I used to take the two littlest sons to work with me and put them in a playpen in the waiting room. Many clients commented about how this was probably the most effective rationale for birth control that they had considered. I think this whole scenario was another example of the impact of sexism on my life. The position of secretary-receptionist was held largely by females in 1976, and I'm certain that my husband could not have taken the children to work with him, nor would he have been able to take a day off to care for them. His income was twice as much as mine, so we could not have afforded for him to miss work. Meanwhile, I continued to juggle child care, work demands, and household duties. Some nights I was so exhausted that I couldn't even remember going to bed.

David died in 1979 at age 33. I was 29, a widow, with three young sons to raise. It became imperative for me to find a better-paying position, so I returned to a dream: an advanced degree.

The larva stage: being and becoming

I went back to college and earned a Master of Social Work degree. While I was working on that degree, I worked part-time as a cost accountant and part-time as a home-based tutor for the public schools, and I cleaned the grill at the local Dairy Queen at night—from 2 A.M. to 4 A.M. I would probably be arrested today for neglect because I left my three sons home alone during the times I cleaned the grill. Cleaning the grill allowed me to avoid free lunches for my school-age son and allowed a little fun money for the kids, such as a weekly McDonald's drive-through.

In 1986, I began teaching part time at a four-year liberal arts institution. I worked full time as a school social worker and part time as a medical social worker. My position at the college gradually increased to full-time, tenure track. My starting salary was $18,600 annually. I felt rich compared to all of the time I had earned part-time income, but in reality I was still not being paid as much as my husband had been paid in 1979, without an advanced degree. I worked at this institution for six years before deciding to leave. My reasons for leaving were tied to issues of sexism.

- I was forced to work on my Ph.D. by contract, while a male in the computer science department had no such restrictions.
- The school hired a male athletic trainer with just a bachelor's degree, at a salary that was $6,000 greater than mine was after six years of service (according to the faculty grapevine).
- I served on six committees, I taught four classes per semester, I had four preparations, and I was both a freshman advisor and an academic advisor. I had asked to be relieved of some of my committee work because I was driving quite a distance to night classes twice a week, and my mother had a stroke and I was the only surviving child to see to her care. I was told, "You're just the kind of person we want interacting with our students. There are people on this campus who we don't want near our students." My annual review usually included comments such as, "Needs to learn how to say no."

Thinking that my experience in higher education was probably universal, I left college teaching in search of another career. I moved to a community about an hour away and assumed a managerial position for a weight-loss center. The year was 1992.

Getting wings: the butterfly stage

I connected on a personal level with Bob, a man I'd known in high school. He seemed charming, witty, attentive, and stable. Bob had been my mother's real-estate agent for nearly five years, and we had talked frequently over the course of those five years. We began our serious relationship in early 1992 and married in September 1992.

Within the first month of our marriage, Bob held me captive in his home. Basically, I was supposed to stay home, cook and clean, and be ready for his return from a hard day's work. He secretly sold the items I had in storage and did not allow me to have car keys; however, two of my sons were teens, and both had cars. My oldest son was in college in another city. Since my sons were in school, I tried to find a job. If I had an interview, Bob would call me before and after my scheduled appointment. I found part-time employment as a home-health, quality-assurance technician. The area where we lived was fairly isolated and had a high rate of rural poverty, so jobs were scarce. I could not afford my prescription medications, and Bob would not put me on his insurance. He would not allow me to call my mother unless I paid for the call because it was long distance.

I remember clearly the day I asked if I could have a can of Diet Coke that I had purchased. Something snapped inside me, and I began laying the ground-work to leave. I began to save every cent I could, and I investigated the cost of renting a U-Haul truck to move our remaining items. I could not have pre-dicted how soon I would have to use this information, though. Before my plan was fully in place, we needed to leave for our safety.

My youngest son was in another state at a choir retreat with a school group. My other son and I were home with Bob on a rainy fall evening. Bob had just bought a purebred chocolate lab. He was trying to housebreak the puppy. The puppy had just gone outside in the rain, but when Bob brought her back in-side, she squatted and urinated on the floor. This infuriated Bob, and he began shaking and hitting the puppy. My son asked him to stop, and Bob aggressively turned on my son, threatening him in no uncertain terms. I intervened, put myself between them, and told my son to go to the car. We left immediately with only the clothes on our backs. We stayed overnight at a motel in the near-est town and rented a truck the next morning. We didn't know where we were going until we were forced to give a destination. I have no siblings and had no other family nearby. We returned to the place where I had originally taught col-lege courses. We were homeless. We put our items in storage and stayed with friends until we collectively earned enough to rent our own home. The year was 1993. I had stayed with Bob nearly a year.

I again began teaching as an adjunct at that college, and both sons worked part time to help with expenses. They both eventually graduated from high school. My oldest and middle sons completed college. I returned to college and completed my Ph.D. in 2000. I was a telemarketer and a college admissions rep-resentative to support myself and assist my younger son as much as I could.

CONCLUSION

It is an undeniable truth that one's sex at birth—biology—begins a process of so-cialization resulting in one's gender—the social role. In the 1950s, being male or female resulted in clearly defined social roles. As a female born during the 1950s, I didn't see very many choices for myself. As a result, I did what I thought I was "supposed to do"—I followed role-appropriate behaviors. Sexism is unequal treatment because of one's sex. Because of institutionalized sexism, my life story plays out in several important ways. First, my retirement income will not be the equivalent of a male counterpart because my salary has been less. This smaller "nest egg" will be reflected in both my personal retirement and my Social Se-curity income. I will have to work longer and save more than my male coun-terparts with equivalent professional training and jobs. Second, my education and training did little to balance my opportunities in the face of institutional in-equality. I was powerless as an individual; however, I believe that positive change can happen with organized groups of educated individuals.

While I was writing this chapter, a colleague and I had a brief discussion of my use of the term *sex* as opposed to *gender*. He thought that I should be using *gender* because social implications are at issue. The point in my choice of terms is that the human biological level of sex has influenced my destiny. Gender, on the other hand, is what I can make of my life from this point forward. My colleague then questioned my use of the term *female,* saying he thought it was more empowering for women to identify as *woman* than as *female* (I am woman, hear me roar). My response to him was that I spent most of my life being "just a *woman,*" doing "*woman's* work." Now, I prefer to think of myself as a human who happens to have been born female, and all possibilities are open to me as a result. My basic biology is fundamental to my personal empowerment, no longer a limitation.

Biology is not destiny, and using biology as destiny should not be allowed to govern the expectations for women or men. My personal and professional growth has taken place across time. Recognizing and combating sexism has not been an overnight development. It is a journey I'm still taking. As for my sons, their life experiences have allowed them to become very supportive and nurturing males, husbands, and fathers. As teenagers and young adults, they witnessed the inequitable salaries I received. They did not have positive male role models in their lives, and they each missed that sort of interaction in unique ways. The oldest son now has two children and values very much the time that he spends with them. He remembers times when he and his brothers were ill at the same time, and there was just mom to tend to their needs. He finds it incredible that one person could do what needs to be done. He cooks, he cleans, he irons—he does whatever he needs to. The middle son missed having someone to show him how to throw a football and change the oil. Even though I played catch with him, I didn't have the knowledge to throw a perfect spiral. He recently told me that he blamed me for that for a long time. Now that he is married and a first-time home owner, he realizes that throwing a perfect spiral was not as important as learning how to budget time and money, and hearing, "I love you." He never fails to tell me that his wife is extremely grateful to me for raising a son with no fear of talking about his feelings. My youngest son is also married. He treasures his life partner, makes a great beef and broccoli stir fry, and openly cries if he feels he needs to. He is still struggling with choices about his life's work. Because my sons experienced firsthand the results of sexism on my life and theirs, they have vowed not to repeat patterns of inequality.

DISCUSSION QUESTIONS

1. Explain how "blonde jokes" are sexist. Someone in your usual crowd begins telling a blonde joke. What do you do?

2. What are the reasons that a woman might stay in an abusive relationship? How do these reasons relate to sexism?

3. Can men be feminists?

4. If women don't recognize that they are victimized by sexism, how might it be pointed out to them? Should this be pointed out?

5. How does pornography contribute to sexism?

6. Is it sexism to have assigned role responsibilities based on sex? Why or why not?

7. In what ways has your sex shaped your life?

REFERENCE

Bernard, J. (1989). The good-provider role: Its rise and fall. In A. Skolnick and J. Skolnick (Eds.), *Family in transition: Rethinking marriage, sexuality, child rearing, and family organization* (6th ed., pp. 143–162). Glenview, IL: Scott, Foresman and Company.

✳

Part II

Issues Related to Privilege, Oppression, and Discrimination

13

Assumed Privilege

A Double-Edged Sword

ALLAN E. BARSKY

BACKGROUND

According to cliché, "You don't know what you've got until it's gone." This seems to be true in the case of social privilege. If you are born into society such that you are fortunate to benefit from mainstream or majority status, you are less likely to be aware of social privilege than if you come from an oppressed or minority background. In my situation, I did not know what I had until I slowly came to the realization that I was part of an oppressed minority group. In fact, the oppression was so strong that I hid my minority status for many years, living in fear about what life would be like without privilege.

I am 42 years old, White, male, Canadian, able-bodied, employed, and well educated. In other words, I have a background that has afforded me many privileges. I have not had to endure ageism, sexism, racism, ableism, and so on. Educationally and career-wise, many doors have been open that I have generally taken for granted. Yet there are two areas of my life in which perhaps I am not quite so privileged, though some say I am twice blessed (Balka & Rose, 1991).

As a Jewish person who grew up in a small prairie city with few Jews, I have experienced a number of forms of discrimination throughout my life. As the only non-Christian in my classes, I was expected to recite Christian prayers and songs, participate in Christmas pageants, and eat food that went against family traditions. Although our family did not keep strict rules of kashrut (religious dietary laws), I still remember a Christmas party at which I bit into something and said it was the strangest beef I had ever had. My friends laughed at how I did not even know what ham was. I can still feel the blush in my face, even though I did not really have anything to be ashamed of. There were times when teachers acknowledged my Jewishness, but that was often worse than when they ignored it. Once I was asked to play Jesus in a school play because Jesus was Jewish and so was I. Initially, I wondered whether this meant they wanted to crucify me. The play was not as traumatic as I thought it might be, but it did reinforce that I was different, not quite fitting in with everyone else. Another memory that still haunts me is being asked to sing a Chanukah song at the Christmas pageant. I think the teacher meant to be sensitive to my religion, but once again the experience felt alienating and embarrassing. I also remember being asked questions about the "Old Testament," with the teacher assuming I would be an authority on this because I was Jewish. I wanted to say, "What do you mean, Old Testament? There is only one testament." It seemed easier to comply rather than to confront. Most of my classmates had little knowledge of Judaism, so most of their insensitivities could be chalked up to ignorance rather than intentional meanness. One told me that I could not be Jewish because I did not have horns. Another told me his parents would not let him come to my house because we were Jewish, although he did not know why they had this rule. Others used the phrase "I got jewed" (meaning cheated) without even knowing this was an offensive term. In spite of these incidents, my overall experience of being Jewish has been quite positive. I have felt strongly supported by my family and by the Jewish communities I have been associated with. With few exceptions, my opportunities to make friends, to be admitted to educational programs, to participate in cultural events, and to get jobs have not been limited by my being Jewish. Though Christian privilege still exists in Canadian and American society, more and more opportunities seem to be open for non-Christians.

My other experience of being a minority is a bit more complicated. I am gay and believe that being gay is something I have always been. However, being gay is not an aspect of myself that I was always aware of. From my earliest recollections about sexuality in my childhood until into my early adulthood, I assumed I was heterosexual—I lived a heterosexual life, and I benefited from living with an assumed heterosexual identity. I was free to date women and be seen with them in social situations, without fear of being harassed verbally or physically, and without fear of losing a job, family, friends, or other support systems. At the time, I was not aware of the privileges I had. As I came to realize my identity as a gay man, however, all of this privilege came into doubt. I had to make some decisions about the life I would lead, the risks I would take, and the privileges I would have to leave behind.

THE PRIVILEGE OF THE CLOSET

When people ask me about my being in the closet, most assume that this was a horrible part of my life. In hindsight, parts of this closeted lifestyle were horrible—living in fear about being found out, not wanting to disappoint or embarrass my parents, doubting who I was, living a double life, feeling as if I was living a lie, wondering whether suicide was the answer. For several years, however, my closet was actually quite a comfortable place to live.

Although I was gay, people assumed I was heterosexual, and I benefited from heterosexual privilege. Most of my mannerisms, interests, clothes, and so on were not typically gay. In grade school, I was sometimes teased for not being the most coordinated or athletic kid, particularly during competitive team sports. But I was not the last one chosen for the team or the one who was called "fag" or "fairy." In retrospect, perhaps I should thank a couple of classmates for taking much of this abuse because I could have just as easily been the recipient. As someone who generally fit in, I could talk hockey and football, play sports, drink beer, party, and do most of what "ordinary guys" did with their peers. Although I was somewhat shy and awkward with dating, that did not identify me as gay because many young straight men go through a phase of being shy and awkward when they are dating women.

Although I was surrounded by homophobia and heterosexism, I was not aware that those biases had any direct relevance for me. I was still deep in my closet, even if I was called a fruit or mocked for having long, curly hair, and this teasing did not go to my identity because I still thought of myself as a "normal person." I hardly ever discussed sexuality—homosexual or otherwise—with peers or family. To avoid the embarrassment of having to talk directly about these issues, my parents strategically placed an old edition of the book, *Everything You Always Wanted to Know about Sex, but Were Afraid to Ask* (Reuben, 2000), on a bookshelf where each of their two pre-teenaged sons could read it, in case we had questions we wanted to ask. This was the first professional literature on homosexuality that I had ever read. Like most pre-1980s psychological literature on homosexuality, this book alluded to homosexuality as an illness. At the time, I did not know it was telling me I was pathologically disordered. In fact, the book seemed quite progressive.

My only other familiarity with gays came from Hollywood movies, such as *Dog Day Afternoon* or *Cruising,* in which gays were portrayed as promiscuous, dangerous, and deviant. I accepted that there was something wrong with being gay, and that it was something that required either punishment or curing. It was not until later in my life that I began to understand the oppressiveness of the media and of traditional mental health views on gay, lesbian, bisexual, transgender, queer and/or questioning (GLBTQ) individuals.

Throughout my adult education, I had very few role models, teachers, or professors who were gay-positive. Although law schools and social-work schools are more progressive today, many of my courses and textbooks still viewed homosexuality as immoral (something to be punished) or pathological (something to be treated and cured). The one professor who everyone "knew" was gay made deprecating remarks about gays, supposedly in jest. These jokes did not bother me. They were not mocking me because I was still not identifying myself as gay. Although some professors spoke of social justice issues for GLBTQ people, the curricula focused on sexism, racism, and cultural discrimination. I bought into the rhetoric and internalized the view that individuals who are GLBTQ choose their social condition and therefore do not fit into the same category as other oppressed groups.

As I began my professional career, still single, the comfort of my closet was starting to break down, and I had to make some choices—would I continue to live life as if I were heterosexual, or would I start to admit to myself and others that I was gay, with all the risks that would entail?

BEGINNING THE PROCESS: COMING OUT TO MYSELF

For myself, as for many other GLBTQs, coming out is a gradual process, including coming out to oneself, to the gay community, to straight colleagues at work, to straight friends, and finally, to family members. Each stage of coming out can be filled with fear and anxiety (Smith, 1997). For heterosexual adolescents and young adults, exploring sexuality can be a scary stage of life, fearing how the other person will respond to you and whether you will be "good enough" in spite of your inexperience. Yet as a heterosexual, society sends many positive messages telling you that intimacy with a person of the other sex is good, fun, and even expected. There are also many positive role models. For gays, many societal messages still tell you that same-sex intimacy is wrong, corrupt, dirty, or sick. When I had my first sexual and intimate encounters with other men, these were the messages I carried with me. Internally, something felt wonderful about this intimacy, but I also experienced an overwhelming sense of shame and guilt. I tried to rationalize, "Yes, I've had sex with men, but I can't be gay. I'm not effeminate like them. I'm just a bit shy with women."

Though I was not aware of this at the time, many social forces encouraged me to remain in the closet. As long as people assumed that I was straight, I would continue to be accepted by my family, my friends, my employers, and even people who hardly knew me. In other words, I could access heterosexual privilege, so long as I played the game. I had a close friend whose parents cut him off from their lives when they discovered he was gay. He was emotionally devastated for several years. This could have been me. Most people from minority backgrounds are a minority within the community but not within the family. But I felt alienated in my own family, afraid to ask for support from those who loved me most, out of fear of losing them altogether.

Professionally, I had many experiences that challenged the safety of my assumed heterosexuality. Having pursued careers in law and social work, I was supposed to be an advocate for social justice and promote equality for those in vulnerable situations. If I was too scared to advocate for myself, even within my own family, how could I be effective as an agent of social change for others?

MAINTAINING PRIVILEGE OR RISKING SELF-DISCLOSURE

In one of my first social-work jobs, I worked with street youth, 14- to 24-year-olds who had either run away from home or been forced out of their homes by their families. Many of these clients were gay, lesbian, bisexual, transgender, queer, or questioning. I felt incredibly queasy about working with these populations, still apprehensive that I was only starting to work through my own issues. I felt hypocritical trying to help GLBTQ clients feel better about themselves while I was still hiding so much about myself. On one hand, I risked losing the safety bubble of my assumed heterosexuality if I started to come out to my clients. On the other hand, I knew that being authentic with clients is one of the cornerstones of effective therapeutic practice.

Perhaps the most critical incident of my professional career came when a client presented to me in crisis, crying, perspiring, and trembling. Through a long and confused story, he divulged that he was gay, that he was just outed to his friends on the street, and that he would rather die than face them. Although he had slept with a few men, he did not have any gay friends or support systems. Incorporating what I knew from crisis-intervention training (Hammelman, 1993), I went through the protocols for suicidal ideation screening and intervention. He had a specific plan for killing himself—jumping in front of a subway—so I knew there was a high level of risk. Of Rogers' (1957) three core conditions for effective psychotherapy, I offered the client empathy and unconditional positive regard, but not genuineness. I felt that the client responded well to the understanding and respect that I demonstrated, but I also felt that had I been more authentic with the client and with myself, I could have offered much more. I wanted to let him know that he was not alone in his pain—that I had also felt the fear of being rejected by family and friends. Yet, how could I tell him this when I was still living in fear and not confronting it myself? I rationalized that I should not use the counseling situation to work through my own issues, so I should not disclose. I knew deeper down that I had internalized societal homophobia so deeply that I could not risk coming out to the client, even though he was gay and in need (Barsky, Barsky, & Laverdiere, 2000).

I tested the waters of coming out with people who I assumed had no connection with my family, friends, and co-workers. The easiest places to do this were in foreign cities and at gay venues in neighborhoods that were far from where I lived. I could continue to live as a heterosexual and enjoy the privileges this entailed, while beginning to develop relationships with people in the gay community. As I began to see more and more openly gay people, I started to visualize a realistic possibility of coming out. I would often ask people for their coming-out stories, expecting to hear the worst, but more often than not hearing a narrative of triumph or freedom. My images of gays as being bashed, discriminated against, rejected, and destined to a troubled life were being replaced with stories of people who had accepted their destinies as being gay, who had gone through varying experiences of discrimination and rejection, and who ultimately were finding that being out and living without heterosexual privilege was far better than living a lie.

I still feel somewhat anguished for putting my parents through a period of misery when I came out to them. They also had to come out to friends and family about having a gay son. When I was in the closet, they did not have to be concerned about people's reactions to their son, who they saw as a source of pride. Once I came out, that privilege was lost. Who knew how people would react to news of having a gay son? They already questioned whether they were to blame. Interestingly, they never questioned whether they were to blame for the fact that their other three sons were heterosexual.

ASSUMED PRIVILEGE NO MORE

I have worked through many of my issues, accepting that each time I come out to someone I am taking a risk that a heterosexual person would not experience. Although many of my experiences have been positive, I continue to experience oppression in many realms of my life. I have had neighbors who would not speak with me because I am gay. I have had friends who cut me off from their lives when they found out I am gay. My partner cannot get health coverage through my university because the State of Florida does not recognize our Canadian marriage or our domestic partnership, even though it is registered with our county. Strangers ask about our daughter's mother and respond with bewilderment when we say that our daughter has two fathers. I have been chased by drunken teens and harassed by police because they thought I was gay. My partner's stepfather broke up with his mother because she allowed me into her house. I have had students accuse me of being "anti-Christian" because of my inclusion of GLBTQ content in the curriculum. Each of these incidents hurt me, making me feel angry and sad at times, but sometimes even more determined to do what I can to make life easier for those GLBTQ people who come after me.

As a social-work professor, I include GLBTQ content in my courses (Barsky, 2000; Bowser, Auletta, & Jones, 1993; Hartman & Laird, 1998; Martin & Hunter, 2001; Perez, DeBord, & Bieschke, 2000; O'Neil, 1999; Roberts et al., 1994; van Wormer, Wells, & Boes, 2000) because infusion of GLBTQ content in the curriculum has been found to reduce homophobic attitudes of social-work students (Lim & Johnson, 2001). I use inclusive language, such as "intimate partner" rather than "husband or wife" to promote language that validates the existence of GLBTQ people, rather than deny it. I use examples from my own experiences with doctors, social workers, and other professionals who had no clue I was gay and were therefore unable to help me with issues related to my gayness and the homophobia I was experiencing. Many GLBTQs are afraid to access help for serious concerns, including suicidal ideation (Tremblay & Ramsay, 1997), substance abuse (Howard & Collins, 1997), and domestic violence (Lundy & Leventhal, 1999; Mallon, 1998). I stopped seeing a doctor, for instance, whose intake questionnaire asked if I were homosexual; I feared how he would react if he found out I was lying and wondered what would happen to my health insurance if the provider found out. Using relevant examples from my own life not only demonstrates pride in who I am, but gives GLBTQ students permission to talk about their experiences with homophobia, in class or privately. I also invite students of other diverse backgrounds to relate their experiences with privilege and oppression. The class members learn to appreciate one another's experiences with privilege and oppression, which helps everyone to be more empathic and supportive when they are working with clients with similar issues.

I still catch myself, once in a while, fearing what others will think or do if they suspect I am gay. I know that accepting heterosexual privilege by not revealing myself to others can be a double-edged sword: Included with the benefits are costs, and these costs are simply too high.

APPLICATION

Consider the following scenario. Shauna is a recently hired assistant professor in a Women's Studies department at a liberal-arts college. During her first year, Shauna has received positive teaching evaluations, published two research articles in credible journals, and taken a lead role in the department's curriculum redesign. What her department does not know is that Shauna was born as Shawn. Shauna had male-to-female sex-reassignment surgery shortly after she graduated from high school. She decided to start her life anew, which meant moving to a new town and not telling anyone about growing up transgendered.

Shauna has a number of reasons to fear disclosure. She lives in an area in which the majority of the population is very conservative in terms of religious and social perspectives. The laws of her state do not protect transgendered people from discrimination in the workplace or otherwise. She has not received tenure. She has heard other faculty in her department make disparaging remarks about gays and lesbians, and she believes that the head of her department would nix her tenure if the faculty discovered her secret. Still, she has no proof that disclosure would impede her career.

Chris, a colleague from the psychology department, knows Shauna's history, having grown up with her. Chris tells Shauna that she needs to disclose her transgenderism to her department and to her students. According to Chris, Shauna is being dishonest. Chris and Shauna both see themselves as feminists, meaning that they believe "the personal is political" (Saulnier, 1996). Accordingly, Chris suggests that Shauna's transgenderism is not just a private issue, but also an issue that needs to be raised publicly to enhance awareness and social justice for all transgendered people. Shauna feels conflicted. How would you help Shauna with the following questions:

1. What aspects of social privilege has Shauna benefited from by being assumed to be non-transgender?

2. What are the potential risks to Shauna if she gives up the invisibility of her transgender background?

3. What are Shauna's legal, ethical, and moral obligations concerning disclosure?

4. Under what circumstances, if any, would it be appropriate for Chris to out Shauna against Shauna's will (Mohr, 1999)? Because Chris has grown up in a situation of privilege, how can she truly understand the oppression Shauna might face if she comes out or is outed involuntarily?

Consider the following questions from the viewpoints of Shauna (personally and professionally), the liberal arts college, the students, and general society.

1. Are the obligations of a professional any different if the person comes from another oppressed group (for example, a lesbian or a light-skinned person with African American ancestry)? If so, what might justify the differences?

2. Do the answers to these questions depend upon whether the professional is a university professor, a social worker, a psychologist, a primary school teacher, or some other type of professional?

Consider the next two questions as they relate to the author of this chapter.

1. Reflecting back over the chapter, what aspects of the author's experiences surprised you? Why do you think these were surprising?

2. How could other professionals in the author's life have helped him with the coming out process?

REFERENCES

Balka, C., & Rose, A. (Eds.). (1991). *Twice blessed: On being gay or lesbian and Jewish*. Boston: Beacon Press.

Barsky, A. E. (2000). Archie's adoption (role-play exercise on advocacy involving a gay client). In A. E. Barsky, *Conflict resolution for the helping professions* (pp. 253–255). Belmont, CA: Wadsworth.

Barsky, A. E., Barsky, S. A., & Laverdiere, A. (2000, August). Crisis intervention with a gay Irish American man: Social work and interprofessional responses. In E. Geva, A. E. Barsky, & F. Westernoff. (Eds.), *Interprofessional practice with diverse populations: Cases in point*. Greenwich, CN: Greenwood.

Bowser, B. P., Auletta, G. S., & Jones, T. (1993). *Confronting diversity issues on campus*. Newbury Park, CA: Sage.

Hammelman, T. L. (1993). Gay and lesbian youth: Contributing factors to serious attempts or considerations of suicide. *Journal of Gay and Lesbian Psychotherapy, 2*(1), 77–89.

Hartman, A., & Laird, J. (1998). Moral and ethical issues in working with lesbians and gay men. *Families in Society: The Journal of Contemporary Human Services, 79,* 263–276.

Howard, B., & Collins, B. E. (1997). Working with lesbians and gay men. In S. Harrison, & V. Carver (Eds.), *Alcohol and drug problems* (pp. 293–318). Toronto: Addiction Research Foundation.

Lim, H. S., & Johnson, M. M. (2001). Korean social work students' attitudes towards homosexuals. *Journal of Social Work Education, 37,* 545–555.

Lundy, S. E., & Leventhal, B. (1999). *Same sex domestic violence: Strategies for change*. Thousand Oaks, CA: Sage.

Mallon, G. P. (1998). *We don't exactly get the welcome wagon: The experiences of gay and lesbian adolescents in child welfare systems*. New York: Columbia University Press.

Martin, J. I., & Hunter, S. (2001). *Lesbian, gay, bisexual and transgender issues in social work: A comprehensive bibliography with annotations*. Washington, DC: Counsel on Social Work Education.

Mohr, R. D. (1999). *Gay ideas: Outing and other controversies*. Boston: Beacon Press.

O'Neil, B. (1999). Social work with gay, lesbian, and bisexual members of racial and ethnic minority groups. In G. Y. Lie & D. Este (Eds.), *Professional social service delivery in a multicultural world*. Toronto: Canadian Scholars.

Perez, R. M., DeBord, K. A., & Bieschke, K. J. (2000). *Handbook of counseling and psychotherapy with lesbian, gay, and bisexual clients*. Washington, DC: American Psychological Association.

Reuben, D. (2000). *Everything you always wanted to know about sex, but were afraid to ask*. New York: Bantam (1st ed., 1969).

Roberts, H., Gonzales, J. C., Harris, O. D., Huff, D. J., Johns, A., Lou, R., & Scott,

O. L. (1994). *Teaching from a multicultural perspective.* Newbury Park, CA: Sage.

Rogers, C. (1957). The necessary and sufficient conditions of therapeutic personality change. *Journal of Counseling Psychology 25,* 91–103.

Saulnier, C. R. (1996). *Feminist theories and social work: Approaches and applications.* Binghamton, NY: Haworth.

Smith, A. (1997). Cultural diversity and the coming out process. In B. Greene (Ed.), *Ethnic and cultural diversity among lesbians and gay men.* Newbury Park, CA: Sage.

Tremblay, P. J., & Ramsay, R. (1997). Gay and bisexual male youth: Overrepresented in suicide problems and associate risk factors. Presented at Third Bi-Regional Adolescent Suicide Prevention Conference, Breckenridge, CO. Available on World Wide Web at: www.virtualcity.com/youthsuicide/colorado.htm.

van Wormer, K., Wells, J., & Boes, M. (2000). *Social work with lesbians, gays, and bisexuals.* Boston: Allyn & Bacon.

14

"Who, Me? White?"

The Process of Acknowledging and Challenging Racial Privilege

HELEN G. DEINES

UNDERSTANDING AND EXPERIENCING
WHITE PRIVILEGE: HELEN'S STORY

My first week at college taught me an unexpected fact—I do not look Mexican. I grew up in San Francisco, the daughter of a Mexican mother and an Irish father. In my circumscribed immigrant neighborhood, everyone knew me as I knew myself—as both Elena (at home, a little Mexicana with braids) and Helen, one of a motley assemblage of children becoming Americans.

When I moved 30 miles away to attend Stanford University, my social identity changed practically overnight. What a mess! At 18 years old, for the first time in my life, I was identified as White. I learned that most Americans equate fair skin and unaccented English with White and simply refuse to accept what to them is a contradictory term, *Mexican,* or even *Mexican American.*

This is not a story about passing—in 1960, I didn't even know that term. I tried to explain who I was "really," and I devised my own convoluted process of racial coming out. Most people, however, did not pay much attention to my efforts to explain myself. Over the years, I continued to grapple with building some clear sense of who I was, sometimes boldly asserting my Mexican roots, but at other times simply being unable to find a graceful way to challenge others' assumptions about my Whiteness. Two incidents stand out for me as pivotal to my identity development and my understanding of privilege.

Story one

I left California after college, moving successively further away from the part of the country where Mexican heritage is widely understood. In 1996, by then a social work professor in Louisville, Kentucky, I participated in the Lilly Conference on College Teaching at Miami University of Ohio. I walked across campus in a soaking rain to hear Trinity University's Distinguished Professor of Humanities, Arturo Madrid (1996), present a paper on Latino history. I was unsure of my motivation to hear the speech. I just knew it was sufficiently important to me, personally, to justify a thorough drenching.

I listened, for the first time, to my reality being described as an objective academic topic. Madrid used the words I had grown up with and long ago forgotten or suppressed—the demeaning *pachuca* (a poor street kid, and my mother's greatest insult, as in, "Elena, dress like that and people with think you are a *pachuca!*"), the mystifying *californianos* ("We are descendants of the Spanish conquistadors, you know!") rather than the charged *mexicanos* (the not-quite-respectable mixture of Spanish and "Indian"). Madrid's voice was slow and sad, I thought, when he used the homogenized, meaningless Hispanic. None of us, after all, ever came to the United States from a country named "Hispania"; we who are Latino/a carry the cultures of Puerto Rico, Cuba, Mexico, Ecuador, Spain, Chile, and so many more—each unique and each worth naming to the persons whose life the country shapes.

Most important, he described my interior life—that of a woman who looks White, carries an Anglo name, speaks Spanish like a four-year-old, but is nonetheless a Latina. He described the lives of people I had never envisioned—people who looked Mexican or Puerto Rican or Guatemalan, had Spanish surnames, but spoke no Spanish and grew up in totally Anglo cultures; nonetheless, they identified as Latinos and Latinas. I wept throughout the talk, realizing for the first time that my own confusion was a common experience among Latino/as in the United States. These were tears of relief. I felt expansive, deeply connected in a whole new way to people whom I had never met. Yet I also felt a fleeting sense of shame that I was so self-absorbed that I was blind to others' struggles. At that moment I did not realize how my Whiteness had exempted me from others' realities.

When I spoke with Madrid after the presentation, he responded to my emotional intensity and promptly gave me the Web site for the written text of his speech, so that I might easily revisit all the new ideas. I left the hall feeling weightless. I no longer saw my confusion about identity as a personal failing. I was now confident that my individual struggle would be eased by awareness of faceless sisters and brothers who walked through similar challenges.

At the end of the conference, I returned to Louisville, committed to finding ways to reclaim my Latina roots. I began reading Latino/a authors. An anthology of growing-up stories by Mexican American children (López, 1993) included narratives very much like my own, and a Latino/a studies reader (Delgado & Stefanic, 1998) introduced me to complexities of identity I had never considered. The famous Richard Rodriguez (1982, 1992), whose writings explore how his brownness has shaped his life, was educated just as I by the Sisters of Mercy and Stanford. Yet Rodriguez (1982, p. 130) notes that he "was the student at Stanford who remembered to notice the Mexican American janitors and gardeners working on campus." I had not.

As I became increasingly focused on my Latina identity, I studied Spanish and made plans to travel to Colombia as a human rights observer. I wanted to "try out" a Latin culture, but I was not quite ready for Mexico. A pervasive uneasiness suggested that "who I was" was not a simple matter.

Story two

Only a few months after the Lilly Conference, I was having lunch with an African American colleague. We were bemoaning the disrespect we experienced as women of color. I ached as I heard her description of being dismissed as "just one of those affirmative-action hires." She listened quietly as I described my frustration at repeatedly coming out to colleagues and students, who most often responded by denying my claim of being Latina or joking about what might be an apt metaphor for a woman who is White on the outside and Brown within. My friend was silent for a few seconds, finally saying, "But you always have the choice."

WHAT "HAVING A CHOICE" MEANS AND WHERE IT LEADS

My friend's simple observation was what transformative educators (Mezirow & Associates, 2000) identify as a "disorienting experience," an event that causes a shift in one's most basic paradigms. Suddenly I knew that how I named myself mattered not a bit because the world saw me as White. I had, in fact, lived with all the advantages that accrue to Whites in American society. As I look back on the experience of leaving home for college, I realize that I knew I was White long before I acknowledged that I was White. Like any 18-year-old going off to college, I worried about many things—that I would not be smart enough, that I would be the poorest person in my class, which I was, or that I would be the only Catholic in a Protestant world. Yet I have no memory of thinking that I would look or sound different than my classmates. For all my conscious thoughts about being Mexican, I knew in an unspoken, deeply visceral way that I would "fit." Race was not a worry.

That pattern has continued throughout my life. When a police officer stops me while I'm driving on the expressway, I assume I must have been speeding; racial profiling need never occur to me. I enter every professional job interview free to focus solely on my qualifications, never diverted by having to manage ethno-racial differences—people in power almost always look just like me!

Diane Goodman (2001) cogently describes the situation, ". . . oppression operates on the basis of how society (the privileged group) views and names individuals, not necessarily on the basis of how people define themselves" (p. 7). This is the insidiousness of privilege. I need not seek advantage. It is conferred through the ways in which our society distributes and uses power. Exercising privilege also requires no personal meanness. Silence and/or inaction maintain the status quo in which some are always unconsciously "ahead of the game."

My stories bear the "fingerprints" of privilege. Goodman (2001, pp. 25–31) describes three ways of thinking that she finds common among individual members of advantaged groups—lack of awareness of their dominant identity, denial of the existence of oppression, and a sense of entitlement to the advantages they usually experience. In retrospect, I realize that my gender, status as a child of immigrants, and nurturance in a social justice-oriented family masked my sense of Whiteness. I felt like an outsider, so I was quite oblivious to my identity as a member of dominant White society. Although my family ensured that I was aware of injustice and oppression, we never identified ourselves as the oppressors! Finally, I smugly nurtured in my heart a sense of being entitled to all the good experiences, opportunities, and relationships in my life. Did I have the advantage on an unequal playing field? Never!

My ultimate "white privilege" is to choose when and where to be a woman of color. Root (2000) offers a poetic "Bill of Rights for Racially Mixed People" that includes these lines: "I have the right to identify myself differently than strangers expect me to identify . . . to identify myself differently from how my parents identify me . . . to identify myself differently in different situations" (p. 121). Although in my mind I have always been Latina, I consciously decide, just like any person who comes out, when to disclose my hidden identity. I try to be honest and practical, disclosing appropriately as friendships or collegial relationships develop, but not bothering grocery clerks with my heritage. I justify selective "secret-keeping by omission" as avoiding gratuitous debate. It was only after my colleague's comment about choice that I realized I was also protecting myself from painful discussions about whether I am "really" Mexican. I have the ultimate white privilege—I need never engage in America's contentious discussion of race unless I so choose. I am an active, yet sometimes unaware, participant in the racist "system of advantage and privilege which accrues to those considered White" (Basham, Donner, & Everett, 2001, p. 158).

That, given a choice, I most often opt to describe myself as Latina should not be surprising. Goodman (2001) observes that people cling tenaciously to the disadvantaged dimensions of their identity (the place where they have known hurt) to defend against seeing themselves as advantaged in comparison with other groups. For example, White women tend to emphasize their gender, gay men their sexual orientation, and so forth.

To recognize myself as White has been an explosive piece of knowledge. Hardiman and Jackson (1997) suggest in their theory of social identity development that all of us begin as children with a sense of naiveté about race. Our culture teaches us the unwritten rules of domination and subordination. Eventually, we encounter landmines of contradictions that lead us to question, as I often do in my classes, "If we are all created equal and if we all are free to live the American dream, why are there so few people of color in my neighborhood . . . or my child's classroom . . . or leaders in my professional organization?" Ultimately, if eyes and ears stay open to contradictions and there is opportunity for value-focused reflection, individuals resist the long-standing "givens" that maintain the inequities that pervade our lives. Sustained, active resistance is possible only when one recognizes one's own place in maintaining systems of domination.

CONCLUSIONS AND LESSONS LEARNED

In this narrative, I have shared my struggle to recognize and challenge my own white privilege in a multiracial society. Antiracism education experts present my reality in coldly objectifying terms: "The already complex nature of racism is complicated further for people who identify themselves as biracial and whose families include both agents and targets [of oppression]" (Wijeyesinghe, Griffin, & Love, 1997, p. 85). My narrative is a more personal account, using

Elena's/Helen's story to demonstrate the common human dynamic of clinging to an image of self as disadvantaged, oblivious throughout to one's own privileges and place in maintaining systems of domination (Goodman, 2001).

Considering my personal stories in the context of multicultural education and practice, I find two consistent applications. First, as social identity develops and changes through interactions across the life span, change agents need a "long haul" view in promoting individuals' recognition of their own privileges. I focus my work on precipitating those disorienting experiences and building spaces safe for exploration of the threatening world of relative advantage and disadvantage. I highlight the disturbing elements in student or client stories, poetry and fiction, videos, as well as multicultural exercises, encouraging participants to move in their own time through dis-ease. Immediate epiphanies are neither required nor encouraged. I reward critical, reflective thinking and tenacity in staying in the struggle.

Second, I believe that simply recognizing privilege is an insufficient measure of competence in the helping professions. Actions that dislodge longstanding patterns of domination and subordination are required. I foster skills in raising questions, visioning alternative ways of working and living together, and acting intentionally to resist injustice. My goal over that long haul is to foster a spirit of discomfort about life's inequities, uneasiness that calls forth sustained reflection, and, ultimately, deliberate action to unravel pervasive webs of privilege.

DISCUSSION QUESTIONS

1. Have you told your own racial and ethnic stories? With whom have you shared them? How have they responded? Have you ever gone "below the surface" with a colleague, considering what difference your race makes and how other facets of your identity interact with your race?

2. When do you notice Whiteness? Do you assume that it equates with a European heritage? How do you ask White people about how they see themselves?

3. When, if ever, do you discuss white privilege in your direct practice with clients? Have you ever suggested privilege as a topic for supervision or for "over-coffee" conversations with co-workers?

4. How do you respond to the feelings associated with a serious discussion of race—guilt and shame, anger, fear, and anxiety? Are you willing to take the personal risks involved in openly confronting your part in maintaining both racial oppression and white privilege?

5. How do you invite your clients to recount and explore the critical incidents that shape their sense of personal and social identity?

6. In an era of managed care and outcome-focused practice, how can you reserve time for in-depth reflection about race as a crucial dimension of individual and social functioning?

7. Does your agency or professional association include white privilege in its diversity trainings? If not, how can you help them provide a safe forum for sustained exploration of the realities of and challenges to white privilege?

8. Case study: Angela is a 45-year-old attorney referred to you for counseling for depression related to a recent diagnosis of Stage 2 breast cancer. During her second session with you, she reveals that she is a lesbian in a 7-year-long relationship with a local health professional. Angela describes her feelings this way: "It's not fair! I've worked hard my whole life, tried to do everything that's expected. I've struggled with my sexual orientation, put up with my brothers' verbal harassment, and faced the fact that my family church doesn't want me! I volunteer in the community and help out my parents. I don't deserve this and I can't go through any more!" Imagine Angela as a White client; where would race fit in your treatment plan? What if she were a woman of color?

REFERENCES

Adams, M., Bell, L. A., & Griffin, P. (Eds.). (1997). *Teaching for diversity and social justice: A sourcebook.* New York: Routledge.

Adams, M., Blumenfeld, W. J., Castañeda, R., Hackman, H. W., Peters, M. L., & Zúñiga, X. (Eds.). (2000). *Readings for diversity and social justice: An anthology on racism, antisemitisim, sexism, heterosexism, ableism, and classism.* New York: Routledge.

Basham, K. K., Donner, S., & Everett, J. E. (2001). A controversial commitment: The anti-racism field assignment. *Journal of Teaching in Social Work, 21*(1/2), 157–174.

Delgado, R., & Stefanic, J. (Eds.). (1998). *The Latino/a condition: A critical reader.* New York: New York University Press.

Goodman, D. J. (2001). *Promoting diversity and social justice: Educating people from privileged groups.* Thousand Oaks, CA: Sage.

Hardiman, R., & Jackson, B. W. (1997). Conceptual foundations for social justice courses. In M. Adams, L. A. Bell, & P. Griffin. (Eds.), *Teaching for diversity and social justice: A sourcebook* (pp. 16–29). New York: Routledge.

López, T. A. (1993). *Growing up Chicana/o.* New York: Avon Books.

Madrid, A. (1996, April). *Juntos y revueltos: The U.S. Latino population at the end* of the twentieth century. A paper presented at the Schomburg Memorial Lecture, Mount Holyoke College, Mount Holyoke, MA. [On-line] Available: http://www.mtholyoke.edu/acad/latam/schomburgmoreno/juntosweb.html

Mezirow, J., & Associates. (2000). Learning as transformation: *Critical perspectives on a theory in progress.* San Francisco: Jossey-Bass.

Rodriguez, R. (1982). *Hunger of memory: The education of Richard Rodriguez.* New York: Bantam Books.

Rodriguez, R. (1992). *Days of obligation: An argument with my Mexican father.* New York: Penguin Books.

Root, M. P. P. (2000). A bill of rights for racially mixed people. In M. Adams, W. J. Blumenfeld, R. Castañeda, H. W. Hackman, M. L. Peters, & X. Zúñiga (Eds.), *Readings for diversity and social justice: An anthology on racism, antisemitism, sexism, heterosexism, ableism, and classism* (pp. 120–126). New York: Routledge.

Wijeyesinghe, C. L., Griffin, P., & Love, B. (1997). Racism curriculum design. In M. Adams, L. A. Bell, & P. Griffin (Eds.), *Teaching for diversity and social justice: A sourcebook* (pp. 82–109). New York: Routledge.

15

No Parece

The Privilege and Prejudice Inherent in Being a Light-Skinned Latino Without an Accent

EDWARD A. DELGADO-ROMERO

INTRODUCTION

I am a light-skinned Latino with no (Spanish) accent. My parents were born in Colombia, South America, and I was born in the United States. I am 100 percent Colombian, a Latino, a Hispanic, and a person of color. However, because my appearance and speech do not meet the stereotypical expectations of other people, I am often exempt from the prejudice and oppression that other people of color face. Worse, at times people will try to confide and involve me in their racist thoughts and beliefs. I am not quite invisible nor am I a chameleon. Struggling with privilege and prejudice, inclusion and exclusion has given me insight into the complex nature of the sections of privilege, ethnicity, race, and oppression.

PROFESSIONAL CONTEXT

I am a licensed psychologist; my doctorate is in Counseling Psychology. I am an assistant professor in Counseling Psychology at Indiana University, Bloomington, after having worked at the University of Florida Counseling Center for five years. I consider myself a "self-taught" multicultural counseling psychologist, given that my doctoral program offered only a 6-week seminar on multicultural issues. I am indebted to Dr. Beverly Vandiver (who was then a counseling-center psychologist) and the pre-doctoral internship at Michigan State University, especially the Multi-Ethnic Counseling Center Alliance (MECCA), for helping to advance my training in multicultural issues.

PERSONAL BACKGROUND AND CRITICAL INCIDENTS

My skin is not really that light. My son, who is half-Colombian and half-Dutch/Irish/English/Russian/Norwegian mix, has skin so fair that it seems translucent. His eyes are blue, as were mine when I was born and before they changed to brown. My skin is light brown, darker than White but not quite brown or black. My parents, whose strong Spanish accents subject them to prejudice to this day, drummed any trace of a Spanish accent out of me. My parents saw their accents as a source of shame, and they made certain that their children would not stand out as "different." Thus, visibly and audibly, people do not often identify me as being Latino or Colombian. This perception is not limited to White people; many times, other Latinos and even other Colombians do not think I look Latino. This hurts the most.

> I was walking around the streets of downtown South Bend, Indiana, during the international festival, wearing my Colombia T-shirt that symbolized my newfound pride in my heritage. A young Latina woman approached me and asked, "*¿Colombiano?*" I eagerly answered, "*¡Si!*" She looked at me, wrinkled her nose, and said, "*No parece*" (you don't look like it). And then she faded into the crowd, leaving me alone with my shame and anger.

Often people will mistake me for Italian or Arabic, if anything, but mostly, it seems, my ethnicity is invisible, often leaving me feeling left out of both majority White and Latino cultures. I have often been so distressed by this cultural invisibility that I have asked my mother whether I was adopted, whether she is "sure" that I am Colombian. She is offended every time I ask her. Being ethnically ambiguous (in my case being able to pass for White) has its privileges. I can go where I want without the fear many people of color have regarding how they might be treated.

Although I grew up in Atlanta, Georgia, my exposure to other people of color (outside of my immediate family) was limited. I lived in a predominantly White suburb and attended predominantly White (middle-class) Catholic schools. The nuns who taught me in grade school were socially progressive, and they taught me to desire social justice. We learned about the Civil Rights movement and were taught not to hate others based on the color of their skin. When we left the safety of our suburban school to visit the Martin Luther King Center in downtown Atlanta, we had to pass through poor neighborhoods to get there. Everyone in those neighborhoods was African American, and they stared at me in my new school bus, full of White nuns and priests, White teachers, and White friends in their Catholic school uniforms. I began to feel guilty; this was not Martin Luther King's dream.

My hard-working mother kept me anchored in reality. We did not have much money because my father would spend money faster than he could make it. I knew that attending Catholic school was tenuously dependent on my mother being able to earn enough money babysitting, sewing, and cleaning other people's houses. My father would have sent me to the dreaded public schools in an instant. My father firmly believed that his children should assimilate to U.S. culture, and to him that meant we should be White. He also encouraged me to turn down minority scholarships for college (including a letter from Harvard inviting me to apply based on my PSAT scores and minority status). Instead I took out more than $50,000 in student loans to attend a prestigious institution where elite Southern families sent their children. His perspective mirrored that of others.

"Ed, you don't want to go to such and such college; it's not very good," my guidance counselor said. I knew "not very good" meant too many Blacks went there and therefore the college was second rate. Southerners have a secret, coded language to avoid the appearance of being racist. "Plus, you want to get into college on your own merits, not due to some minority scholarship." I wonder whether she told that to athletes, or to children of alumnae? I knew the answer.

Every day I was confronted with the privilege that my college classmates felt was as natural as air. For example, my roommate was a descendent of one of the founding families of Atlanta, and he was literally a millionaire. However, the large iron gates that surrounded the school reminded me that not everyone was welcome on campus. I began to wonder what I had done to deserve this privilege. What was so special about me that I deserved to be at this overwhelmingly White private university while, literally steps from the university gates, was a city that was 60 percent African American? Furthermore, surrounding this urban, African American city were small farming communities that were stringently segregated by race. I felt guilty for living in my privileged world while people beyond the gates, including my mother (my father had finally left us when I went away to college), struggled to make enough money for food to eat. The following is an incident I experienced while attending the private university.

My college girlfriend took me to her small hometown to introduce me to her family. When she introduced me to her grandmother, the matriarch of her family, she said, "This is Ed; his family is Spanish, from Spain." Her grandmother nodded in approval, and later I found out that she was pleased that I was not Mexican and thus not a migrant worker. I was Spanish, therefore European, therefore White, and therefore, acceptable.

I went from a small private school to a large private Catholic school for my graduate studies. Despite qualifications that were equal to or better than my classmates, I was viewed by many people as an "affirmative action" admission (not qualified but a minority) or a Spanish/European (academically qualified but not a "real" minority), or my ethnicity was ignored altogether (a White guy with a Spanish surname). Consequently, many people would "trust" me enough to share their real opinions regarding racial matters. I do not think that people were trying to be offensive or malicious in telling me their real opinions. Rather, I think that they were so comfortable with me that they considered me a person with whom they did not have to be politically correct. For me, part of my privilege was hearing what some White people really thought.

A colleague congratulated me on my graduate minority fellowship. "Good for you," she said. "You aren't even a real minority! I mean, you don't speak broken English or have an accent!" I think she genuinely meant to congratulate me on what she saw as a way for me to manipulate the system.

While I was shopping for fruit at my local grocery store, an elderly White employee giving out samples of kiwi struck up a conversation with me. She noticed that I was looking at the avocados and stated, "Those are from Mexico." She then looked around to make sure no one else could hear her. "A lot of things in the U.S. are from Mexico, if you know what I mean. I feel sorry for those poor Mexicans. I used to live on the border of Texas and Mexico, and I tell you, it's sad. Plus most of those Mexicans are on dope."

This knowledge often made me suspicious about the motives of Whites, especially as I sensed that it was only a matter of time before I became a target.

In graduate school, I was taught about social justice, feminism, and equity. My clinical training motivated me to take a closer look at myself and at the themes in my life. I realized that I needed to come to understand myself as a person of color, because for many years I had let others define me and be the judge of whether or not I was a "real" person of color. However, this was a painful process. For example, at a local conference, I was invited to a "students of color only" meeting. I went begrudgingly and left as soon as possible. The leader of this meeting was an African American student who seemed ready to take on the world. She talked about the need to unify, and our common destiny as people of color. I was scared of her words, but the things she said echoed in my mind for quite some time.

As I continued my clinical training and continued to read about race, oppression, and multiculturalism, I began to make connections in my life, and I began to notice injustice and prejudice that surrounded me. As hard as it was to realize, I had to go no further than to my graduate program to notice inequity. We had no professors of color, few graduate students of color, and limited training in multiculturalism. As a graduate student, noticing these things was difficult. I lacked the power to make any real change, and my status in the program was dependent on the very faculty I was criticizing. Around this time, I read *The Autobiography of Malcolm X* (Haley, 1964), and I began to understand institutional racism and was able to center my feelings about race within a broader context. I became inspired to reclaim my Latino heritage and asked my mother to take me to Colombia. I put a great deal of energy into consciously being Latino, and I devoted my free time to outreach and retention efforts with minority students. As Janet Helms (1990; 1995) might say, I immersed myself in being Latino.

By a fortunate twist of fate, the graduate student who had inspired me at the "students of color only" meeting accepted a job as a counseling psychologist at my university during my third year, and we became instant friends and colleagues. My fervor and energy for multicultural issues were amazing, but my friend could see some of the holes in my identity. Although I was connecting with Latino heritage, I was still very prejudiced, privileged, and homophobic.

"Ed, just because you are Hispanic doesn't preclude you from being prejudiced. Did you know that Hispanics owned slaves, too? You can't exempt yourself from the legacy of slavery by saying you are Hispanic. I mean, Colombia had some of the biggest ports for slave ships. Brother, you have to get yourself together."

She was right. I had too easily identified with the oppressed. In my zeal to appease my guilt for having privilege, I had assumed an identity that was not authentic. "Getting myself together" was and is a continual process of acknowledging my privilege, of not negating having received unearned assets due to privilege, of not so easily identifying with those who are oppressed, of critically examining my authenticity as a person of color, and of ferreting out the more subtle impacts of racism and oppression that linger in my subconscious.

The first step was to realize that consciously giving up my privilege was not the same thing as never having had privilege in the first place. For example, my mother had come to this country with nothing, but her light skin and family connections allowed her to quickly make something of herself in the United States. People in projects such as Chicago's Cabrini-Green, or migrant farm workers picking fruit in Michigan would likely never have the opportunities I had, no matter how hard they worked. This process of self-examination was going to be a lifelong process. A friend mentioned to me that I have an easier time dealing with the White, Spanish, and oppressive side of me than I do accepting the indigenous, racially mixed, and oppressed side of me. This seems to be my growth edge.

PROFESSIONALLY ORIENTED PERSONAL STRUGGLES AND TRIUMPHS

After internship I took a job at the counseling center at the University of Florida where I worked from 1997 until 2002. Moving to Florida from the Midwest was another lesson in privilege for me. Although Florida has a large Latino population, Cubans and South Americans predominate, while Mexican Americans are a small minority, all of which is a stark contrast to many other areas of the United States. Consequently, there exists a hierarchy of Latino heritage, with Mexican Americans consistently being at the bottom. Earl Shorris (1992) referred to this racism within Latino culture as *racismo*. As a result, I had to confront anti-Mexican prejudice and educate students about the political activism of the Chicano movement as a model for Latino activism.

I was not prepared for the tension that existed between African Americans and Latinos in Florida, especially amongst faculty and administrators. It seemed that Latinos were viewed as competing for traditionally African American resources, and African Americans were viewed as wanting exclusive rights to diversity and multiculturalism. The rise in numbers and power of Latinos is a growing political reality, and it seemed to me common sense to build coalitions between minority groups, but many disagreed with me. In the politicized battles over rapidly diminishing diversity resources, it seems that no one emerges victorious.

I became the faculty advisor for the Colombian Student Association (COLSA), and my work with these students gave me a chance to connect with both Colombian and other Latino cultures. I attended Latino cultural events, gave Latino music and dancing a chance (and grew to love it), improved my Spanish, read Latino literature, and watched Latino movies. I learned to insist that people use both of my surnames, which surprisingly forces people to view me differently. These things helped me feel more authentic as a Latino, regardless of what others thought. More often than not, people now identify me as a Latino, if not always a Colombian. Having other Latino friends to share my struggles and to compare notes also has helped me a great deal.

A main part of my work at the University of Florida Counseling Center was outreach with Latino students. I found that the multicultural literature does not offer much guidance in understanding and working with Latino clients, especially with those who are not from the demographically dominant groups (that is, Mexican American, Puerto Rican, or Cuban). In particular, I was unsatisfied with Latino racial/ethnic identity models (Delgado-Romero, 2001) that seemed to be too general to be of much use. Similarly, relatively little is known about bilingual therapy and few programs offer training to bilingual therapists. I believe there is much more to be learned about Latino people and the way we are being changed by (and changing) mainstream American culture. The multicultural literature needs to move beyond generalities and deal with the specifics of each Latino culture. For example, I can verify from personal experience that Colombians often differ more from each other than they do from other Latinos. Colombia is an immense country with many ethnic, racial, and cultural variations within its borders, and it is only one of the Latino countries.

CONCLUSION

"NO SPICKS FOR PRESIDENT"—Graffiti painted on the side of the Institute of Hispanic/Latino Cultures on the morning of student-government elections in response to the first Latino presidential candidate, who was also one of my students.

The misspelled racial slur caught me by surprise. I had grown comfortable within my enclave of Latino friends and the small but powerful Latino student community. There was a sense of excitement as my student ran for student-body president. He was the first Latino candidate for the influential student-body-president position (the president directly controlled an eight million dollar budget), and there was hope that he could win.

The result of the slur was emotional and political upheaval. For the first time in their lives, many of the Latino students felt unsafe and singled out because of their ethnicity. Many people became "minorities" for the first time that day, especially those who had lived all their lives in predominantly Latino cities such as Miami. It seemed that because of recent numerical and political gains, Latinos were the new targets for backlash.

I wondered whether I had made the right choice in choosing to identify so strongly with my Latino heritage. I wondered whether my life and that of my half-Colombian son would have been easier if I had just continued to pass for White and had lived a life wherein my Colombian heritage was an interesting factoid, but otherwise not important.

As I prepared to speak at the student-led rally in response to the racial slur, I looked out into the crowd. There were faces of every color and race; there were gay men and lesbians; and there were White people. All were united in a sense of common outrage and purpose. At that moment, I knew I had made the right choice and that, through examining my deep-seated prejudices, internalized racism, and homophobia, I was providing an example for others. Then I spoke. . . .

DISCUSSION QUESTIONS

1. If you had a client or colleague who was struggling with cultural/ethnic invalidation, how would you deal with it?

2. You might be more prepared to deal with oppression than privilege; what might be some of the challenges in helping someone deal with privilege (especially if you don't have that privilege yourself)?

3. What happens when people tell you what they really think—when politeness and political correctness are stripped away, and anger and resentment surface? Can you work productively with these beliefs/feelings?

4. How prepared are you to work with Latino clients from different ethnic and national origins? What kinds of resources do you have, and what kinds of resources might you need?

5. Does working through privilege have to be a struggle? The author implies being "comfortable" is a negative thing. Do you have to be uncomfortable to examine privilege?

6. With so many differences within groups, how can we effectively teach multicultural competence?

7. Is multicultural competence a goal, or an ever-evolving attitude?

REFERENCES

Delgado-Romero, E. A. (2001). Counseling a Hispanic/Latino client—Mr. X. *The Journal of Mental Health Counseling* (Special Issue: Counseling Racially Diverse Clients), *23*, 207–221.

Haley, A. (1964). *The autobiography of Malcolm X.* New York: Ballantine Books.

Helms, J. E. (1990). *Black and White racial identity: Theory, research and practice.* New York: Greenwood Press.

Helms, J. E. (1995). An update of Helms's white and people of color racial identity models. In J. G. Ponterotto, J. M. Casas, L. A. Suzuki, & C. M. Alexander (Eds.), *Handbook of Multicultural Counseling* (pp. 181–198). Thousand Oaks, CA: Sage.

Shorris, E. (1992). *Latinos: A biography of the people.* New York: W. W. Norton & Company.

16

Oppression of the Spirit

Complexities in the Counseling Encounter

DIBYA CHOUDHURI

INTRODUCTION: SHANIA

Shania sat before me, face turned obstinately away, looking out the window, her eyes both distant and angry. I leaned forward to make the plea I had made too many times before. "Shania," I said, "I know you can do it. I know how intelligent you are; all you have to do is try, but you're giving up before you even start!" This conversation was part of a familiar dance we would do throughout the academic year. We would have a productive counseling session in which she busily planned out her schedule, organized her time, and made commitments. Then, during the next session, she would disclose that she had not followed through on those promises and would retreat into silence when I pursued her. I felt sure she could succeed; she seemed sure she would fail.

Shania was a sophomore in the university, institutionally identified as African American. She was a grudging member of the Black Students Association, an enthusiastic but erratic member of the Women of Color group, and passionately attached to the Multicultural Center where I worked as a counselor. Academically, she traversed heights and chasms. Each semester she would start out with As and end up with Incompletes from sympathetic professors who wanted to give her a chance but didn't get much work from her. She received failing grades from professors too busy or too disinterested to notice the emotional chaos in which she was enveloped. When Shania was interested, she was dazzling, with great flashing eyes and beaming smiles, her heart on generous display. She was obviously intelligent, with a facility for taking passionate and insightful part in discussions of multiculturalism. Her faculty noted her brilliant contributions to class discussions but bemoaned her lack of follow-through in producing written work. Indeed, upon first acquaintance, Shania seemed an ardent, committed, and intelligent young woman of unlimited potential. When she crashed, as I later discovered, the results were oftentimes late-night phone calls from her, threatening suicide. After her first year, Shania had been put on academic probation and was mandated to see me for counseling. I had recently graduated from my master's counseling program, and Shania was one of my first clients. I desperately wanted to help her live up to the potential she so obviously had.

INTRODUCTION: DIBYA

I am an Asian Indian woman and a first-generation immigrant. I arrived in this country for college at 17 years of age with my family left behind in India, and I was quite happy to make it on my own. I had always been rebellious, fervent in my support of socialist ideals, and encouraged by my family's tolerance of my activism.

When I came out of 4 years at an Ivy League women's college, I was committed to issues of diversity. There, I had been one of those students who chanted slogans such as "Racism is a disease." We marched and protested, and fought for the institution's divestment in South African business and support of apartheid and for increased ethnic minority representation among the faculty and staff of our college. After college, I continued working in an academic setting, administering a community-service program. This employment kept me in touch with human services. I continued to work with people in homeless shelters and domestic-violence clinics, and on suicide hotlines. I decided to go on to graduate work to formalize what I felt was my intrinsic passion to help.

My graduate program in counseling honed my counseling skills and gave me some theories that I alternatively questioned and accepted. For instance, while I loved the empowerment and respect inherent in the person-centered approach, I also felt intuitively that this approach might not work well with clients who might be in survival modes. I pursued my interest in multicultural counseling with little support or guidance from faculty. I read widely, following the work of scholars such as Pedersen, Sue, Ivey, and Arredondo, and would often find my faculty unfamiliar with or unaware of the issues I then raised in classes. I attended workshops and conferences at which I got some of the training, and I used my electives to take classes in women's studies and anthropology. In spite of my efforts, I was woefully unprepared for Shania.

SHANIA REVISITED

Theoretically, I framed Shania's issues in a social and familial context (McGoldrick, Giordano, & Pearce, 1996). The narratives we form about the ethnic histories and group identities from which we emerge pattern how we organize to meet the changing contexts of our environment. In a sense, we are lived[1] by the stories of our race and place. Our stories inform us in togetherness and separation.

---

[1] This is a postmodernist metaphoric phrase implying that unlike the notion of individuals approaching their lives independently, the social contexts and histories we inherit have far greater agency than we admit—we may not live them so much as they live us.

Shania's father was African American, and she identified her mother as Native American, although she was unclear about the particular tribal affiliation, which is often critical to establishing identity (Sutton & Broken Nose, 1999). The first 10 years of Shania's life were spent on a reservation, but when her mother died, she was moved to a major city and placed with female relatives of her father.[2] She grew up in poverty and was handed from relative to relative. In spite of the obstacles associated with poverty and her unstable living arrangements, Shania was able to attend college on a full academic scholarship. However, this college was a majority-White institution located in a cosmopolitan but small and mono-cultural town, very different in community from both the reservation of her childhood and the urban surroundings of her youth.

Shania had absorbed the attitudes of women from her Native American nation, women whose position was of greater flexibility and power than in dominant society (LaFromboise, Berman, & Sahi, 1994). I believe that culturally Shania often gave the wrong cues and was subtly contradictory—looking African American, but acting in ways her African American peers didn't understand. When disturbed, she retreated into cold silence rather than reacting in the expected manner of "in-your-face" confrontation.

Constantly confronted and frustrated by the issues associated with being a woman of color on a predominately White campus, Shania was likely in the throes of reconstructing her racial and ethnic identity. The Racial/Cultural Identity Development Model developed by D. W. Sue and D. Sue (1999) acknowledges similar patterns of adjustment to cultural oppression experienced by many members of minority groups, regardless of specific ethnic identity. In this model, the individual moves through five stages of development as he or she strives to come to terms both with the demands of the majority culture and the culture of origin, and with the oppressive relationship between them. The stages delineated are conformity, dissonance, resistance and immersion, introspection, and finally, integrative awareness (Sue & Sue, 1999).

Shania seemed to be in the resistance and immersion stage, with her passionate endorsement of minority-held views and her blanket rejection of dominant society values. Her anger toward White society, her conflicted empathy toward other groups of color, and, most importantly, her reactivity were key identifiers to place her in this stage. One of the significant issues in such a stage is developing an identification with and immersion in one's own reference group of origin. However, Shania's struggles in this stage seemed complicated by confusion about the reference group available to her. In this majority White, mono-cultural community, Shania's visible appearance identified her as African American, even though her inner ethnic and cultural reference group was Native American. She struggled with her connection to the Black Students' Association and the African American community because she felt like an outsider.

---

[2] In African American families, often the female kin will be responsible for child-raising rather than the man whose offspring it is. He may offer financial support from time to time, but it is the grandmother and often older aunts who take over the day-to-day responsibilities. In Shania's case, she never actually spent much time with her father who migrated frequently all over the country.

However, given her commitment to activism and her upbringing by her father's family, she did not want to be perceived as rejecting the African American community. At the same time, trying to find a reference group that was similar to her inner experience was difficult, given the distance of her original kin.

Based on messages she had received from her father's family, she feared she would also be considered an outsider among Native Americans because of her appearance. Physical appearance has often been a central part of social relationships, and this is particularly true for women. The physical ambiguity of perceived difference in appearance for mixed-race women can be particularly painful as a central part of self-worth (Root, 1994). Confronted by such dilemmas, Shania lashed out at everyone, sabotaging both her academics and her relationships. As Houston (1985) framed it in her poem about her own "Amerasian" mixed identity, Shania had, "a soul composed of wars, mixed pride, and agony" (as cited in Root, 1994).

THE COUNSELING PROCESS

Shania and I worked together for a year in counseling. I began our work by providing a space in which she could speak. There were many silences, sometimes lasting half the session, but those I could take in stride, given the cultural encounter (Herring, 1999). In my office, I had arranged the chairs so either one of us could look out the window to the trees beyond, and Shania would spend long moments contemplating the vista while I tried to attend without staring intrusively (Sutton & Broken Nose, 1999). When she was particularly upset, she would take a shawl I had hanging and cover herself with it, as if in a cocoon. She would often miss sessions or come late. These times would be followed by the times when she contacted me every day with anguished refrains that evidenced her disintegrating emotional state.

Whenever there were such opportunities, I tried to bring her into contact with some of the local Native adults I knew who played leadership roles in the Native community. Many responded to her with warmth; but here, too, she alternated between reaching out and withdrawing.

During a particularly harrowing period, when most of our interaction consisted of her either being silent or accusing me of not caring, I tried storytelling (Herring, 1999). Using the Ericksonian model of storytelling (Wallas, 1985), I carefully constructed for her a fantasy about a school in which a young girl learns to be a puppet master, only to discover to her shock that she and all those around her have strings attached to them. They, too, are puppets. I detailed the girl's angry, shamed, and destructive responses and then led into her realization that the strings went both ways. She could dance to others' manipulations, or she could use her connectedness to influence in turn and be interdependent. We didn't delve into the story or analyze it, but after that, she seemed somewhat more thoughtful and less reactive. In our journey together, however, we seemed as lost as before.

My work with Shania brought my competence into question. Essentially, no matter how empathic I tried to be with her, I felt personally let down by her because I could not see why she was failing. I knew that she had encounters with racism on this predominantly White campus; but then, so did I. I had been followed and threatened, both verbally and physically. Through our sessions, I learned that Shania had conflicts with many of the other African American students, especially the men. In my mind, I framed the conflicts as her attempt to self-sabotage and alienate her own support group. My internal litany, especially obsessive after our counseling sessions, sounded something like, "Why can't she focus on the good stuff instead of the bad?" or "Why can't she let it go when a certain young black man talks about women derogatorily?" or "Why can't she hear that they aren't targeting her. . . ?"

In spite of my apparent lack of success, Shania kept coming to our sessions with a willingness to give me and our counseling relationship another try. Perhaps she knew that, despite my judgments and critical attitude (relatively visible despite the patina of my person-centered approach), I did care about her and believe in her. Where I failed her was in translating my awareness of the sociocultural conflicts she brought with her into a clinical approach that was effective.

DIBYA REVISITED

What I left out of this clinical description was the exploration of my own privilege and oppression, a process that might have enabled me to understand Shania's impasse more clearly. Because I used my own identity as a woman of color as the focal point for understanding and interpreting her behavior, I assumed that Shania's emotional issues were based on the day-to-day harassment women of color face. When she related examples of being overlooked in class by the professor, or of being asked whether she had really done the assignment by herself, I responded with understanding, but also with some underlying impatience. In my thoughts, shaped by my own internalized oppression, I asked, "After all, wasn't this par for the course? One simply had to be twice as good to withstand the criticism." In doing this, I failed to notice the profound differences between us, differences my understanding could not encompass. One important difference between Shania and me was that for the first 17 years of my life, I did not live in a society in which I was the minority. I was raised middle-class and came from a caste background that gave me privileged access in my home country to almost everywhere I wanted to go. These differences in historical and lived experience profoundly affected the interactions and understandings that I brought into our counseling sessions.

As an immigrant of color, I understood the impact of racism in the present U.S. society, but I had little experiential understanding of racism as a generational force that operated to punish and confirm status. India, by its own history, still struggles with the impact of 200 years of colonization by the British and the legacy of internalized oppression that seeks paleness in its women, adeptness at Western cultural norms to denote competence and achievement, and infinite adaptability to oppressive conditions. My own internalized oppression led me to admire White people, because my attitude toward them was that they were absent conquerors who had left an admirable heritage. I internalized the "immigrant's optimism" and belief that struggle brought reward—the belief that if a person does everything twice as well as another, success is an inevitable outcome. After all, many others, including myself, have worked hard and become successful. I often wondered why the next person, in this case Shania, couldn't follow suit. My perspective of "I did, so why can't you?" caused me to overlook how messages of success have been defined by White, middle-class society for people of color in the United States. For some people of color, particularly Native Americans, the defined success may require directions that conflict with cultural lifestyle orientations (Tafoya & Vecchio, 1999).

I wanted Shania to succeed because she was a woman of color with whom I felt kinship; I wanted her to overcome obstacles because I cared; and I thought she could do it because I had. I had no emotional understanding of the paralyzing traps she was in, traps in which failure and success were one and the same. Although achievement and success were framed as desirable, they were defined in particular ways—as accessible through academic success in college using a language, stance, and process infused with White, middle-class values. If Shania did achieve that success, she faced losing her already-fragile membership in the communities of people of color. She had lost so much in her life already—her indigenous community, her mother, her father, her sense of family, and the norms and values she had come to know. No wonder she resisted when I asked her to risk losing what little she had left.

RESOLUTIONS: SHANIA AND DIBYA

At the end of her sophomore year, Shania told me that she was dropping out of school and planned to return to New York. I struggled with her decision, for she relayed no sense of future plans or purpose to go along with her decision. I foreshadowed a life of drifting that might end sharply, given my knowledge of her self-destructive attempts. I dreaded that I would someday hear that she had ended up in a series of positions that took no account of her amazing intelligence and generous spirit—or worse, that she had committed suicide. I felt a lack of competence in my abilities and viewed this act as failure by both of us, even though I argued and fought with her and for her far more than I ever had with any other client. Nevertheless, she still left.

Two years after Shania left for New York and at a time when I was leaving my work site to go on to a doctoral program, I received a letter from Shania. In it, she detailed an incredible journey in which she had returned to the city, but then had gone on to return to the reservation. She had made contact with some of her mother's relatives and reconfirmed her roots. She also ended up working with a youth-at-risk program. After having those experiences, she believed that she was ready to continue her education. During that time, she had been successfully taking classes at a local college to finish a degree in education, and she intended to get a graduate degree in social work so she could go back and work on the reservation.

In her letter, she wrote that many things I had said to her during our counseling sessions were making more sense now, but she had needed to be at home to hear them properly. She did not elaborate with examples, so I can never know which of the many things I said to her stayed and which faded (and I suspect we might each have chosen different examples when pointing to critical moments). She finished with saying that although we had had our "fights," she wanted to let me know what was happening in her life because she knew I had cared. I cried when I read that letter. My tears were for the thankfulness I felt for her triumphs, as well as for my own sense of relief and competence.

CONCLUSION AND LESSONS LEARNED

It has been many years since the experiences discussed here, but I have never forgotten the lessons. I am determined to stay conscious and humbled. To be framed in the role of expert who passes on the knowledge of multicultural counseling to others is a shaky endeavor. I realize we have much to learn about the convoluted nature of oppression and the resistance of privilege to self-scrutiny. The generations of learning and misinformation have deep roots, which can bear poisoned fruit that we ingest without ever knowing we are doing so. Knowing the theory of cultural competence is rarely sufficient for knowing the practice. Our own perspectives and worldviews, no matter how scrutinized through classes, theory, and academic experiences, still hold potency when we are challenged to reach across and be respectfully present and engaged with "an Other."

In counseling, it is in the spirit that we perceive the impact of oppression: the defeat and the despair, the self-hatred and the sabotage, the disjunction and alienation. In other roles, we can advocate and struggle against systems, but in the counseling relationship itself, I believe it is essential to work with the noxious messages that sicken the spirit. Effective multicultural counseling goes beyond theoretical knowledge of the stages of racial identity development (D. W. Sue & D. Sue, 1999) and a "culturegram" awareness of cultural customs (CultureGrams, 2003). To infuse one's counseling and truly recognize the multicultural nature of every encounter is to become committed to interrogating the self in multiple contexts. If we can look at oppression as a powerful systemic force that shapes our worldviews, status, history, and experience, we must acknowledge that it permeates our practice. Every encounter invokes some aspects of oppression. The degree to which we can scrutinize both the client and ourselves and attend to the ways in which each of us brings to the mix our perspective of the world is the degree to which we can perhaps avoid replicating the toxicity of oppression. And because legacies of oppression and privilege are heavy with emotions such as shame, guilt, anger, and resentment, we must be prepared for the emotional upheaval of such scrutiny. Our reward for perseverance is the positive impact that uprooting the legacy of privilege and oppression has on both our clients and ourselves.

DISCUSSION QUESTIONS

1. How might you frame Shania's issues developmentally? Can you decipher ways of self-presentation that might be traced to her various cultural constituencies?

2. Are there any theories on multicultural counseling that might be helpful in practice with such a client?

3. In working with a client such as Shania, what issues of your own oppression and privilege might you need to explore and bracket?

4. What might the counselor have done here that could have been more helpful to Shania?

5. As a counselor, how can you manage your frustration and disappointment when a client is not helped?

REFERENCES

CultureGrams (2003). *CultureGrams: The nations around us, world edition.* Lindon, UT: Ferguson Publishing.

Herring, R. (1999). Counseling with Native Americans and Alaska Natives: Strategies for helping professionals. *Multicultural aspects of counseling series 14.* Thousand Oaks, CA: Sage.

LaFromboise, T. D., Berman, J. S., & Sahi, B. K. (1994). American Indian woman. In L. Comas-Diaz & B. Greene (Eds.), *Women of color: Integrating ethnic and gender identities in psychotherapy* (pp. 30–71). New York: Guilford Press.

McGoldrick, M., Giordano, J., & Pearce, J. K. (1996). *Ethnicity and family therapy* (2nd ed.). New York: Guilford Press.

Root, M. P. (1994). Mixed-race women. In L. Comas-Diaz & B. Greene (Eds.), *Women of color: Integrating ethnic and gender*

identities in psychotherapy (pp. 455–478). New York: Guilford Press.

Sue, D. W., & Sue, D. (1999) *Counseling the culturally different: Theory and practice.* (3rd ed.). New York: John Wiley & Sons.

Sutton, C. T., & Broken Nose, M. A. (1999). American Indian families: An overview. In M. McGoldrick, J. Giordano, & J. K. Pearce (Eds.), *Ethnicity and family therapy* (2nd ed., pp. 31–44). New York: Guilford Press.

Tafoya, N., & Vecchio, A. D. (1999). Back to the future: An examination of the Native American holocaust experience. In M. McGoldrick, J. Giordano, & J. K. Pearce (Eds.), *Ethnicity and family therapy* (2nd ed., pp. 45–54). New York: Guilford Press.

Wallas, L. (1985). *Stories for the third ear: Using hypnotic fables in psychotherapy.* New York: Norton.

FURTHER READINGS ON WOMEN OF
COLOR PERSPECTIVES AND PRACTICE

Adleman, J., & Enguidanos, G. (Eds.). (1995). *Racism in the lives of women: Testimony, theory, and guides to antiracist practice.* New York: Harrington Press.

Anzaldua, G. (Ed.) (1990). *Making face, making soul = Haciendo caras: Creative and critical perspectives by feminists of color.* San Francisco, CA: Aunt Lute Foundation Books.

Anzaldua, G., & Moraga, C. (Eds.). (1983). *This bridge called my back: Writings by radical women of color* (2nd ed.). New York: Kitchen Table, Women of Color Press.

Bulkin, E., Pratt, M. B., & Smith, B. (1988). *Yours in struggle: Three feminist perspectives on anti-semitism and racism.* Ithaca, NY: Firebrand Books.

Comas-Díaz, L., & Greene, B. (Eds.). (1994). *Women of color: Integrating ethnic and gender identities in psychotherapy.* New York: Guilford Press.

Flores, M., & Carey, G. (2000). *Family therapy with Hispanics: Toward appreciating diversity.* Boston: Allyn and Bacon.

hooks, b. (1984). *Feminist theory from margin to center.* Boston: South End Press.

Hull, G. T., Bell Scott, P., & Smith, B. (Eds.). (1982). *All the women are White, all the Blacks are men, but some of us are brave: Black women's studies.* Old Westbury, NY: Feminist Press.

Jordan, J. V. (Ed.). (1997). *Women's growth in diversity: More writings from the Stone Center.* New York: Guilford.

Kim, E. H., & Villanueva, L. V. (Eds.). (1997). *Making more waves: New writing by Asian American women.* Boston: Beacon Press.

Lorde, A. (1984). *Sister outsider: Essays and speeches.* Trumansburg, NY: Crossing Press.

McGoldrick, M. (1998). *Re-visioning family therapy: Race, culture, and gender in clinical practice.* New York: Guilford Press.

Mohanty, C., Russo, A., & Torres, L. (Eds.). (1991). *Third world women and the politics of feminism.* Bloomington: Indiana University Press.

Romero, M., Hondagneu-Sotelo, P., & Ortiz, V. (Eds.). (1997). *Challenging fronteras: Structuring Latina and Latino lives in the U.S.: an anthology of readings.* New York: Routledge.

Rothenberg, P. (2000). *Invisible privilege: A memoir about race, class, and gender.* Lawrence, KS: University Press of Kansas.

Seeley, K. M. (2000). *Cultural psychotherapy: Working with culture in the clinical encounter.* Northvale, NJ: Jason Aronson.

Sue, D. W., Ivey, A. E., & Pedersen, P. B. (1996). *A theory of multicultural counseling and therapy.* Pacific Grove, CA: Brooks/Cole.

17

Acculturation and Identity

Intra-Ethnic Distinctions Among Mexican Americans

GENARO GONZALEZ

INTRODUCTION

I have taught psychology for 15 years in the same South Texas area where I was born and raised, on the border with Mexico. If your cognitive road map conjures up San Antonio, you must imagine driving directly south for another four hours, into *deep* South Texas.

During the past decade, the region has become one of the fastest-growing metropolitan areas in the country, yet it remains one of the poorest and least educated. My university more or less mirrors our demographics: of our 14,000 students, about 85% percent are Mexican American.

Being a native son, the psychology department hoped that I might serve as a role model. And at a time when minorities are sometimes hired with only their race or surname to substantiate their status, my cultural credentials were authentic. My first years were spent in a family of migrant workers who followed the harvest across state lines. After my parents' divorce, my life became less nomadic but still mired in poverty. Even after my mother remarried, my stepfather's wages as a taxi driver in a small-town barrio barely matched her sporadic earnings in produce-packing sheds and fieldwork.

Both my father and stepfather were indifferent to my college plans, and my mother's illiteracy could do little to counter their inertia. The region's dismal track record for supporting minorities in higher education did not help either, and after two years in the institution where I now teach, I left for California, where I eventually completed my doctorate in psychology. I turned down better teaching possibilities in order to return to this region and its university. Prior to my current position, I had also taught for several years in central Mexico to improve my Spanish and cultural awareness.

At first glance, my background would seem an ideal match with the student population. Certainly my personal history would not seem unusual for those of my generation. Nor is it that different from the backgrounds of first- or second-generation students who currently live in *barrios* or *colonias* (outlying, unincorporated communities with substandard housing). But most of my Mexican American students now come from middle-class homes where English is often the language of choice. So, rather than resonating, my story comes across as a quaint tune. Despite our ethnic bond, my observations of growing up in the same place but at a different time and in different circumstances often elicits discomfort or defensiveness rather than ethnic solidarity. Perhaps their desire to gain acceptance in mainstream society requires that they ignore reminders that Anglo-Americans might not welcome them with open arms. Thus, the disconcerting anecdotes of past local discrimination that I include in my Social Psychology classes, along with discussions on in-group prejudices based on skin color, make more than a few squirm uncomfortably.

I incorporate these anecdotes because any meaningful study of the Mexican American experience must examine prejudice and stratification, both historical and actual. But a disturbing number of my students dismiss these issues as irrelevant, although in truth a subtle, complex denial seems at work. The uneasy nature of that underlying dynamic is a central aspect of this chapter.

More specifically, I shall try to show how acculturation, by encouraging a blanket adoption of mainstream values, also ends up promoting mainstream prejudices against Hispanics. As a psychologist, I am interested in the inner conflicts and doubts that this process may create in Mexican Americans, especially with respect to identity. Further, I shall explore the relationship between assimilation and privilege—how increased acculturation often goes hand in hand with added privilege, psychological as well as material. Indeed, a major incentive for acculturating is the accretion of social status. But as we shall see, one by-product of this process may be in-group prejudice. Finally, I shall touch on the occasional irony and paradox that comes with acculturation and privilege; for instance, acculturated Mexican Americans may find themselves on the "privileged" side of the stratification equation yet may end up as spokespersons or role models for the less privileged in their group. Such a redefinition of their status may force them to confront anew the culture they thought they had left behind, as well as their uncertain relationship to the non-privileged members of their stigmatized group.

ACCULTURATION AND ITS DISCONTENTS

Although intrigued by findings that on average our Mexican American college students were quite "Americanized" (Cuellar, Arnold, & Gonzalez, 1995), I first attributed the phenomenon to the changing times. The success of the Civil Rights struggles spearheaded by my cohorts and me had paved the way for an acculturated generation who prefers English to Spanish and envisions endless opportunities ahead. My occasional reflections in my Mexican American psychology class of barrio life and migrant camps were a far cry from the middle-class world that most of my students and I now inhabit.

Before proceeding further, however, some aspects of acculturation, a central construct of this chapter, must be clarified. Acculturation, as first formulated in the literature (Redfield, Linton, & Herskovits, 1936), described the process that occurs when two cultures come into contact. It does not presume that an acculturating individual will necessarily lose her original culture while adopting the new or host culture; when the latter does occur, the result is assimilation. In practical terms, though, for ethnic groups during our country's history, acculturation and assimilation have generally gone hand in hand, regardless of which side one takes in the culture wars. That is, those who promote pluralism and diversity lament the loss of the native culture. Those who advocate a melting pot agenda lament that the shedding of the native culture and the acquisition of the host culture does not occur as fast or as thoroughly as they would like. For that reason, despite the conceptual differences, I shall use the two terms interchangeably.

Similarly, I am using the concept of identity in its broader, generic sense, including elements of self-esteem and self-evaluation. Various investigators (Cross, 1987; Rotheram & Phinney, 1987) have shown that ethnic identity is a complex construct, and that its relationship to acculturation and assimilation can be subtle and even relatively independent (Keefe & Padilla, 1987). However, these important and interesting nuances are beyond the scope of this chapter. I have chosen instead to examine identity in a more generic manner while still focusing on cultural themes and ethnicity.

I admit that my observations of what happens to my students are influenced by the nature of my own immersion into the larger society. While my contact was gradual, many of my students grew up in families already well immersed in the mainstream language and culture. And while the lack of Latino success stories during my youth may have limited one's horizons and aspirations, it did make for a more clear-cut ethnic identity: Anglos were the "haves," we were the "have-nots." By contrast, today's ethnic stratifications are blurred, with Mexican American role models in greater abundance, especially those in the public eye. What goes unsaid is that the crossover performer or politician either expunges many of the ethnic elements from his public persona or lacks them from the start, since by definition a crossover success must appeal to the mainstream. Usually this is not evident to my students, since the ethnic angle of the role model that is highlighted and promoted is often obvious (for example a Spanish surname), yet trivial (only a surname). The end result is a simulacrum; yet for many of my students this is fine, since the recipient role model carries the imprimatur of the mainstream society. Here one can return to the earlier distinction between acculturation and assimilation, adding that while acculturation is largely a personal choice, successful assimilation requires that the larger society give the go-ahead through opportunities and access. Thus, for true assimilation, acculturation is necessary but not sufficient.

How then, does one assimilate? Through imitation, of course, and like other forms of social learning this typically occurs through observation and interaction. But in a geographic area where barely 20% percent of the population is White and where even that small proportion tends to live within its own ethnic enclave, opportunities for observation and interaction can be problematic. One possibility involves vicarious or virtual interaction, in the form of the constant multimedia portrayal of White America that enters almost every Hispanic home on a daily basis. Yet these sources depict a very distorted picture of mainstream America. Even "reality programs" portray the larger society in a way that is closer to hyper-reality. The result is that a border Mexican American growing up in an insulated environment ends up emulating the caricatures from the popular media. The corrective influence that might come from real and meaningful interactions with Whites is often absent.

Acculturation can have another unfortunate consequence. Mainstream views of Mexican Americans are often pejorative, so in seeking to enter that world my students are pressured to incorporate negative views of themselves, of family, and of friends.

Although I am not a clinician, my psychology credential is incentive enough for students to drop by my office to talk about matters that usually transcend academic concerns. Once the discussion takes a turn for the personal, anxieties and insecurities over acculturation are not far behind. One familiar scenario with Mexican American coeds centers on family tensions and, with slight variations, follows a pattern. She lives with her family, but the father disapproves of her weekend activities and returning at late hours. The mother, trying to mediate, merely antagonizes the father and exacerbates the conflict.

Only gradually does the student see the clashing cultural dynamics. On the one hand she craves the independence of those media American coeds she seeks to emulate. Yet she also wants the emotional support and stability that comes with remaining under her parents' wing, without realizing that such support comes with a price—following her father's rules, based on bedrock cultural attitudes. Oftentimes she simply tries to dismiss that world as antiquated and out of touch with modern times.

Although I hear such complaints frequently, for most of these young women an objective analysis of the situation is neither obvious nor automatic, since their premises are based on nonconscious ideologies (Aronson, 1972, p. 178). She sees her need for personal privacy and independence as utterly natural; unfortunately her father sees *his* demands in the same way. The result is a recipe for culture clash, with neither side realizing the implicit cultural assumptions of his or her respective views.

EDUCATION AND THE EXACERBATION
OF INTRA-ETHNIC DISTINCTIONS

The theme of education is crucial to understanding both acculturation and identity among Mexican Americans. In fact, acculturation is re-education—by the host culture. Although this new enculturation involves much informal and implicit learning, a large part is, in fact, formal. Educational institutions are therefore crucial to acculturation and assimilation.

With "visibly identifiable" minorities such as Mexican Americans, one must realize that the things that distinguish them as such—that make them visibly identifiable—are characteristics such as skin color and facial features. Being ascribed characteristics, there is little the person can do to erase them. By contrast, educational attainment and its concomitant acculturation, resemble more closely an achieved status. As such, it offers the possibility of attenuating or minimizing one's minority status. It is no accident that efforts to allow Latinos fuller participation in mainstream society have an overwhelming emphasis on higher education. Beyond the obvious tools that this provides, such as knowledge and skills in the sciences or the arts, one must not underestimate its importance of "Americanizing" (that is, assimilating) the individual into a more homogenous cultural mold.

In addition to physiognomic criteria, Mexican Americans face other factors that accompany discrimination. For instance, even those with light complexions or more European features might still be "aurally identifiable" due to distinct accents or limited English vocabulary. Here too, however, education offers a way out, with its emphasis on language fluency.

The significance of education as a cultural stamp of approval may be difficult for White Americans to appreciate. After all, their formal education is largely an expansion of the cultural history, language, and attitudes already embedded in their early enculturation. For many Mexican American students, however, education provides a ticket into a culture that views them as quasi-Americans.

Just as importantly, a higher education legitimizes them to themselves. For many Mexican Americans, the payoff goes beyond the material. A college degree symbolizes their entry into mainstream culture. It does not merely accredit their grasp of the arts and high culture, it validates their ability to navigate American lowbrow culture. Much has been made of the fact that the average college curriculum, far from being culture-free or culture-fair, often places those with non-mainstream enculturation at a disadvantage. For instance, Anglo instructors may pepper their lectures with American idioms and with references to popular culture. And yet this very same biased nature adds to the college diploma's worth. For some Mexican American students, it affirms their enculturation into popular culture, including the latest fads and phrases making the rounds in mainstream America.

OTHER FACTORS THAT AFFECT IDENTITY

If I have painted a somewhat dismal portrait of the cultural orientation of Mexican American students at my university, one must remember that many do not resemble this generalization. Moreover, it is discouraging only if one advocates true cultural diversity and not simply the hollow paeans to pluralism one hears in academia, where cultural icons are trotted out on designated days while pluralism is left to languish the rest of the time.

To an extent, my concern lies in the eye (or ear) of the beholder. When I told a White colleague how quickly cultural awareness was eroding among my students, he first seemed genuinely puzzled, then countered that he almost always heard Spanish in the halls. I had to point out how often I *didn't* hear it, adding that perhaps his not being bilingual makes him overlook and forget the familiar (English) while remembering the foreign (Spanish).

The loss of cultural awareness and identity is all the more striking considering that our university is less than a half-hour drive from Mexico. It is probably worse the farther north one gets from ground zero, the border. Yet that proximity may paradoxically accelerate our acculturation. One reason is that Mexican American students here, despite their efforts to acculturate, are still more likely to understand and speak Spanish than those beyond the border area. Not that our students have greater cultural pride than others elsewhere; we simply live in Mexico's backyard, so our exposure to its language and culture is overwhelming. An exodus of immigrants sees to it that the language and traditions are replenished continuously. This translates into a kind of cultural surplus rarely seen beyond the border. Whereas Mexican American youth elsewhere may find themselves fighting to retain diminishing traditions, our own students may unwittingly see themselves amidst a cultural excess, and therefore entitled to squander some.

Yet were they simply shedding elements of their ethnicity due to a cultural glut, one would not encounter the cultural disparagement so often seen and heard. Here too our proximity to Mexico plays a key role, since many find it difficult to identify with a mother country whose own people appear to be leaving in droves. To a social scientist, the reasons for the emigration are obvious—poverty, coupled with lack of opportunities. But many of our students, like much of the larger society, view these deficits as inherent conditions or characteristics rather than causes. The end result is a pejorative perception of anything "Mexican," including their own ethnic origin.

A variation of this can be an intra-ethnic pecking order. For instance, a number of my native-born pupils criticize or disparage Mexican-born students (naturally, after first stopping to ascertain that *I* am not foreign-born). But the prejudice does not end there. A first-generation victim may in turn point out that she lives here legally, while so-and-so does not. I have even talked to undocumented workers in the community who acknowledge their status, yet quickly add that they hold jobs, but their neighbors down the block are "not only illegal but on welfare."

This dichotomy of cultural adoration and cultural disdain fits Spicer's (1977) model of ethnic identity: individuals exposed to a culture with superior material benefits tend to embrace it openly. For instance, Spicer points out that such was Rome's prestige in the ancient world that its conquered subjects sometimes viewed their new status as a step up. Similarly, I regularly encounter immigrant "overshooters" who ape every mainstream fad and bend over backwards to appear more Anglo than Anglo-American. In such an uneven playing field, their original culture is bound to lose prestige (Royce, 1982).

Unfortunately, acculturation may also encourage such individuals to adopt negative stereotypes about their group. So although recent Mexican immigrants bring positive in-group stereotypes, over the long-term they internalize the negative stereotypes of the larger society (Dworkin, 1965; Buriel & Vasquez, 1982).

Juggling these prejudices requires considerable cognitive contortions. One favorite strategy with my students is to footnote their pejorative attitude with more positive exceptions (that is, themselves). Although research on this subtyping model (Webber & Crocker, 1983; Kunda & Oleson, 1995) centers on the prejudices of majority groups, I frequently find a self-subtyping variation among my students. While acknowledging that many Mexican Americans are poor and/or ill-educated, the acculturating individual carves out a more exclusive and desirable sub-category, referring to himself as Latino or Hispanic (supra-categories, actually). In sum, the person rationalizes that although he technically belongs to the stigmatized group, he nevertheless differs from the stereotype.

CONCLUSIONS AND A CAVEAT

Teaching at a university with a historical commitment to Hispanic students, I undoubtedly stress higher education for us. Yet my personal and professional observations also suggest that this view might be at cross-purposes with promoting ethnic awareness and identity. Even educators who have no qualms with assimilation must address the argument that as Mexican Americans move away from traditional values, they become more prone to deviancy and other social ills (Buriel, 1984). Offering college courses that validate diversity may help, but the token effort at most universities makes one wonder whether this really makes a difference. Ideally an additive approach to acculturation could provide the tools and skills to succeed without relegating one's original culture to ridicule or irrelevance. In reality, though, we promote an educational process that impedes an affirmation of indigenous cultures.

A central theme of this book examines discrimination from the perspective of the privileged and/or oppressor. The draft of my original chapter contribution dealt more explicitly with the porous barrier between oppressor and oppressed—specifically Hispanics who first find themselves on the receiving end of discrimination, but later, through education and acculturation, join the ranks of the privileged. This is not without cultural conflict and role strain. In fact, the issue is not limited to Mexican Americans who make a successful mainstream transition. As others from disadvantaged groups (for example, women and other discriminated minorities) make similar transitions in substantial numbers, each may face a crossroads with respect to his or her identity. They often realize that rather than leave behind their status of visible minority, they now have a mutated status—*privileged* visible minority. This includes those whose new privilege anoints them as role models or as cultural contextualizers who work as ethnic go-betweens. The irony is that instead of lessening their cultural identity, it becomes even more salient. In this chapter, I examine not the end result—a privileged status—but the acculturation process leading to that, including conflicts over identity that may carry over into the new status.

In the trenches of the current culture wars, this sometimes translates into personal acts of resistance. For instance, some of my Chicano colleagues pay lip service to pluralism but fail to follow through with congruent conduct. I have tried to do otherwise. Rather than let my first language wither, I forced myself to improve it in Mexican classrooms, before firing squads of unforgiving undergraduates. Similarly, my refusal to neutralize (or perhaps neuter) my name ethnically elicits disapproval at times, and not only from Anglo-Americans. I have done likewise with my child's name, realizing that it might narrow her options, not only within the mainstream but among assimilated Hispanics as well.

And yet, whenever I hear Hispanic parents call out to their children with the hyper-Anglicized names that are all the rage in our community (Roberts, 1996), I try to restrain my cultural condescension. It is difficult to fault a parent who believes—and with reason—that the strategy will enhance his child's chances in our country. I try also to remind myself that faulting them is a bit too facile, since my own brand of acculturation has already afforded me a certain degree of affluence. Still, I wish it were possible to convince them, along with my students, that one can master a second culture with minimal loss of her first one, or of her identity.

DISCUSSION QUESTIONS

1. The previous account describes a region where the minority status group is numerically the majority. Discuss how rather than producing a paradise free of prejudice, many Mexican Americans in the community practice their own brand of stereotyping. Explain what pressures, insecurities, and influences (for example, proximity to Mexico's poverty) might motivate them to do this.

2. Malcolm X once remarked that mainstream society's greatest crime against African Americans was to teach them to derogate themselves. How might a similar argument apply to Mexican Americans with respect to their views of their own culture? What anxieties and emotional conflicts might be found in an acculturated person who, in "passing" from a stigmatized status to a more privileged one, tries to distance himself through a pejorative dismissal of his own cultural origins?

3. In some respects the internal "culture (civil) wars" that Mexican Americans often experience are merely domestic variations of a drama played out globally among groups that are undergoing contact with American culture. Describe current or historical examples of other cultural groups who have undergone cultural conflict in dealing with another culture, either directly or indirectly (for example, through films or the Internet).

CASE SCENARIO AND DISCUSSION

A graduate student conducting an interview in a Mexican American barrio asks how its residents view mainstream America and how they believe it, in turn, views them. In one comfortable home, the head of the house replies that although they may have experienced prejudice from Whites, he is still proud of the fact that everyone in the house is native born, unlike the family at the end of the block. At that very next house, the interviewer is told that although others may look down on them for being first-generation, at least they are in the United States legally, unlike the family two houses down. Upon being interviewed, that third family in fact admits to its undocumented status but quickly adds that at least they are all hard workers, unlike the family across the street, which is not only undocumented but on public assistance as well.

1. In this scenario, discuss the statuses (generation level, employment, etc.) around which the intra-ethnic prejudice is crystallized.

2. Scapegoats are easy targets of discrimination due to their relative lack of power. How does the pecking order in this scenario support this?

3. Discuss how the first individual interviewed responds to being viewed as a target of prejudice. Compare this to an approach that considers the larger social forces that help create the prejudice in the first place.

REFERENCES

Aronson, E. (1972). *The social animal.* San Francisco: W. H. Freeman and Co.

Buriel, R. (1984). Integration with traditional Mexican-American culture and sociocultural adjustment. In J. L. Martinez, Jr. & R. H. Mendoza (Eds.), *Chicano psychology* (pp. 95–130). New York: Academic Press.

Buriel, R., & Vasquez, R. (1982). Stereotypes of Mexican descent persons: Attitudes of three generations of Mexican Americans and Anglo American adolescents. *Journal of Cross-Cultural Psychology, 13,* 59–70.

Cross, W. E. (1987). A two-factor theory of black identity: Implications for the study of identity development in minority children. In J. S. Phinney & M. J. Rotheram (Eds.), *Children's ethnic socialization: Pluralism and development.* Newbury Park, CA: Sage.

Cuellar, I., Arnold, B., & Gonzalez, G. (1995). Cognitive referents of acculturation: Assessment of cultural constructs in Mexican Americans. *Journal of Community Psychology, 23,* 339–356.

Dworkin, A. G. (1965). Stereotypes and self-images held by native-born and foreign-born Mexican Americans. *Sociology and Social Research, 49,* 214–224.

Keefe, S. E., & Padilla, A. M. (1987). *Chicano Ethnicity.* Albuquerque: University of New Mexico Press.

Kunda, Z., & Oleson, K. C. (1995). Maintaining stereotypes in the face of disconfirmation: Constructing grounds for subtyping deviants. *Journal of Personality and Social Psychology, 68,* 565–579.

Redfield, R., Linton, R., & Herskovits, M. J. (1936). Memorandum on the study of acculturation. *American Anthropologist, 38,* 149–152.

Roberts, S. (1996, March 3). Forget Jose. There's an America of Kevin's and Ashley's aborning. *The New York Times,* p. E3.

Rotheram, M. J., & Phinney, J. S. (1987). Definitions and perspectives in the study of children's ethnic socialization. In J. S. Phinney & M. J. Rotheram (Eds.), *Children's ethnic socialization: Pluralism and development.* Newbury Park, CA: Sage.

Royce, A. P. (1982). *Ethnic identity: Strategies of diversity.* Bloomington: Indiana University Press.

Spicer, E. (1971). Persistent identity systems. *Science, 4011,* 795–800.

Webber, R., & Crocker, J. (1983). Cognitive processes in the revision of stereotypic beliefs. *Journal of Personality and Social Psychology, 45,* 961–977.

18

Unmasking Within-Group Prejudice

A Case Study

FELICE LICHAW AND MARYA HOWELL-CARTER

This narrative was written by two people: Felice, a supervisor in a community-based counseling center, and Marya, her supervisee. Their story highlights the impact of internalized oppression and the revelation of internal attitudes through good supervision.

INTRODUCTION: FELICE

I come from a Jewish, lower-middle-class family. My mother emigrated from Czechoslovakia with her family when she was quite young, and most of my maternal grandmother's family was killed in the Holocaust. My father was a first-generation American (United States) whose father had been persecuted as a Jew in Poland and Russia before World War I. I am the daughter of this union.

Having spent the majority of my 20-year career working with clients whose cultural contexts differed from my own, I was well down the road toward understanding the role of culture in treatment when I met Marya Carter, then a second-year doctoral student. She had applied for an externship at our agency, a private, not-for-profit, community-based youth-service agency. The agency serviced a large and diverse area of Chicago, including a historical port of entry for immigrant populations. The students at the high school closest to our location spoke a mix of 102 languages. Our primary population was African American adolescents and their families. I was looking for a student who would be available to interact within our clients' diverse cultural contexts. Marya was searching for a site at which to complete her externship, and she had an interest in working with youth and families of color.

In our first interview, Marya presented herself as an open, enthusiastic, and idealistic young woman. She looked fresh. She seemed surprised by some of my questions, but she gamely answered them, particularly the one I asked all students about what brought them to the agency and what they wanted to get out of the experience for themselves. I can't remember exactly what Marya said about her motivation for working in our agency. It might have been something about fulfilling the need to give back to her community or wanting to learn more about working with youth and families, but it was sufficiently self-motivated for her to be offered an externship.

INTRODUCTION: MARYA

My father is African American, born in the 1920s of southern parents who migrated north to find work during the years following World War I. He married my mother, the daughter of a Caucasian German farm family in Central Michigan, in the late 1960s. I was born in Detroit, not long after the fires of the 1967 race riots destroyed much of our city. As I grew up, my father from time to time warned me about the legacy he perceived to be mine. "You are a Black woman; you will always be at a disadvantage. To be successful, you have to work harder and be smarter than everyone else."

I believed my father and identified with his admonitions—that is, Black women must do more and do it better, and they will never be given anything for free. What my father didn't realize was that, because of my light skin, I was insulated from many of the harshest realities Black women face.

When I decided to enter the field of psychology, I made the commitment to work with people of color. As the time for choosing training experiences approached, my graduate-school peers chose field placements in the affluent, White, and Jewish communities of Chicago's North Shore. I assumed that, being Black, I wouldn't feel comfortable in those settings, and that the people in those settings might not feel comfortable with me. I wanted to gain experience in a community of "my people," a community with "real problems," a community that needed someone like me—an educated, socially conscious, Black clinician.

My requirements for choosing a clinical placement were shaped by an additional assumption that I made about myself: that being African American, I could not exercise prejudice. Although I had been protected from the most blatant expressions of prejudice, I thoroughly understood the history of pain and disenfranchisement that Black people had endured as subjects of one of its forms—racism. I assumed that this awareness would protect me from engaging in any form of prejudice or discrimination.

UNDERSTANDING THE EXPERIENCE
OF PRIVILEGE—COMING
TO CONSCIOUSNESS: MARYA

When I began my externship, I was totally unaware of the ways in which dominant cultural stereotypes had infiltrated my thinking about African Americans and other people of color. I am now aware that the American myth of the meritocracy had pervaded my thinking. I had not yet examined how the ideal of meritocracy had been distorted by racism and other isms. Despite my academic and family training about discrimination, I believed that those who are not successful are flawed by illness, poor work ethic, or a misunderstanding about the requirements for success. I thought that in becoming a therapist I would help the people of my community combat their "flaws" and achieve success.

I began my externship with Felice at Alternatives Inc. in the fall of 1991. During the first weeks there, my work seemed to be going well. I was making efforts to connect with my clients, and it appeared that they were engaging in the therapeutic process. However, as time progressed, clients stopped regularly attending their therapy sessions with me. I became frustrated with their sporadic attendance or non-attendance and started to look for an explanation.

The psychodynamic perspective I had learned at my White, upper-class university informed me that my clients were being resistant. In contrast, during supervision, Felice attempted to normalize the experiences I was having. We discussed the agency's client population and the factors that make non-attendance, sporadic attendance, and attendance only during acute crisis common. We also began to explore ways to change client expectations about attendance, and counter the resistance sometimes associated with non-attendance. Yet I remained unclear about what kept certain clients engaged in the therapeutic process and not others, and uncertain whether I was providing an appropriate therapeutic environment.

Looking for role models, I began to more closely examine the attitudes and practices of other therapists working at the agency, and I noticed that my colleagues were not all equally skilled. While some were open, conscious, and sensitive in regard to the cultural contexts of their minority clients, others were ignorant, even offensive. I judged these to be poor therapists: People whose upbringing, race, and education limited their worldview and prevented them from connecting with our client population. At the same time, I realized that I shared something with this group. We had the same pattern of no-shows, cancellations, and premature terminations. I began to experience a growing dissonance between how I viewed myself and how my clients might be viewing me. As my recognition of my problem grew, so did my anxiety and confusion.

REFLECTIONS ON CHANGE: MARYA

Like the therapists I was so quick to judge, I realized that I too had failed to engage my clients by not creating a safe space where their experiences, strengths, and culture defined the context in which change occurred. Instead, I was attempting to replicate the values of the world in which I lived—particularly values around promptness, openness, and parenting. Without being fully aware of it, I expected my clients to tune into my values, and to adopt those values as their own. I was replicating the experience of invalidation that they faced in their everyday lives.

I was an extremely reluctant supervisee as I struggled to understand why I was not having the success that I had expected. As the hour for weekly supervision approached, I experienced a pervasive feeling of heaviness accompanied by nausea. I attempted to avoid supervision by being late or "forgetting," and I gained a temporary reprieve from self-examination by diverting attention to my "acting out." The reason for my symptoms was the dissonance I experienced during supervision. I was being challenged to see my clients as whole people who were successful and productive in ways that I, as a product of the dominant culture, did not accept. I was being asked to view my clients not as the victims I perceived them to be, but as people living within a particular set of circumstances to which they responded adaptively. They were doing the best job they knew how to do. I could not yet see my clients' strength, resilience, and integrity, a view that would enable me to effectively assist them in creating change.

The feeling in the pit of my stomach before every supervision session also came from the discovery that my cultural assimilation had been so pervasive that I was having difficulty meeting the expectations of my supervisor. Recognizing my middle-class status and embracing middle-class values made me different from the clients with whom I worked and impeded the therapeutic process. I also found it difficult to accept that a White, Jewish woman—both descriptors are important to me, given the history of interaction between these groups as I experienced them growing up in Detroit—had more insight into, and understanding of, the effects of economic deprivation and racism than I had. Fortunately, I was sufficiently engaged in the learning process to continue with supervision even though the dissonance it created was quite uncomfortable.

ENGAGING IN THE PROCESS
OF CHANGE: FELICE

While Marya was working through this phase in her identity development, I was thinking about how I could help her to understand the context of the clients she was working with. Although it was true that Marya was biracial and had been raised in a predominantly African American community, it is equally true that there is a great deal of variability within African American communities (Ibrahim, 1991), and that relative privilege within does exist. She seemed to have a background that engendered that relative privilege. I knew that she had done her undergraduate work at a prestigious university and had won a fellowship for graduate study there. This led me to believe that in high school, she had achieved a degree of academic success that surpassed most, and that she also had managed to sustain her excellence through four years of undergraduate study to win a fellowship. When Marya and I began to work together, I did not yet understand how the dynamic of relative privilege would unfold within the process of her professional development.

It seemed to me that the best way to help Marya understand our clients and explore her own privilege was to acquire information regarding her context. When we began supervision, I attempted to establish a "safe" relationship. Establishing a safe relationship with a trainee is much like establishing a safe relationship with clients in therapy. The supervisor is required to maintain an attitude of acceptance and willingness to engage with the trainee's experiences, knowledge, mistakes, and criticism. If the expectation of the supervisor is that trainees will work within the contexts of their clients, the supervisor has to model this by working within the context of the trainee. Establishing a safe relationship also involves both setting norms for what is appropriate for discussion in supervision, and having clear role expectations with the accompanying role accountability.

I communicated some important ground rules to Marya at the beginning of the relationship:

1. Cultural identity is a valid and valuable tool for establishing connection with others.

2. It is important to accept and respect your own culture as well as others' cultural identities.

3. Discussion of cultural background, differences, and expectations is normal both within the context of the supervisory relationship and within the therapeutic relationship.

4. Respect for clients' cultural contexts is an important tool in establishing relationships.

5. Understanding context is an important part of understanding people's culture.

6. All cultures are adaptive in the sense that they are made up of components that help people get the work of living done.

7. Some adaptive cultural components may have outlived their usefulness yet still remain parts of the culture. These parts are usually referred to as dysfunctional.

8. Cultures' dysfunctional components offer valuable information about history and current functioning, and through implication, possible roads toward change.

Underlying these ground rules was my assumption that Marya came to our agency with her own set of experiences, beliefs, and assumptions about the world around her and the people in her world. These assumptions formed the framework that she would use in creating relationships. I asked Marya countless questions in an attempt to assist her in making her assumptions explicit. Explicit assumptions are more easily clarified and more easily shaped to include novel situations. I set out to assist her in developing an awareness of her own values, beliefs, and assumptions, with the intention of facilitating both the engagement process and her own counter-transference issues.

I was aware of the differences in our cultures and was deliberate in my attempts to understand and bridge the gaps in our culturally based understanding. I was curious about Marya, as I am curious about most people, and let my curiosity guide me in the process of uncovering the gaps and making connection.

I came to supervision aware that there is no single correct way of doing things or of seeing the world, and with the hope that I would model a good example within the supervisory relationship for working in treatment. I encouraged Marya to try new things and to make mistakes. I also encouraged confusion—in my experience the precursor to change. My goal was to assist her in ferreting out her "truths," and to challenge those truths when I saw them interfering with her efficacy in the development of therapeutic relationships. This formed the basis of our supervisory process. There is risk involved in this method—the student may be intolerant of dissonance or may not be developmentally or emotionally ready for change. Happily, Marya was ready to engage in this process. The stage had been set for her to begin to explore her identity as a therapist working with poor minority populations.

INTERNALIZATION OF CHANGE: MARYA

Clinical supervision furthered my understanding of my role with clients and my awareness of my own privilege. It helped me to see that I had been using my own cultural experience to infer my clients' cultural context. Although many things about Felice and her personal style spurred this change, the aspects of supervision that had most influenced me were the inquiries she made during supervision. She asked "How" questions about my clients, as well as about my own context and racial identity.

Felice asked me for information about how my clients experienced the world, and how their life experiences had affected them. Quite often, these were questions that I had never considered. I had learned to ask the "What" questions such as "What were the client's experiences?" Once I knew "what," I thought that my theory of psychopathology and my own ability to reason would provide me with the answer to "how" events had affected the client. Coming from a doctoral program that rarely addressed multicultural issues, I had not been encouraged to counsel idiographically. According to Ridley (1995), "The idiographic approach underscores the need to understand the personal meaning held by the client as a particular person, not simply as a representative of certain groups" (p. 83). By believing that I knew something about my clients because I was a person of color, I was ignoring individuality and  within-group variation. As Ibrahim (1991) points out, "Treating any person as a stereotype of his or her cultural group violates the person's individuality and may lead to premature termination, with minimal therapeutic effectiveness, and possible negative outcomes regarding the client's perceptions of the counseling . . . profession" (p. 14).

The early stages of a therapeutic relationship consist largely of information gathering, assessment, and goal setting—what people's experiences have been, what those experiences mean about them, and how the process of treatment will proceed (Cormier & Hackney, 1987). After meeting with clients in these early phases, I would return to my desk, think through the information a client had given me, and connect that information to the problem that had prompted the client to seek therapy.

For example, if an adolescent client reported that his mother was abusing drugs, and that many of his friends were in a gang, I made the assumption that these factors were significant in his choice to be gang-involved. Gang membership provides adolescents with a substitute family. Based on this logical, research-based, well-intentioned understanding, I would create treatment goals and decide on a treatment approach. Before Felice inquired, I did not routinely ask a client how he or she interpreted life events or how those events had influenced the client's decision-making. My cultural encapsulation was so powerful, my socialization so great, and my education so narrow that I believed that I already knew the answers.

At the beginning of my externship and supervisory relationship, I was excited about the treatment-planning work that I had done for those clients, because I *thought* I understood them, particularly those African American clients who I perceived as culturally similar to me. However, as time progressed and attendance waned, so did my excitement. Fortunately, Felice's questioning of me regarding how life events had shaped my clients, and her insistence that I answer with what *they* had said about how life had shaped them and the meaning *they* made from their own experiences (rather than with assumptions and theories), prompted me out of my role as the expert who knew more about my clients than they knew about themselves. I began to understand why clients had cancelled, failed to attend appointments, or terminated therapy altogether.

My growing insight led to many discussions about the difficulty I experienced in asking clients the questions that were so critical to my forming a complete understanding. Often, I failed to ask the questions because I assumed I already knew the answers. As I learned to consciously question, to allow my curiosity to lead me, I had to constantly remind myself that the clients are the experts about themselves and their experiences. My work as a therapist is to assist clients in discovering their own paths toward change.

MARYA'S LEARNINGS AND CONCLUSIONS

During supervision, I was asked how my life experiences had shaped who I was. This questioning led to conversations that made explicit my own strongly held cultural values, beliefs, assumptions, and counter-transference issues, and it helped me develop a tolerance for dissonance, ambiguity, and my own mistakes.

Since my work with Felice in externship, I have gone on to teach and train new counselors in multicultural counseling. The experiences that she and I shared in that formative year shaped the approach I have taken in training students to be culturally competent. This approach is consistent with the recent literature about multicultural competence in counseling (Arredondo & Arciniega, 2001; Vinson & Neimeyer, 2000). The Association of Multicultural Counseling and Development (AMCD) has identified three domains that are crucial in developing multicultural competence in clinicians: Counselor Awareness of Own Cultural Values and Biases, Counselor Awareness of Client's Worldview, and

Culturally Appropriate Intervention Strategies (Arredondo et al., 1996, as cited in Arredondo & Arciniega, 2001). All of these strategies help to reduce the level of stereotyping, reduce the exertion of privilege, and eliminate the imposition of majority culture values that may occur in counseling.

DISCUSSION QUESTIONS

1. How are dominant cultural stereotypes perpetuated by organizational or institutional structures? How might this perpetuation affect an individual's ability to develop awareness about prejudice?

2. What are some of the values you hold that might limit your ability to make connection with clients?

3. When a direct supervisor has difficulty accepting his or her own privilege, how might a supervisee work through his or her own biases? What resources might students draw from to further their cultural competence?

4. How might universities better integrate issues of multiculturalism, privilege, and racial identity development into both their curricula and training experiences?

5. Should universities have responsibility for overseeing multicultural training in off-site training facilities?

6. Although some people are ready to confront their prejudice, others are not. What methods, other than direct confrontation, can help people uncover their prejudice?

REFERENCES

Arredondo, P., & Arciniega, G. M. (2001). Strategies and techniques for counselor training based on multicultural counseling competencies. *Journal of Multicultural Counseling and Development, 29,* 263–274.

Cormier, L. S., & Hackney, H. (1987). *The professional counselor: A process guide to helping.* Englewood Cliffs, NJ: Prentice-Hall.

Dukes, R. L., Maritnez, R. O., & Stein, J. A. (1997). Precursors and consequences of membership in youth gangs. *Youth and Society, 29,* 139–166.

Gibbs, J. T. (1989). Biracial Adolescents. In J. T. Gibbs, L. N. Huang, & Associates (Eds.), *Children of color: Psychological interventions with minority youth* (pp. 322–350). San Francisco: Jossey-Bass.

Ibrahim, F. A. (1991). Contribution of cultural worldview to generic counseling and development. *Journal of Counseling and Development, 70,* 13–19.

Maxson, C. L., Whitlock, M. L., & Klein, M. W. (1998). Vulnerability to street gang membership: Implications for practice. *Social Service Review, 72,* 70–92.

Ridley, C. (1995). *Overcoming unintentional racism in counseling and therapy: A practitioner's guide to intentional intervention.* Thousand Oaks, CA: Sage.

Vinson, T. S., & Neimeyer, G. J. (2000). The relationship between racial identity development and multicultural counseling competency. *Journal of Multicultural Counseling and Development, 28,* 177–188.

19

Personal Compassion and Alliance Building

Observations of an Asian American Professor

MATTHEW R. MOCK, PH.D.

"RACISM. GETTING SICK WASN'T OUR FAULT.
BUT GETTING WELL IS OUR RESPONSIBILITY."

(ANONYMOUS)

A STORY OF AN INCIDENT I OBSERVED

One day, after teaching a graduate psychology class, I went to a major department store to do some gift shopping for the holidays. I observed an incident that still stands out in my mind today. Although what I observed from close by took just a few minutes, I can replay it frame by frame as though it were happening in slow motion. Clearly, what I witnessed had an impact on me.

After perusing the departments for a while, I observed a man in his mid- to late-thirties looking in the cases of the jewelry department. The man, appearing to be Asian American, had also caught my attention because few Asian Americans live in the immediate and surrounding areas. This man was casually dressed and wore a trench coat because it recently had been raining sporadically. He seemed quite acculturated, perhaps even native born. I overheard his conversation with an Asian American woman and a child (perhaps his wife and daughter) agreeing to shop separately for a while. As soon as his wife took the escalator upstairs, heading for another department, I observed the man become keenly focused on some earrings in one of the jewelry cases.

The jewelry cases were situated in a rectangle around the service and purchase area. On this particular day, the department-store salesperson was a woman who appeared to be White and in her mid-fifties. Because it was the holidays, the store and jewelry departments were bustling. After careful scrutiny, the Asian American man seemed to make his decision about his purchase of some onyx earrings and waited in what was now a short line that was forming. He checked his watch. I thought that perhaps he was making certain that he had time to make his purchase before his wife and child returned to the shopping area.

Two other customers, one a man and the other a woman, who both appeared to be White, individually made their purchases. Now the only one left in line, the Asian American man waited for the saleswoman's attention and his turn to be served. However, instead of assisting this man, the saleswoman left the immediate counter and register, and instead went to serve a woman, also White, who had just come to another side of the counter to ask a question. It was as though the saleswoman looked but did not see the man, so she turned away! The saleswoman opened one of the cases at the female customer's request to show her some watches. She then proceeded to assist this customer in making her department-store credit-card purchase, as she had the previous male and female customers. Afterward, instead of returning to the Asian American man at the register, she answered the questions from a man passing through the department. It was as though the Asian American customer was invisible or nonexistent. Despite the fact that these customers were being given attention and service out of turn, the man waited patiently.

Finally, upon returning to assist the Asian American man, the saleswoman made no mention that she had passed him by and put him off. He pointed to the earrings he had carefully selected, indicating that he wanted to also use his store credit card for the purchase. The woman stepped over to the register and swiped the card in the crediting machine, all the while studying the man up and down and carefully scrutinizing his face. After a pause, she came back to the man, requesting his signature on the credit-card slip. To this, he routinely complied. She looked at the signature carefully, paused, and then commented, "I'm sorry. Please sign again." He signed once more, only to have her react with an audible sigh and then request, "I must see your driver's license or some other form of identification." In response, the Asian American man looked at her somewhat perplexed, but after a brief pause cooperated anyway. After collecting his driver's license, stepping away and studying it against his store credit-slip signature, the saleswoman returned from the register. By this time, a small line had formed behind the man. The saleswoman said firmly in a lowered voice, drawing the man closer, "Please sign again. Only this time, make an effort to sign it like your license!" Clearly more flustered, the man complied once again, but first commenting, "I did not see you request this of the prior customers. And is showing a picture identification store policy?" To this, the saleswoman iterated her stance for a "careful" signature. She responded assertively to him, but with careful, slowed, and purposely formed words, as though he might not understand English. Hoping to draw the man closer to her to not be within earshot of others, she spoke as though she were sharing a secret with him. At a near whisper, she said in a patronizing tone, "Please, sir. This is for your own good!" Following this brief dialogue, the interaction finally broke off with the man hurrying away at last with his purchase, once again searching for the time on his watch.

REFLECTIONS AND CONSIDERATIONS

After reading this story, many of you will appropriately express some form of shock or disbelief at the way this man was treated. Others of you will recognize this type of treatment as personal to your own experience. Some of you will assume that there must be more to the story than was witnessed and recounted, for such blatant mistreatment does not occur without a reason. Still others of you may not associate this treatment with racial discrimination at all.

Consider *your* response. Also consider the following questions, some of which you may have asked yourself after reading this story: *How do you know the salesperson was discriminating against this Asian American man? Was this really a racist interaction? Was it about skin color or appearance, tone of voice, gender, facial expressions, or perceived socioeconomic status, or was it something about this man's assumed attitude? Would it have made a difference if there had not been the earlier slights, invisibility, or acts of disrespect, dehumanization, or marginalization?* Finally, consider other questions you had that could be added to this list.

AN IMPORTANT REVELATION

There is an important sidebar to my story and its concluding events. I was actually not just an idle witness to this event. I did not just observe this from afar. *This was an actual event that happened to me. I was that Chinese American man, in the department store, with my family, shopping like other families do. I felt the saleswoman had discriminated against me.*

By way of self-introduction, I am a third-generation, Chinese American, heterosexual man. I earned my bachelor's degree in psychology, with a child and education focus, from Brown University, and master's and doctorate degrees in clinical and consulting psychology from the California School of Professional Psychology in the California Bay Area. I grew up bicultural in the company of many siblings, with few material or monetary resources, but with textured life experiences that enriched my growth and development. I recall that our family was one of the few Asian American families in the entire community, especially during my early, formative years.

Professionally, for more than 15 years now, I have been director of Family, Youth and Children's Mental Health in Berkeley, California, a program that provides services to the poor, working poor, or those often most marginalized. One of my other major roles is that of system-wide ethnic services and cultural competency coordinator for the City of Berkeley.

Also, as a professor of psychology and director of the Cross Cultural Counseling program in the Graduate School of Professional Psychology at John F. Kennedy University in Orinda, California, I am committed to imparting knowledge to graduate students in ways that enrich their multicultural perspectives and their contributions to social justice. I give invited workshops and talks nationally and abroad.

As a Chinese American family, one of our core values is teaching and learning about compassion and empathy toward others. Living in the Bay Area of California, we are never lacking in situations that remind us of the great importance and imperatives of striving toward equality in how we, and others, are treated. Knowing and telling personal stories past and present, and creating future possibilities for us as a family are extremely important. I try to impart some of these stories as inspirations for my workshop attendees or graduate students. Whether it is in my personal or professional life, I feel I am addressing issues of combating racism and discrimination on a daily basis. Sometimes, personal and professional experiences closely interweave.

"THE REST OF THE STORY"

There is an addendum to my department store story. As I left the store and felt the coolness of the outside air, I had a moment of clarity and inner strength. I questioned what had happened in just a few minutes' time. I paused to think about who I am and what I stand for: I am a professor and somewhat prominent multicultural psychotherapist who advocates for equality and social justice for others. I am a husband and a father. I am teaching my young daughter to speak up for herself as well as for others. I know all too well the historical legacy of Asian American mistreatment, and what things might be done to help stop the cycle of discriminatory interactions. I thought to myself: For my daughter Rachel, my family, for others, and for myself, I cannot let this incident go by without having my voice heard. Now the coolness of the outside air contrasted with the warmth of my face and mounting, renewed spirit.

With these internal, yet firm and grounded feelings hard to put into exact words, I trudged back into the large, bustling department store, past the fancy displays, sparkling boxes of costume jewelry, and holiday-wrapped colognes and perfumes. As I got closer to the jewelry counter, the saleswoman with whom I had interacted had been joined by another saleswoman. The added representative was now helping customers on the opposite side of the counter to make their purchases. The saleswoman with whom I had interacted seemed to be counting receipts and perhaps preparing to take a break. As I walked toward her counter, she recognized me immediately and leaned toward me although somewhat cautiously from a safe distance. Summoning up my feeling of being more grounded and strong inside, I assertively said to her, "In that interaction before, you were not respectful to me. First, you passed me by as though I was invisible. Then you treated me differently than you treated other customers. As a professional, I sign many things. I question if you ask all of your customers equally for their signature multiple times, and for their identification or license, and then respond to them as you did to me. I did not appreciate your condescending demeanor. Please think about this." Although I kept a clear, calm, firm yet steady voice, her face registered some shock and dismay. If I had to guess, I think her reaction was because I had actually taken time to address her about what had happened. Feeling satisfied with my verbal assertion, we then parted ways.

Upon realizing that I was a bit overdue to meet up with my wife and daughter, I turned from the counter, taking a few quick steps away. Sweeping through the narrow aisle of holiday merchandise, my open trench coat caught some of the neatly displayed and stacked boxes of jewelry pins, tumbling all of them to the floor. Pausing to pick up the mess I had just made in my haste, I half-wondered if the saleswoman in witnessing this would mistake my actions and have her finger on the phone ready to call security. Suddenly, after apparently witnessing much of what had transpired, a White female customer knelt down beside me and helped me pick up the few remaining small boxes. Kneeling side-by-side, she gently said to me, "I saw what happened to you. I was shopping, too, and I was a few customers behind you in line. The way she treated you was not fair or right. I am sorry. I will also say something on your behalf." We stood together briefly sharing small smiles of personal, connected acknowledgement. I thanked her simply before we parted. To this day, when I think about this scenario, I feel warmth at the *personal compassion* of this anonymous woman, her words, and our nonverbal connection. I recognize an ally. We choose our battles and sometimes who will participate in the struggle. While I have gone to the store management in similar situations, during this one I let go to have an ally carry on where I left off. This partial ending brings me hope and renewed energy, even optimism.

CONNECTING OUR STORIES
OF PERSONAL COMPASSION

We each have multiple identities, including ethnicity, gender, race, sexual orientation, religion or faith, professional status, abilities, and others. To be aware of which of these statuses earns us relative power and influence in different contexts is essential. These interactions of enacted power become manifest in our lives in many ways. We can also understand ways to teach and learn what might be done in similar situations (Adams, Bell, & Griffin, 1997; Creighton & Kivel, 1992). I share my personal scenario with the saleswoman, but I end with the female customer who took the time to help me as an ally, to emphasize the fact that even small acts of *personal compassion* have larger meanings in collective efforts to achieve social justice. Not only do the events themselves, but sometimes even the invalidation that can occur in the retelling, perpetuate feeling hurt. Small slights, like small nicks or cuts, lead to feelings of pent up rage or perhaps more appropriately, *outrage* for the continued injustices. It is critical for individuals to begin exercising *personal compassion,* getting others to understand at a deep, personal level what it means to be treated differently, and to understand how differential treatment is related to power and privilege (McIntosh, 1988; Pinderhughes, 1989), and to the conscious or unconscious perpetuation of acts of racism, discrimination, and oppression. We have to consider strategies to constructively address negative acts of others. For me, empowering people with a sense of hope and the ability to take personal action are the true meanings of what it means to be "PC"—*not* to be *politically correct* but instead to be *personally compassionate* (Mock, 1999; Mock, 2002). It is with small acts of one individual, and the combined personal acts of hundreds that we can construct lasting alliances toward change.

FINDING OUR OWN PERSONAL COMPASSION TOWARD ANOTHER

The events of September 11, 2001, had a profound impact on us all. Like many people, I cancelled many flight plans right after that date, thinking about the planes that were used as projectiles to bring down the towers of the World Trade Center in New York City, and all the people inside. I had been home watching television as that tragedy unfolded. I had tried to coordinate efforts through my clinic and school programs to help children and families cope with all the feelings of profound sadness, fear, anger, loss, confusion, and anxiety.

Nonetheless, as weeks passed, I was able to fly once again. On one of these trips to give a workshop presentation, I found myself on a full flight of passengers. As we all settled in, I noticed that one of the last individuals to get seated was a Middle-Eastern-appearing woman slightly younger than I. She sat two rows in front of me in a window seat. The flight proceeded without anything unusual, except midway through, when there was a slight bit of turbulence.

Shortly after this turbulence began, the Middle-Eastern woman got up from her window seat as though to go to the restroom at the rear of the plane. She walked briskly with downcast eyes. I noticed several people around me looking up from their reading or talking, acknowledging her passing. After several minutes, she returned. However, as the flight proceeded, she asked to be excused by her neighboring passengers once again to use the restroom. She had tissues in one hand and appeared to be dabbing at her face. After some moments of seemingly collective silence among those around her, she returned once more. The flight proceeded as expected, with the usual courtesies from the flight crew; and as the plane descended toward landing, the warning to be seated and secure seat belts was announced. A short time after the pilot made this announcement, the Middle-Eastern woman arose quickly once again, hurrying to the rear cabin restroom, this time carrying a small purse. Heads turning, several passengers seemed to take additional note, as did one flight attendant. After some moments ticked by, the flight attendant went to check on the woman. Finally, the woman emerged, returned to her window seat, and the plane landed with a near-perfect, smooth touchdown.

What had just happened? Why did I, and others, feel as we did? Was what several of us fellow passengers felt collectively yet silently "normal" under the circumstances? Was feeling uncomfortable, or at least questioning, a reflection of fear, mistrust, or needing to be protected? How should we have voiced our concerns? And finally, what might the woman have been feeling, and was she aware of how others reacted? I silently toiled over some of these and other questions as we got off the plane, walking on to get our baggage.

As we claimed our luggage coming off the turnstile, I noticed the Middle-Eastern woman a few passengers away from me. We picked up our bags at about the same time and then proceeded to the passenger pick-up area outside. After sitting there side-by-side for a few awkward minutes, I finally broke the silence to say "hello" and make small talk. Within a few minutes, we had a readily flowing conversation, first about trivial matters of the day, and then eventually to national and worldwide events. She told me how she too had been affected by the tragedy in New York, by the violence and loss. She had resided in the Bay Area of California all of her life, and her parents had lived there for more than 20 years. Shortly after September 11th, she was cautioned by some of her Muslim neighbors about wearing clothes more readily identifying her as Middle-Eastern or Muslim. Her elderly mother, shopping one day as she usually did at her neighborhood grocery store, had her cart run into by another woman, supposedly as an "accident." She stopped shopping unless another family member accompanied her. A Muslim neighbor had also had an obscene gesture and verbal taunts made at her by teenagers as she was in her car at a stoplight.

With each of our rides due to arrive shortly, our conversation came around to her behavior on the plane, of how she got up several times. She went on to explain how she had to get up numerous times with an upset stomach. She constantly felt the pressure of all eyes focusing on her, not just throughout this flight and other previous ones, but also by airport security who had carefully screened and checked her and her luggage twice before she boarded. She even told me that at times recently she had a bloody nose, perhaps due to increased stress and feeling the silent yet highly palpable tension of those around her.

As we talked and shared our stories, I felt a moment of closeness and commonality with this relative stranger. I expressed how bad I felt and how hard it must be for her, especially when others do not take time to acknowledge her or her feelings and experiences. I told her how I was glad that we had made brief contact to introduce ourselves to each other, to share brief snippets of each other's stories especially in the context of tense times. What she shared next I will not forget. She expressed thanks for my taking time to speak with her, to check in about her welfare, and to engage her sincerely as a fellow human being with thoughts, feelings, and family history. She felt troubled with the silence of others, but validation through our brief yet meaningful engagement. Finally, as my ride arrived, we parted with short acknowledgements, and each headed home.

Later that evening, upon reflection, I experienced a mixture of feelings. At first, I felt bad for being one who experienced moments of tension on the flight. I also felt good for having taken the risk to engage this woman, which allowed us to get to know each other briefly and allowed me to share my feelings of personal compassion toward her and her family's experiences. Last, and perhaps most important for me, I was reminded how being an ally or successfully engaged with another person, even for a few precious moments, means taking risks, breaking from anonymity, finding and giving humanity, being aware of cultural humility, and discovering commonality across differences. That night, in the warmth of my home, reading with my daughter until she fell asleep, I felt hopeful.

CONCLUSION

I give multicultural workshops, presentations, and trainings to a wide array of people, from graduate students to seasoned health and related professional audiences who are primarily in mental health and related fields nationally and internationally. No matter how many times I present the material or how large the audiences are to whom I give workshops on diversity and social justice, I often encounter forms of the same three questions. The first question is "Is fighting racism and oppression for equality primarily the work of people of color or of White people?" Another often asked question is "The history of discrimination and oppression in the United States is so long and hard, and I am just one person. What can I do to make a difference?" One other common question might be "What does someone need to do to make a difference when racist acts are still prevalent, covert and overt, and at so many levels of our society?" Although these questions are common, moving toward answers is a continuous challenge.

Similar to what occurs in my classes, I hope the following teaching points have been articulated in this chapter:

1. Racism and discrimination have an impact on all people, no matter how much individuals have seemingly attained professionally.

2. Fighting racism, discrimination, and oppression for social equality is a battle for all of us, not just one person or group.

3. We all need allies in this hard, ongoing struggle.

4. I am committed to take the daily position that "linking arms" strengthens stances against social injustices. I feel that not only should we take such a stand, but we must do so for our survival. We must move beyond simple political correctness to deep personal compassion leading to a better world for all present and future humanity.

DISCUSSION QUESTIONS

1. Discuss what you look to in order to decide whether someone's actions are discriminatory or not. At what point might you have determined that the saleswoman's behaviors were discriminatory toward the man?

2. Discuss the Asian American man's going back into the store. Do you feel he did enough to address the issue? What might he have done differently? If you were the man, what would you have done? Would you have done more (that is, go to management directly) or not? If not, why not?

3. Discuss the interchange from the perspective of the saleswoman and the man.

4. For the woman who was identified as an ally, what would you have wanted her to say to the store manager? What elements of her comments would be respectful of the man and be most beneficial?

5. What do you imagine might have been some of the thoughts or experiences of the saleswoman to get her to act the way she did?

6. For the two people who were targets of mistreatment in the earlier scenarios, what kinds of conversations would you have with them?

7. The scenarios can have additional aspects of focus including gender, immigration status, class, language, and race. Please discuss.

REFERENCES

Adams, M., Bell, L., & Griffin, P. (1997). *Teaching for diversity and social justice.* New York: Routledge.

Creighton, A., & Kivel, P. (1992). *Helping teens stop violence.* Alameda, CA: Hunter Press.

McIntosh, P. (1988). *White privilege and male privilege: A personal account of coming to see correspondences through work in women's studies (working paper no. 189).* Wellesley, MA: Wellesley College Center for Research on Women.

Mock, M. (1999). Cultural competency: Acts of justice in community mental health. *The Community Psychologist, 32*(1), 38–40.

Mock, M. (2002). Cultural sensitivity, relevance, and competence in school mental health. *School mental health handbook: Strategies for successful implementation.* Baltimore, MD: Kluwer Press.

Pinderhughes, E. (1989). *Understanding race, ethnicity and power: The key to efficacy in clinical practice.* New York: Free Press.

20

Going Through Cultural Barriers in Counseling

RUTH CHAO

INTRODUCTION

As a minority[1] in the counseling psychology profession, I have met diverse cultural obstacles in my daily counseling. Culture and language differences are often interpersonal barriers that I have been challenged to turn into bridges.

My experience began at a practicum in a university counseling center. As a "non-White" counselor-trainee, I faced issues of "Whiteness" on a daily basis. The program advocated multiculturalism; however, my supervisor was White, as were most professors, more than half of my peers, and most of my clients. As an Asian female in a Ph.D. program in the United States, I became used to thinking of psychology as "made in the West," and I thought I was at home in Western psychology until I met Mary.

CRITICAL INCIDENT

As part of my counseling practicum, Mary, a White, female client, came to me with issues associated with body image and romantic relationships. As she looked askance at me, I could tell by her body language that she was taken aback by having me, an Asian, assigned as her counselor. She affirmed my suspicions by saying, "But I don't think you would understand me. You are an Asian, and I'm not. I'm afraid you would judge me with your Asian, conservative values. I want a White female counselor."

Besides being suspicious of my inability to understand her culturally, Mary gave hints of worrying about my language ability. Specifically, she kept apologizing for using slang, idioms, and other culture-bound expressions. During our conversation, I repeatedly assured her that I thoroughly understood her words and their meanings. When those assurances didn't convince her of my understanding, I asked her if my accent disturbed her and was keeping her from accepting me as her counselor. At that point, she acknowledged a clear

---

[1] Being a minority person, I identify myself more with minority people than with the White majority. The following pages present me both as a minority person and as a counselor.

understanding of my English and instead stressed her concern about my "possibly conservative cultural values." She then expressed her desire for a White, female counselor with values similar to hers. I was shocked numb at this counselee's rejection of me and her request for another counselor. I intuitively searched inside me for a way to respond to this client's judgment of my cultural background as a way to dismiss my qualifications in spite of my academic and counseling credentials. Because I could not change my birth or my accent to demonstrate my empathy and willingness to help, I was at a loss about knowing what to do with *myself.*

At this personally intimidating moment, I searched in my mind for resources to help me with this challenge. I ransacked my memory for readings on multicultural counseling, but unfortunately I found no "magic formula" to help me. However, I did remember what I was taught; that is, that a counselor's self-awareness of cultural values and backgrounds is an essential component in his or her multicultural competence. And so, after this session, to further my reflections on multicultural competence, I absorbed myself in multicultural literature. Because my encounter with this client was predominately based on race and culture, I sought out the meaning of "multicultural competence." I poured over Sue, Arredondo, and McDavis's (1992) guidelines about "culturally skilled counselors" and compared myself with the examples they gave and with their suggestion that a culture-sensitive counselor has moved away from cultural naiveté to become aware and sensitive to his or her own cultural heritage. I felt competent with that guideline, because I already knew and felt how Asian culture differs from White, Western culture, and I recognized how much Asian culture had shaped my worldview.

Another guideline offered by Sue, Arredondo, and McDavis (1992) states that culture-sensitive counselors know how oppression, racism, discrimination, and stereotyping affect their work. Yet, my scenario was different from the ones described in the literature; it was not the counselor who was stereotyping and being racist, but the client. I continued searching these guidelines for support, but found nothing, no research or literature relevant to how a counselor of color might counsel a White client when such cultural and personal issues arise.

Later when I met with my supervisor, she asked if I was angry with Mary. Surprising as it was to the supervisor, I was not angry with Mary because my experience with her was typical of interactions I have had with the majority of White people, clients or no, I had encountered. Far from trying to resolve personal anger that was non-existent, I was focused on how to work through therapeutically the challenge Mary brought to the session; that is, the task of working through cultural differences between an Asian counselor (myself) and a White client (Mary), to effectively accomplish the therapeutic assistance to the White client.

In most cases, counselor-counselee dyads are White counselors working with clients of color (Daniels, 2001), yet the reverse relations—counselors of color with White clients—do exist and are on the increase. Counseling trainees of color now occupy 30 percent of the membership in counseling psychology (Alexander, Heineman, Zarin, & Larson, 2002). Current multicultural theories facilitate White counselors in addressing their issues of racism and privilege when counseling clients of color, but counselors of color are given little if any help in working through their prejudices or their clients' prejudices. Counselors of color need to be culturally sensitive as well, struggling as they do *differently* from their White counterparts, and differently among themselves, in their quest to be culturally sensitive. I needed a theoretical guide to help me to help my client. My search of the literature, however, turned up few resources on this dilemma.

CULTURAL DIFFERENCES IN COUNSELING

Recognizing that most psychological principles derive from the West (Sue, 2001), I found no clear answers in Western counseling strategies. I turned inward to my own culture and upbringing for wisdom from the paradigms of Chinese sages (for example, Mencius) and other cultural paradigms (for example, Taoism, Buddhism) that inspired psychotherapy (Hayes, 2001). Somewhat intuitively, I fell back on my own culture and the significance of heartfelt concern for others—the "heart that cannot bear others to suffer . . . seeing people hungry, I am hungry; seeing people drowning, I am drowned" (Mencius 1A7, 4B29, in Lau, 1984, 171). I also followed what Zen/Taoism says, "Don't push the river" (Chuang Tzu 19/22-24, in Graham, 1981).

In my initial session with Mary, I accepted her rejection as it was—not manipulating her distaste of me into my advantage, but following along and wrapping her rejection with empathy. I expressed my concern about her distrust of me and I *accepted* her comments calmly without degrading my professional dignity or position. I took her suspicion seriously and questioned her on her own ideal of a "White, female counselor."

In this situation, another factor that worked to our therapeutic advantage was that I did not take her criticism personally. As my Asian culture suggests, "Try our hardest and accept what comes, not prejudging future consequences." Yet another positive factor at work here was that my Asian culture also encourages letting go of "right" and "should," to be open and accommodating. Falling back on such old Asian values, I was ready to accept whatever my client questioned and criticized in the session with me.

Without guaranteeing that I would counsel her to find a suitable White, female counselor, I promised Mary that I would bring up her concerns at a supervision meeting. I tried hard to let her know that her distrust was also my concern. Although her suspicion and distrust hurt me, what I cared more for was her distrust as related to her needs. She was the center of my concern in that session. Seemingly touched by my good intentions, she decided to stay with me for one more session.

CONCLUSIONS AND LEARNINGS

It is ironic that as I fell back on my cultural roots, the very factor of interpersonal obstacle provided an occasion for ubiquitous, compassionate empathy and acceptance of common humanity. Eventually, I was able to make a connection between my Asian sentiments and Western counseling skills; that is, listening, reflecting, accepting, and being client-centered. I realized that what was part of my response to accepting my client's reactions was also in line with what Teyber (1992) pointed out, ". . . not [to] act on initial impulse, which was trying to assure the client of therapist's competence and ability to help. . . . [I]t is even more essential to listen and respond to the client's concerns when ethnic/cultural differences exist between the therapist and client (p. 61)."

My living in two cultures—American and Asian—has provided me some fresh perspectives on cultural differences in counseling. My session with Mary and other similar experiences have taught me that cultural similarities and differences interweave to compose our complex world. Western insights on counseling today (for example, Teyber, 1992) and ancient Asian thoughts—what Chinese thinkers said so many centuries ago—can and should *mutually* echo, complement, and validate. This discovery of multicultural inter-enrichment vastly enriches and expands my counseling horizon.

Over time, mutual feelings of openness and serenity seeped into the sessions Mary and I shared. My anxiety and nervousness from her critical judgment shifted to calm, genuine acceptance. Mary also began to change. My accented English seemed to have turned less forbidding and more understandable. She found that my Asian upbringing would not prejudge her or shut her out. She laughed heartily as she watched me role-play her anger at her boyfriend, an imaginary interaction that showed her that I intimately and personally understood her anger, sorrows, and frustrated hopes. Slowly, we both came to experience a sharing of serious honesty precisely through our cultural differences. She felt that I took her in, that I took her concerns with genuine seriousness. We both became motivated to build our cultural barriers into a bridge. We both began to *accept* our differences as we learned to understand—both each other and her initial mistrust. I learned to infuse my Asian cultural upbringing into my Western counseling strategies.

Such is one of many examples of intercultural experiences that have already vastly expanded and enriched my counseling. Cultural differences are not hurdles, but potential bridges—bridges to togetherness and mutual understanding.

DISCUSSION QUESTIONS

1. How do you cope with clients' stereotypes on your cultural background? Do you challenge clients or confront their stereotypes, or do you prefer not to address their stereotypes?

2. How do you integrate your cultural background with your professional training? Have you ever noticed yourself trying to blend your cultural wisdom with professional skills? Or do you think we counselors need to stick to our professional skills alone?

3. How do you connect yourself to your clients when you come from a culture different from theirs?

4. Do you think it important to be aware of our own cultural backgrounds? Why? If not, why not?

5. There are at least two types of cultural differences in counselor-client relations—(a) White counselors with minority clients, and (b) minority counselors with White clients. How similar are these two types to each other? How different are they each from the other?

6. What cultural barriers do you notice when you work with clients? How do you and your clients deal with them?

7. How do cultural differences influence counseling? Do you think cultural differences enhance or impair the counseling process? How? Why?

REFERENCES

Alexander, C. M., Heineman, C. J., Zarin, M. S., & Larson, L. (2002). Admission criteria to APA-accredited programs in counseling psychology over 10 years: Reflections of the specialty's values. *The Counseling Psychologist, 30,* 135–148.

Daniels, J. A. (2001). Conceptualizing a case of indirect racism using the White Racial Identity Development model. *Journal of Mental Health Counseling, 23,* 256–268.

Fuertes, J. N., & Gretchen, D. (2001). Emerging theories of multicultural counseling. In J. G. Ponterotto, J. M. Casas, L. A. Suzuki, & C. M. Alexander (Eds.), *Handbook of multicultural counseling* (2nd ed.). Thousand Oaks, CA: Sage.

Graham, A. C. (1981). *Chuang Tzu: The inner chapters.* London: George Allen & Unwin.

Hayes, P. (2001). *Addressing cultural complexities in practice.* Washington, DC: American Psychological Association.

Lau, D. C. (1984). *Mencius. Two volumes.* Hong Kong: The Chinese University Press.

Lin, Y. (1948). *The wisdom of Laotse.* New York: Random House.

Sue, D. W. (2001). Multidimensional facets of cultural competence. *The Counseling Psychologist, 29,* 790–821.

Sue, D. W., Arredondo, P., & McDavis, R. J. (1992). Multicultural competencies and standards: A call to the profession. *Journal of Multicultural Counseling and Development, 20,* 64–88.

Sue, D. W., Bernier, J. E., Durran, A., Feinberg, L., Pedersen, P., Smith, E. J., et al. (1982). Position paper: Cross-cultural counseling competencies. *The Counseling Psychologist, 10,* 45–52.

Sue, D. W., Carter, R. T., Casas, J. M., Fouad, N. A., Ivey, A. E., Jensen, M., et al. (1998). *Multicultural counseling competencies: Individual and organizational development.* Thousand Oaks, CA: Sage.

Sue, D. W., Ivey, A. E., & Pedersen, P. B. (1996). *A theory of multicultural counseling and therapy.* Pacific Grove, CA: Brooks/Cole.

Teyber, E. (1992). *Interpersonal process in psychotherapy: A guide for clinical training.* Pacific Grove, CA: Brooks/Cole.

21

Tales from the Heart of Dixie

Using White Privilege to Fight Racism

Wearing baggy gray sweatpants and an old sweatshirt with large pockets, I recently walked into a knitting supply store. An air filtration mask covered most of my face. I explained that I was looking for stocking stuffers, and the clerk politely took me to a separate room filled with small items that would have easily fit into my many pockets. She showed me around a bit and left me alone there to browse.

This is a typical experience for me as a White woman. I wear a mask, similar to those worn by people who mow lawns, because of my disability, Multiple Chemical Sensitivity. Each day I walk into businesses wearing my mask, and on many occasions, I think how different my experiences in those businesses might be if I were a Black man instead of a White woman. Frankly, I wonder, if I were a Black man, would I have been mistaken for a robber and shot?

I am a disabled, White, lesbian professor in the Deep South—an identity that sometimes gives me mental whiplash, alternating as it does between disadvantaged and privileged group memberships. However, it is most often from my privileged status that I am able to combat racism.

Lacking certain privileges some of the time probably helps me to recognize those instances when I do benefit from unearned privilege (Treitel, 2000). Thus, my being female, lesbian, and disabled may make my white privilege easier to recognize, because the notion of veiled discrimination or subtle advantage is not foreign to me. Akamatsu (1998) points out that those who have not experienced oppression may have a difficult time letting go of the myth of the level playing field. I have no illusions that we live in a meritocracy, and so I have perhaps found it easier than some to recognize my own privileges. I do not see myself as unique or especially meritorious in my anti-racism work. I recognize that I fit the typical pattern of Whites who fight racism, described by Treitel (2000): I have been aware of injustice since childhood, recognize myself as a member of an oppressed group, and have long been involved in social justice movements. Perhaps most importantly, I view my work as an expression of my values (Treitel, 2000). Thus, I see my use of my faculty position to work against racism not as an act of charity, but as an act of integrity, which is its own reward.

Kappen (2001) points out that both persuasion research and social-identity theory predict that members of an in-group (in this case, myself as a White person) will have more power to help other members of the in-group to recognize their own privilege. She indeed found that White speakers were more effective in helping White listeners to recognize their own white privilege. Thus, in some instances, I, as a White counselor educator, may likely have more influence than my colleagues of color in helping White people understand the subtle acts of racism people of color experience every day.

STORY ONE

When I was first apartment hunting in Alabama (which the license plates still proclaim to be the "Heart of Dixie"), I asked my colleagues if they knew of any apartments for rent. Someone sent me to look at a delightful and remarkably inexpensive carriage-house apartment. I was about to take it, when the land-lady mentioned it had been vacant for several months. I expressed surprise be-cause it was such a nice place. She responded, "Yes, but I can't advertise it. If I did, the nigras would be over here in two shakes." Stunned, I started backing out, explaining that I don't rent from racists. Realizing she was losing her chance to rent the place, she hastened to explain, "It's not that. You see, it's fur-nished. You wouldn't want to sleep in a bed that had been slept in by a Black man, would you?" I said, "No, I wouldn't care, and no, I don't understand," and sped away. If not for a slip of her tongue, I would have rented a lovely apart-ment for far below the going rate, while my Black colleagues were paying far more for less desirable units.

My experience in almost renting the carriage house was a clear and overt example of white privilege, but later that same week I may have been the re-cipient of white privilege that was much more subtle when I visited a large property management agency to look at the "apartments available" board. The receptionist at the property management agency observed my search, asked me what I was looking for, and then told me about a duplex that had "just become available." She said it was a really nice place, and because they didn't want un-dergraduates trashing it, they were just telling people "like me" about it. I as-sumed she meant professionals or older adults. Since then, I have come to wonder whether she would have told me about the duplex if I had been a young Black faculty member instead of a young White faculty member. I loved that place, but I will always wonder whether it was good luck that I found it, or white privilege. Discussions of such (unanswerable) questions demonstrate the sometimes elusive nature of privilege.

The cost of being Black in the housing market was again made clear to me by an African American doctoral student whose accent does not betray her eth-nicity on the phone. When she responded by phone to a house advertisement that did not list the rent, she was quoted one price, but when she showed up in person to see the house, the rent was suddenly $100 a month higher. Her price for that little bit of extra pigmentation amounts to $1,200 a year in disposable income, which over the course of several years would amount to a down pay-ment on a house. This same student told me that while she was attending col-lege in another state, the Black fraternities and sororities circumvented another discriminatory housing practice by developing a cooperative system whereby

Black women would seek apartments for Black men. Otherwise, apartments were nearly always "just taken" when the men arrived. In this case, Black men lacked the privilege to find housing for themselves because of prejudices held by apartment owners.

I also cite research to show that discrimination in housing is still rampant. For example, fair-housing audits continue to show high levels of discrimination, with African American auditors routinely being told units are not available, when in fact they are (Reed, 1991). Government audits in 76 cities showed rates of discrimination against Black auditors ranging from 10 percent to 90 percent in various cities, with the average being 46 percent. Therefore, in a typical locale, Black apartment hunters have perhaps half as many apartments to choose from as Whites do.

STORY TWO

Several years ago, I was in a group that was considering two job applicants: one Black, one White. A White colleague said that although both candidates were qualified, he "just felt more comfortable" with one of them (the White candidate). I pointed out that if we make hiring decisions based on our comfort, we will likely perpetrate unintentional discrimination because we all tend to feel most comfortable with people who are similar to us in demographic characteristics such as race, gender, sexual orientation, and social class. Others agreed, and we ended up hiring the African American candidate. After the meeting, the only African American person present thanked me for my comment, saying that if I hadn't pointed out the issue, she would have had to. Unlike her, I had the unearned privilege of being able to make the point without seeming defensive. I still paid a small price because a few of the faculty saw me as a troublemaker, but my price was considerably less than hers would have been.

THE POWER OF ALLIES

Allies are sometimes more successful than targeted populations in changing attitudes because of the allies' privilege as members of the dominant group (Kappen, 2001). When I give lectures on lesbian, gay, bisexual, and transgendered (LGBT) issues in counseling, psychology, social work, education, and religion classes and challenge the students' views, I am seen by homophobic students as biased and self-serving. In contrast, a heterosexual ally who challenges their views might create more cognitive dissonance for them. Homophobic students' reactions to the ally's pro-gay attitudes might go something like, "Hmm . . . I respect and identify with her, yet we disagree on this issue"; or "I thought only queers and militants were for gay rights, yet my instructor who has a husband is gay-affirmative. . . . How confusing!" (See Liddle & Stowe, 2002.) The words of allies are perhaps more difficult for homophobic listeners to write off, thereby provoking prolonged thought and the opportunity for more in-depth analysis before the listeners accept or reject the information. For example, I believe my most powerful and successful lecture on this topic was successful not so much because of my own contribution, but rather because of the heterosexual course instructor's later discussion of my presentation (see Liddle & Stowe, 2002). During the class discussion the week after my presentation, the students at first reported only anger and discomfort. However, by the end of the discussion, facilitated by the instructor who is a heterosexual ally to the LGBT community, there was evidence of substantive attitude change. Several students, who had initially reported outrage at being forced to listen to a gay-affirmative lecture that they felt was antithetical to their religious values, ended up saying things such as "I've completely changed my mind." It seemed that by having a safe place to explore their discomfort, and perhaps by seeing the instructor and other relatively gay-affirmative classmates as role models, these students were able to incorporate the information from my lecture in a way they could not have without the help of these allies.

Another advantage allies have in confronting prejudice is that they are more likely to witness some forms of prejudice than are members of the oppressed group. As an out lesbian, I am seldom confronted by open hostility. Perhaps this is because most people tend to be polite about their prejudices, at least when they are around people they know belong to those groups. However, people are not so circumspect when they are unaware that a member of that group is present. For example, a group of workers (one of whom was a closeted gay acquaintance) came to make a repair in my office. The workers were very polite to me, but I later heard from my gay acquaintance that the minute they were out of earshot, they started making derogatory remarks about my sexual orientation. My friend did not dare speak out against this abuse for fear of arousing suspicion that he was gay. He did not share the privilege heterosexuals have—the ability to confront homophobia without fear of discrimination. Because it is legal to fire someone simply for being gay in 37 states, including Alabama (Human Rights Campaign, 2003), my gay friend might have lost his job if he had spoken up. If one of the straight men present had put a stop to the homophobic rhetoric, however, he would not have faced as great a risk.

CONCLUSION

Members of privileged groups can use their privilege to combat discrimination and oppression in both their professional and private lives. The first step is recognizing that privilege and discrimination still exist in our society. The next is deciding to use one's privilege in the service of reducing those injustices. Finally, it takes courage and practice to talk about these issues with one's colleagues and friends. The fact that I face fewer consequences when I act as an ally than would a member of the group being discriminated against, makes me feel an obligation to speak up, rather than waiting for a member of that group to confront the problem. I have had the experience of being an ally and of benefiting from the efforts of allies to the LGBT community. Both experiences have consistently reinforced for me McIntosh's (1988) assertion that one of the most important privileges that dominant community members have is the privilege to confront prejudice without being seen as self-serving. Taking on the role of an ally—deciding in advance that I will not tacitly support injustice with my silence—has helped me find the courage to speak up when opportunities arise.

DISCUSSION QUESTIONS

1. You are spending time with two White friends. One friend tells a joke that you find racially offensive. Your other friend laughs.

    a. What do you do?
    b. Is what you would actually do different from what you ideally wish you would do?
    c. How are your feelings and your anticipated reactions influenced by your own race?
    d. How do you think your own race will influence how you will be seen by your friends?

2. Think of the last time you witnessed prejudice toward a group of which you are not a member. Picture the entire interaction, including what happened afterward.

    a. What was your role in this interaction?
    b. Did you respond constructively (in a way that would promote non-defensive self-examination in the offender)?
    c. If not, what stopped you, and in retrospect what do you wish you had done?
    d. What similar future situations are you likely to face, and what can you do to prepare to respond constructively?

3. When, in the last week, do you think you benefited from privilege (for example, heterosexual privilege, white privilege, or male privilege)?

4. Do you feel any obligation either to give up some unearned privilege or to use your privilege constructively? If so, what forms might your actions take?

5. When have you had to choose between personal comfort and personal integrity? Which did you choose, and what price did you pay for that choice?

REFERENCES

Akamatsu, N. N. (1998). The talking oppression blues: Including the experience of power/powerlessness in the teaching of "cultural sensitivity." In M. McGoldrick (Ed.), *Re-visioning family therapy: Race, culture, and gender in clinical practice* (pp. 129–143). New York: Guilford Press.

Ancis, J. R., & Szymanski, D. M. (2001). Awareness of White privilege among White counseling trainees. *Counseling Psychologist, 29,* 548–569.

Human Rights Campaign (2003). Gay, lesbian, bisexual and transgender workplace issues. [On-line.] Retrieved 4/5/03 from http://www.hrc.org/ issues/workplace/index.asp.

Kappen, D. M. (2001). Acknowledgement of racial privilege, endorsement of equality, and feelings of collective guilt via ingroup versus outgroup influence. *Dissertation Abstracts International, 61*(9-B), 5056.

Liddle, B. J., & Stowe, A. M. (2002). A lesbian/straight team approach to changing attitudes toward lesbian, gay, bisexual, and transgendered people. *Journal of Lesbian Studies, 6* (3/4), 99–108.

McIntosh, P. (1988). *White privilege and male privilege: A personal account of coming to see correspondences through work in women's studies.* Wellesley, MA: Wellesley College, Center for Research on Women.

Reed, V. M. (1991). Civil rights legislation and the housing status of Black Americans: Evidence from fair housing audits and segregation indices. *Review of Black Political Economy, 19*(3/4), 29–42.

Treitel, E. N. (2000). Anti-racist practice by White psychologists. *Dissertation Abstracts International, 61*(5-B), 2785.

22

Yes, I See You're Committed to the Cause . . . But Where's Your Credibility, and Why That Angst?

DAVID MACPHEE

Can a middle-class youth recognize his privilege without being immersed in a low-income environment? Can a White man comprehend racism viscerally if he has not been a visible minority in another culture or witnessed it in action?

BACKGROUND

Two figure/ground experiences in my youth had a formative influence on my perception of privilege. First, I grew up in a small, blue-collar town in Idaho that was dependent on mining and forestry, yet my parents were well-educated professionals. Second, many of the families I knew—all White—were regular churchgoers who believed in the Golden Rule and that God loves all people. Although they might sprinkle everyday conversation with ethnic jokes and slurs, paradoxically they gave to causes that served culturally diverse and low-income people. Most of them were generous and compassionate, and would be offended to be called bigots.

Neither my ethnicity nor social class was obvious to me until I went to a private college where I was less worldly and wealthy. My battered 1954 bread truck advertised to all that I was a "hick from the sticks." I was in daily contact with people of color for the first time, the novelty of which made me uncomfortable. Flashbacks to age 5 bubbled to the surface, when on my first trip to an urban, multicultural city, I pointed to an African American man in the grocery line ahead of us and asked my father, in a preschooler's stage voice, "What's that?"

This naiveté became more self-conscious in graduate school when I became good friends with a Black woman and several Jewish women. Paralyzing internal debates about protocol leaked out in ways that were probably amusing if not appalling. *How much can I ask about what it's like to be Black (or Jewish)? Is it acceptable to talk about prejudice and racism? Is "Jew" a slur, or do I always have to say "Jewish people?" Is it "Black" or "African American?" Am I an ignorant bumpkin or just garden-variety naïve? How can I become less naïve if I don't ask forthright questions? How much should I expect others to rectify my ignorance, even if my intentions are sincere?*

DEVELOPING AWARENESS

A handful of events shaped my perceptions of privilege as well as my commitment to equality and interest in diversity. First, few of my high-school classmates attended university, and all were middle-class kids. The women had to fight much harder than I did for respect and success in school and their careers, especially if they went into law or engineering. I had assumed that I did well in high school because of native intelligence and hard work, not because I was middle class, White, and male. The social comparison processes that happened in college taught me that I had underestimated the role of opportunity structures (Bronfenbrenner & Ceci, 1994), those experiences provided by families, schools, and neighborhoods that allow certain predispositions to flourish. If my White, middle-class parents had not emphasized reading, encouraged involvement in extracurricular activities, and saved faithfully for college, I might have taken a different path in the woods.

Rural life shapes attitudes that are pertinent to everything from voting patterns to consumer habits, as well as perceptions of privilege. Brooks (2001, p. 62) observed ". . . that most [rural] people don't think sociologically. They don't compare themselves with faraway millionaires who appear on their TV screens. They compare themselves with their neighbors" who tend to have a comfortable standard of living. As a result, there is little class consciousness. Attending a liberal arts college compelled me to think about social class for the first time because the framework for making social comparisons was so different there.

Another formative experience was religion. I was privileged to have several ministers who taught a gospel of caring for humanity, but especially for those who are oppressed. My maternal grandparents, both ministers, were outspoken opponents of the neo-Nazis who lived in a compound a few miles from their home. This moral compass was put to the test with other relatives who used the Bible to justify racism and intolerance for gays. Such incidents crystallized for me the hypocrisy of professing belief in Christian principles while bestowing grace on only a privileged few, and that out-groups—all of whom were different from me—are a threat to some people.

My sense of White male privilege was honed by *Masculus hostilis.* This subspecies, the hostile male, vocalizes his displeasure with gender equity and multiculturalism in shrill diatribes (D'Souza, 1991; Schmidt, 1997), and in clippings posted on his office door that defend White male privilege in college admissions, hiring, and the exclusion of women and minority scholars from "The Canon." His table-pounding rants at faculty meetings are directed at women and minorities who he feels are "given" too much that is not earned, and he makes disparaging remarks about faculty research that focuses on gender and diversity. It is anger directed at those who threaten his status, not the angst of self-doubt. What I have learned from a few *Masculus hostilis* colleagues is that equality really does matter; otherwise, it would be a non-issue. Perhaps there would be greater acceptance of the social justice agenda if more of "us" (White males) were outspoken in support of it (see Smith, 1998).

INFUSIONS OF INSIGHT

As my adolescent self-awareness blossomed, I too wanted to be judged by the content of my character, not by my lack of sophistication in navigating a multicultural world with which I had limited experience. This is the nub of multicultural education for those of us from more privileged backgrounds: how to capitalize on interest in the topic—an interest motivated by relevance to one's career or by commitment to social justice—despite feeling inept in knowing how to behave and how to talk about it. When issues of privilege and difference have been relatively invisible in one's personal history, angst and stereotyping are predictable consequences of confronting such topics in the classroom or in social interactions with out-group people (Islam & Hewstone, 2001; Tatum, 1992).

My commitment and angst became more self-conscious when I participated in two curriculum-infusion projects at Colorado State University. The first focused on gender and the second on multicultural diversity. The faculty participants, virtually all White, wrestled with how to *talk*—not just teach—about prejudice, privilege, and the importance of diversity. If we were uncomfortable talking with colleagues who we knew to be committed to the cause, how could we face a class of students who might be dubious about, if not downright hostile to, the principles we espoused?

These projects drew attention to issues of social class and culture, and the undercurrent of power. The intellectual component was invigorating because a few fundamental processes explained disparate behavior patterns across people, class, culture, and time. Yet fieldwork with Hispanic and Native American families (MacPhee, Fritz, & Miller-Heyl, 1996), and with indigenous people in Australia and Belize, left a lasting, visceral appreciation for my privileged status. Inadequate housing and food, limited opportunities, and despondency often were rooted in patriarchy and colonialism, and by birthright I was one of the oppressors.

Despite this growing awareness of power and privilege, though, I have not completely relinquished my belief that the United States is a meritocracy (Akamatsu, 2001; Banaszynski, 2001). I find myself suggesting to students that children from low-income families would have a brighter future if they just worked hard in school and their parents were more involved, which ignores a host of sociocultural forces arrayed against upward mobility (Lopez, Gurin, & Nagda, 1998; Molnar & Lawson, 1984). For example, children of less advantaged class origins need to show substantially more merit than advantaged children to achieve the same level of success as adults (Breen & Goldthorpe, 1999). One lesson for me is that my limited first-hand experience with oppression hamstrings my ability to fully appreciate opportunities denied to others.

Membership in the privileged class has a hidden tax for the diversity educator—the emotional labor can be painful. I attended seminars in which White males were scapegoated for a number of social ills, and a conference workshop at which the only White person in the room (me) was humiliated as a way to "turn the tables." An occasional class went up in flames when a few vocal students were critical of the attention to diversity issues, and I lacked the skill to defuse the tension (see MacPhee, Oltjenbruns, Fritz, & Kreutzer, 1994). Such incidents provoked in me resentment, frustration, and guilt—not exactly virtues. The literature on privilege suggests that these feelings, particularly collective guilt, are normal when in-group members think about their privileged status (Branscombe, 1998). In some cases, such angst may be adaptive because it links consideration of privilege with positive attitudes toward and actions on behalf of social justice (Banaszynski, 2001; Doosje, Branscombe, Spears, & Manstead, 1998).

Credibility can also be a thorny issue for a professor from the privileged class. As a developmental psychologist, I have no formal academic training in women's studies, cultural anthropology, or sociology. On more than a few occasions, I groped for concepts and connections that were not yet second nature, but I found solace in the suggestion that multicultural competence requires professors to abandon their all-knowing façade, and acknowledge their vulnerability and ineptitude (Vacarr, 2001).

More frustrating for me was the opinion of some students and writers that I had no business talking about issues with which I had little direct experience, regardless of my commitment to the cause. Recent commentaries on this issue assert that people from privileged classes must take responsibility for questioning beliefs and practices that support dominance and discrimination (for example, Boyle-Baise, 1995; Jacques, 1997). Research on social persuasion further supports a role for the White, male teacher because attempts to influence others' understanding of privilege are more successful when made by in-group members (Kappen, 2000). It does seem self-evident that a person of dominant identity should refrain from talking about the *phenomenology* of oppression— how it is experienced personally—unless it is prefaced with "Other people report that. . . ." But I don't agree that lived experience is the only legitimate source of knowledge—a form of parochial reasoning (Brookfield, 1987)—even though it can enrich what is taught.

CONCLUSIONS

Why would a White, male professor enthusiastically pursue social justice in the face of such obstacles? Edge (2002) argued that the ability to embrace diversity is necessary to experience compassion, and compassion is a foundation of social justice. Aside from experience with diversity, the impulse for social justice also can be nurtured through community service, religious education, and discussions of moral and ethical issues. As well, certain values coincide with involvement in social justice activities, particularly the importance attached to influencing others and viewing one's work as an expression of beliefs and values (Treitel, 2000).

The conversion experiences I have described may also require some figure/ground contrasts. For instance, can a middle-class youth recognize his privilege without being immersed in either poor or wealthy contexts? Can a White man comprehend racism viscerally if he has not been a visible minority in another culture or witnessed racism—such as slurs shouted from a passing car at a Black friend? Is a husband truly aware of patriarchy until there is marital conflict around his limited contributions to household labor? All of these examples suggest that power and oppression are relatively invisible to the dominant group until that privilege is challenged, and for this reason it is inevitable that multicultural education provokes angst in students and teachers alike.

APPLICATIONS

The following scenario and questions are meant to help the reader think about some of these applications.

Scenario: You are a White, female fourth year English teacher. It is the third monthly meeting of a year-long multicultural education project that will teach instructors how to address issues of diversity, power, and privilege in their classes. The group includes 15 participants from diverse disciplines and different schools/departments, and most are White. All volunteered; they were not coerced by an administrator. By now, you and your fellow teachers are moderately comfortable with one another: Everyone seems okay with sharing personal experiences and opinions.

The first two sessions covered "safe" topics such as project goals, terminology, student and societal demographics, and models of cultural awareness. Today's session is about how to sensitize students to issues of power and privilege. The first hour is devoted to self-exploration exercises that are supposed to help the participants become aware of this multifaceted issue, and the remaining hour will be devoted to instructional methods. But the discussion is rugged. Some of the men are getting defensive because all fingers seem to be pointing at White males for various social ills. Others look perplexed and wonder what all the fuss is about. "I thought this was the land of opportunity," they say, or, "If you work hard enough, you can succeed." You express your doubts that you have the background to talk with authority about these issues in class. This comment triggers an anxious discussion about what will happen if the students feel blamed by the messages or, worse, if they are overtly hostile and accuse the instructor of being politically correct.

1. Discuss how the "invisibility of privilege" might be made evident to professionals (teachers, counselors, social workers, psychologists, human services) from privileged backgrounds. Are there ways to create awareness without also fostering guilt (personal or collective) and defensiveness?

2. Should angst arise in a training seminar, how would you get to the source and how might it be addressed constructively?

3. Is it necessary to have first-hand experience—as a minority, with oppression—to teach with authority? If not, how do you bring these issues alive in the classroom? How might the White males in the group

effectively work toward social justice, and how are students likely to react?

4. A colleague says that he doesn't have the background in sociology or anthropology to address issues related to diversity and social status. How might you respond? What suggestions might you make?

5. How would you defuse a class that is "going up in flames?" Some students are making accusations of political correctness and asking why such issues are even being brought up; others are angry that some of their peers deny there is a problem to be dealt with; still others sit tight-lipped, with arms crossed.

6. Brainstorm teaching strategies that would illuminate ways in which (a) women have less power, and (b) Black youth have less opportunity to achieve. Ideally, these strategies would help to personalize the issues for students (that is, help them empathize), convey accurate information, and/or highlight implications for practice.

REFERENCES

Akamatsu, N. N. (2001). The talking oppression blues: Including the experience of power/powerlessness in the teaching of "cultural sensitivity." *Journal of Feminist Family Therapy, 11,* 83–97.

Banaszynski, T. L. (2001). *Beliefs about the existence of White privilege, race attitudes, and diversity-related behavior.* Unpublished doctoral dissertation, Yale University.

Boyle-Baise, M. (1995). The role of a European American scholar in multicultural education. *Theory and Research in Social Education, 23,* 332–341.

Branscombe, N. R. (1998). Thinking about one's gender group's privileges or disadvantages: Consequences for well-being in women and men. *British Journal of Social Psychology, 37,* 167–184.

Breen, R., & Goldthorpe, J. H. (1999). Class inequality and meritocracy: A critique of Saunders and an alternative analysis. *British Journal of Sociology, 50,* 1–27.

Bronfenbrenner, U., & Ceci, S. J. (1994). Nature/nurture reconceptualized in developmental perspective: A bioecological model. *Psychological Review, 101,* 568–586.

Brookfield, S. D. (1987). *Developing critical thinkers: Challenging adults to explore alternative ways of thinking and acting.* San Francisco: Jossey-Bass.

Brooks, D. (2001). One nation, slightly divisible. *Atlantic Monthly, 288*(5), 53–65.

Doosje, B., Branscombe, N. R., Spears, R., & Manstead, A. S. R. (1998). Guilty by association: When one's group has a negative history. *Journal of Personality and Social Psychology, 75,* 872–886.

D'Souza, D. (1991). *Illiberal education: The politics of race and sex on campus.* New York: Free Press.

Edge, R. (2002). One middle-age White male's perspective on racism and cultural competence: A view from the bunker where we wait to have our privilege stripped away. *Mental Retardation, 40,* 83–85.

Islam, M. R., & Hewstone, M. (2001). Dimensions of contact as predictors of intergroup anxiety, perceived out-group variability, and out-group attitude: An integrative model. In M. A. Hogg & D. Abrams (Eds.),

Intergroup relations: Essential readings (pp. 383–395). Philadelphia: Psychology Press/Taylor & Francis.

Jacques, R. (1997). The unbearable whiteness of being: Reflections of a pale, stale male. In P. Prasad, A. J. Mills, M. Elmes, & A. Prasad (Eds.), *Managing the organizational melting pot: Dilemmas of workplace diversity* (pp. 80–106). Thousand Oaks, CA: Sage.

Kappen, D. M. (2000). *Acknowledgement of racial privilege, endorsement of equality, and feelings of collective guilt via ingroup versus outgroup influence.* Unpublished doctoral dissertation, University of Kansas.

Lopez, G. E., Gurin, P., & Nagda, B. A. (1998). Education and understanding structural causes for group inequalities. *Political Psychology, 19,* 305–329.

MacPhee, D., Fritz, J., & Miller-Heyl, J. (1996). Ethnic variations in personal social networks and parenting. *Child Development, 67,* 3278–3295.

MacPhee, D., Oltjenbruns, K. A., Fritz, J. J., & Kreutzer, J. C. (1994). Strategies for infusing curricula with a multicultural perspective. *Innovative Higher Education, 18,* 289–309.

Molnar, J. J., & Lawson, W. D. (1984). Perceptions of barriers to Black political and economic progress in rural areas. *Rural Sociology, 49,* 261–283.

Schmidt, A. J. (1997). *The menace of multiculturalism: Trojan horse in America.* Westport, CT: Praeger.

Smith, R. W. (1998). Challenging privilege: White male middle-class opposition in the multicultural education terrain. In R. C. Chavez & J. O'Donnell (Eds.), *Speaking the unpleasant: The politics of (non)engagement in the multicultural education terrain* (pp. 197–210). Albany, NY: State University of New York Press.

Tatum, B. D. (1992). Talking about race, learning about racism: The application of racial identity development theory in the classroom. *Harvard Educational Review, 62,* 1–24.

Treitel, N. P. (2000). *Anti-racist practice by White psychologists.* Unpublished doctoral dissertation, California School of Professional Psychology.

Vacarr, B. (2001). Moving beyond polite correctness: Practicing mindfulness in the diverse classroom. *Harvard Educational Review, 71,* 285–295.

23

A Multiracial Unity Group for Graduate Students

BARBARA GORMLEY

CRITICAL INCIDENT

A memorable incident occurred in the late 1990s while I was working on a writing project focused on integrating women's issues with multiculturalism. The purpose of the writing work group was to provide students such as myself an opportunity to meet faculty from other regions of the country with similar interests, to establish mentoring relationships. The women were predominantly White, although the group included a few women of color. Half the women were faculty, including several who were highly influential in our field, and half were doctoral students. During this meeting, Sally, an African American student who was a friend of mine, spoke up about an important issue related to race. She wondered how effectively our final product would address multicultural issues with so few women of color involved. She suggested seeking external consultation from women of color. Not one of the 20 women in the room responded to her comment. The topic shifted to women's issues.

When there was a pause, I, a White woman, reiterated Sally's point. She had asked me to back her up this way if I ever noticed that she went unheard, or I might not have done so. Not only did the group focus on the concern after I brought it up, but a senior member of the group complimented me on "my" idea. Recognizing that I had not attributed the idea to Sally, I told the group that it wasn't my idea and that Sally had suggested it earlier. There appeared to be much embarrassment as many exclaimed that they did not remember hearing her say anything. This was not only a source of great pain for my friend, but also the beginning of the end of a group project that was never completed. Before this event, when people of color told me that their ideas were often credited to White people, I had not recognized the instances when this occurred, nor had I fully appreciated the destructive consequences of invisibility.

For 15 years preceding this event, I had embraced antiracist ideology, challenged my own and others' biases, advocated for Native American and Mexican migrant groups living in my rural area, and presented at conferences on diversity issues. I even won an award for cultural sensitivity in clinical practice. The emotional pain and trauma associated with repeated experiences of racism, however, remained a distant concept even when I heard about it from friends. I specialized as a practitioner in trauma related to violence, but emotional pain associated with race did not deeply affect me. When I went back to school to earn my Ph. D., the emotional process I went through and the people of color I met led me to conclude that the protective emotional shield was White privilege.

FEELING THE PAIN

When I began my doctoral training, there was racial tension within my program. I tried to organize a White Awareness group based on Katz's (1978) model. I had been a member of such a group as an undergraduate in the early 1980s, and I thought such a group would be helpful for me. A faculty member who knew Judy Katz was supportive, but response was poor. White students wanted to lead the group rather than join. I asserted that to be a participant before being a trainer would be helpful, but I lost some participants this way. If I could go back in time, I would ask them what it meant to consider being a participant instead of a leader. Perhaps students needed to examine the issue of power dynamics during recruitment instead of waiting until the group began, especially in light of the fact that I was a first year student trying to recruit senior students. In the end, insufficient interest was expressed to start a group. At one point during my attempt to organize the group, Sally, an African American student, wanted to know why the group was just for Whites. When I responded that the format offered Whites an opportunity to examine biased ideas in a safe environment, she asked how we would know which of our ideas were biased without any people of color present. She had a good point, and this was the beginning of an ongoing, fruitful dialogue. Sally later became my friend and co-facilitated our cross-racial dialogue group that I discuss next.

During my second semester as a doctoral student, a requirement of our multicultural course was to spend 15 weeks observing a cross-racial dialogue group that is one component of the Multiracial Unity Living Experience (MRULE; Thomas, Gazel, & Byard, 1999). MRULE is an undergraduate race-relations program at Michigan State University that emphasizes (a) a grounding in the lives of the student-participants; (b) the role of historical examples; (c) unity in diversity and the role of difference; (d) the centrality of race; (e) social constructions of race; (f) social constructions of Whiteness and white privilege; (g) exploring the dynamics of power relationships; (h) exploring the dynamics of genuine, authentic relationships; (i) the role of dialogue; and (j) the use of participatory action research to sustain, develop, and replicate the program (Gazel, 1999). A discussion group based on these principles is central; however, "field trips" that expose participants to different cultures and activities that require cooperation with racially different others are also paramount. The ultimate goal of the group we observed was to create opportunities for cross-race friendships for freshmen and sophomores. Forty undergraduate students from a variety of races and backgrounds learned to respectfully take risks while discussing difficult race-related topics. The group was moving, and it inspired me to begin working with Jeanne Gazel, one of the group leaders, and several students in my program to organize a Multiracial Unity group for graduate students.

Again, there were strong reactions from students who this time reported feeling left out or judged if they didn't participate. Additionally, Black and Hispanic students recruited to participate did not want too many people from their cohorts involved because of trust issues. As a result, membership was established by word of mouth. Attempts to start these groups elicited strong emotional reactions, and I became a focus of hostility for disgruntled students. One instructor told me that others had failed in similar efforts because they also had become the target of emotion surrounding a long history of racial conflict. My advisor pointed out that, by persevering, I stood up to people's projections and, in doing so, showed people that these projections can be survived. Several students who feared reprisals from faculty for expressing interest in the group observed that this did not happen to Sally or me, and they eventually joined the group.

That semester, the Multiracial Unity group for graduate students began. Jeanne Gazel helped facilitate the first session. She brought three students who volunteered to talk about their experiences in an undergraduate group. The graduate student group had a balanced mix of students of color and White students, females and males, different ages, and different cohorts. The pain Black and Hispanic students expressed and the uncertainty that White students expressed about what to do about race issues moved many to tears. Consequently, we decided to begin by focusing on supporting each other to talk about our current experiences instead of jumping into social action. However, one outcome of these vulnerable conversations was action designed to try to change things within our program.

In the group, we learned to be honest, to take risks, to genuinely examine issues, to dialogue with each other, and to support each other through differences. The members of the group taught me the benefits of making mistakes and seeking new perspectives. I felt the pain of Black and Hispanic students who shared (a) current experiences of prejudice and discrimination, (b) heartfelt tales of wondering whether race influenced the way faculty treated them, and (c) reports that they could not be themselves in our training program. Their stories touched me deeply, and I began to make an emotional connection to race inequity and to dismantle previously held beliefs about an educational system that is dear to me.

Another White member, after listening to the stories of how students of color were treated, said that she would never be the same and that everyone in our program needed to hear these stories to understand what was happening. I wished that everyone could hear these stories, and I felt honored that I had. However, to expect a small number of students to educate the professional community also seemed an unfair burden.

I wanted to be part of the solution rather than part of the problem, and I learned how to use privilege to benefit professional colleagues who do not have racial privilege. Specifically, I can break the silence or speak up about race and oppression when discomfort leads White people to change the topic to gender, or religion, or other personal characteristics that place them in the oppressed rather than the privileged role. I can try to reach those who may be able to hear only White voices. I can support people of color in their efforts to uproot racism and discrimination. I can speak up for those silenced by privilege and credit them for their ideas when others give the credit to me.

As I joined efforts to raise awareness in our training program around issues of oppression, discrimination, and privilege, I also had to work through the repercussions associated with social justice issues. On one hand, I was rejected by some of the White students in a way similar to how African American students were treated. On the other hand, sometimes my voice was heard over Black students who were saying the same thing I was. The complexity of the situation was overwhelming. Being heard was a privilege I would have liked to give up, but silence was a privilege I would not exercise. Instead, as I helped White colleagues see different perspectives, I learned to credit students and faculty of color who for many years before I came along had diligently addressed race issues in our program. When faculty with evaluative power credited me with success in these efforts, I later wondered how much of the credit belonged to a long line of Black students and faculty in the program's history and whether I received the praise because I am White.

CONCLUSION AND LESSONS LEARNED

My efforts to alleviate racial oppression in my immediate environment led to experiences of failure, isolation, pain, and confusion, and feeling as if everything was falling apart. I was credited with tolerating and overcoming these traumatic experiences, but what I suffered for one year seemed more like a vicarious experiencing of a lifetime of trauma or a collective traumatic experience with which many students of color were expected to cope without acknowledgment.

Of greatest importance to me was the genuine contact with students and faculty of color that resulted, a most enjoyable and facilitative aspect of my graduate training. The confrontation, camaraderie, guidance, and friendship of Jeanne, Sally, and others supported my exploration and facilitated a new degree of surrendering privilege. My previous individual efforts to address racial issues seemed insignificant compared with being immersed in a cross-racial community and actively working together. The emotionally connected, community-minded group provided opportunities unavailable in the hierarchical, individualistic, competitive educational structure.

One way students can produce effective dialogue about cultural influences, in spite of commonly experienced fear and anxiety (Constantine, 1998), is to create groups separate from evaluative settings, as we did. Another way is to collaborate with faculty within training programs or academic courses. Ponterotto (1998) recommended that trainees become partners in multicultural training and applauded a shift "from content to process, from knowledge to experience, from quantification to personal narratives" (p. 43). Personal narratives not only are cathartic but also must inform diversity efforts in training programs if we are to understand how student experiences differ by cultural background. In addition, White students need to practice giving up white privilege if they are to be able to work in diverse collegial groups.

There may be limits to how effectively these issues can be addressed in a classroom. Intellectual exercises seldom provoke the powerful effect that arises when the status quo or deeply held beliefs are challenged, and rarely do such exercises incorporate methods for strong emotion to be safely and productively processed. Trainers might expect intellectual decorum or unknowingly push trainees to adopt values like their own rather than encouraging or tolerating a process of exploration. Enhancing awareness, confronting racist attitudes, and providing opportunities for processing related effect are difficult goals for training programs to achieve (Kiselica, 1999). Because of the power differential between faculty and students, trainees may comply with training expectations without expanding their awareness to accommodate other worldviews or changing their professional behavior (Steward, Neil, Breland, & Miller, 1999).

This power differential is especially daunting when a student encounters biased faculty members. Psychologists are ethically required to work to eliminate prejudice and to acknowledge discrimination that affects the psychological well-being of students (American Psychological Association, 1993); however, faculty vary in levels of multicultural awareness, and they are not always aware of discriminatory events. Students might not disclose experiences of racism within their training programs to their faculty, fearing negative consequences, even though students report experiencing racism in training programs when offered indirect opportunities for disclosure (Constantine, 1998). We all may be reluctant to link dynamics that arise to race. "Racism . . . is not a dualistic (i.e., either/or) status but a pervasive, often subtle, set of attitudes that can surface in surprising ways for all of us" (Vasquez, 1992, p. 199).

APPLICATION

Imagine that you are a student in a graduate course with 20 other students. Besides you, the course includes two African American men, one African American woman, one Latina woman, nine White women, and seven White men. The topic is recruiting and maintaining students of color as a means of eliminating discrimination. The instructor states that African American men are not successful in your training program, and there has been discussion among the faculty about not admitting any more applicants of this type. One of the African American men gets up and walks out of the classroom, and he does not return to the course.

1. What are your emotional reactions to the scenario? What kinds of similar or different reactions might the others involved have? What is important about the differences?

2. What kinds of racial power dynamics would you expect in a group with this racial makeup? Are you part of the class' racial minority or majority? Does this position affect your reaction?

3. What are the implications of the power differential between the instructor and the student who left the class? Are there similar and/or different implications of the power differential between Whites and people of color in the room? Do the implications change if the instructor is White, or African American, or of another race?

4. What is the issue? Share your thoughts with others racially different from you, and seek out alternative perspectives. Did your views change? Why or why not?

5. Do you think discrimination or prejudice is being exhibited? By whom? Are there ethical or legal implications to this scenario? Is anyone at risk of being harmed? If so, who is at risk?

6. What would you do in this situation? What would you like to see others do? Which responses to this situation might cause harm or perpetuate prejudice and discrimination? Which responses from Whites maintain or give up privilege?

REFERENCES

American Psychological Association. (1993). Guidelines for providers of psychological services to ethnic, linguistic, and culturally diverse populations. *American Psychologist, 48,* 45–48.

Constantine, M. (1998). Racism's impact on counselors' professional and personal lives: A response to the personal narratives on racism. *Journal of Counseling and Development, 77,* 68–72.

Gazel, J. (1999). Building community through diversity: Theory and practice of the Multi-Racial Unity Living Experience. In R. W. Thomas, J. Gazel, & R. L. Byard (Eds.), *Building community across racialized lines: The Multi-Racial Unity Project at Michigan State University* (Unity Studies Monograph Series, Monograph Number 1). East Lansing: Michigan State University, Urban Affairs Programs.

Katz, J. H. (1978). *White awareness: Handbook for anti-racism training.* Norman, OK: University of Oklahoma Press.

Kiselica, M. S. (Ed.). (1999). *Confronting prejudice and racism during multicultural training.* Alexandria, VA: American Counseling Association.

Ponterotto, J. G. (1998). Charting a course for research in multicultural counseling training. *The Counseling Psychologist, 26,* 43–68.

Steward, R. J., Neil, D. M., Breland, A., & Miller, M. (1999, April). Negative outcomes of diversity training: What can we do? Paper presented at the annual conference of the Great Lakes Region of the American Psychological Association, Columbus, OH.

Thomas, R. W., Gazel, J., & Byard, R. L. (Eds.). (1999). *Building community across racialized lines: The Multiracial Unity Project at Michigan State University* (Unity Studies Monograph Series, Monograph Number 1). East Lansing: Michigan State University, Urban Affairs Programs.

Vasquez, M. J. T. (1992). Psychologist as clinical supervisor: Promoting ethical practice. *Professional Psychology: Research and Practice, 23,* 196–202.

Glossary

acculturation refers to the process that occurs when cultures come into contact with one another. Acculturation does not presume that one culture will eliminate the other, nor that the two will coexist in harmony, although these are certainly possibilities.

ally a person who takes some action to oppose oppression of a group of which he or she is not a member. For example, an Asian American who challenges a racist joke that targets African Americans is acting as an ally to the African American community.

assimilation wherein members of one culture opt to relinquish their own values and traditions in order to adopt those of the new or host culture. Thus, assimilated individuals are not motivated to maintain their original cultural identity.

aversive racism (Dovidio, Gaertner, Kawakami, & Hodson, 2002; Kovel, 1970)—an attitudinal adaptation that results from an assimilation of an egalitarian value system with prejudicial and racist beliefs. In aversive racism as applied to White folks, one consciously endorses egalitarian values and denies negative feelings toward people of color. There is no evidence of blatant discrimination. Racist behavior is often unintentional and attributed to non-racial factors. Despite an absence of racist intentions, racist *outcomes* still occur. Aversive racism results in nondiscriminatory behavior in situations in which doing the "right" thing is obvious, but racist behavior when the situation is ambiguous. For example, Dovidio & Gaernter (2000) found that when both Black and White applicants are weakly qualified for a job, there is no evidence of discrimination in hiring practices. White research participants reject both candidates. When Black and White applicants are both moderately qualified, there is a slight but nonsignificant preference for Whites. However, when Black and White candidates are both *highly qualified,* then a strong preference for the White candidate is seen. The term *aversive* refers to the tension and anxiety experienced by Whites when they are interacting with people of color. It also refers to the aversion that Whites have to the notion that their thoughts or actions might be racist.

bisexual　term for a person who has orientations for intimacy toward both men and women.

closeted　hidden; most commonly used to refer to keeping one's sexual orientation secret; the opposite of *out*.

core conditions　from Rogers' (1957) proposal that there are three necessary and sufficient conditions for therapeutic change: (1) congruence, (2) unconditional positive regard, and (3) empathy. Generally speaking, congruence refers to one's ability to be authentic and genuine in a relationship. Unconditional positive regard refers to nonjudgmental acceptance of another person. Empathy occurs when one enters another person's frame of reference and uses reflection of feeling to communicate an accurate understanding of that frame.

gay　term for a person whose primary orientation for intimacy is toward people of the same sex; progressive literature uses the term *gay* to refer to men and *lesbian* to refer to women, to denote that these are two distinct groups rather than one group being a subcategory of the other group.

gender　based on socialization and sex-role rules, refers to the social construction of how individuals view men and women.

heterosexism　the ideological system that denies, denigrates, and stigmatizes any non-heterosexual form of behavior, identity, relationship, or community (Herek,1990); the system of values that promotes heterosexual relationships to the exclusion of other kinds of relationships (for example, platonic friendships, gay and lesbian relationships); beliefs, behaviors, or systems that discriminate against people who are lesbian, gay, bisexual, transgender, or queer, based upon a narrow view of heterosexuality as normal and healthy, and other sexual orientations and gender expressions as deviant and unhealthy.

homophobia　irrational fear of, aversion to, or discrimination against homosexuality or homosexuals.

lesbian　term for a woman whose primary orientation for intimacy is toward women.

LGBT　acronym used to indicate *lesbian, gay, bisexual, and transgender.*

meritocracy　a society in which people are rewarded solely based on merit. In a true meritocracy, the conditions of one's birth (race, class, sex, etc.) would have no effect on one's chances to succeed.

oppression　(Jaggar, 1983, p. 6)— "Oppression is the imposition of constraints; it suggests that the problem is not the result of bad luck, ignorance, or prejudice, but is caused rather by one group actively subordinating another to its own interest."

out　open; most commonly used to refer to being open about one's sexual orientation; the opposite of *closeted*.

privilege　a right or immunity granted as a peculiar benefit or advantage, often taken for granted by members of dominant cultures.

queer　depending on how the term is used, it could be a derogatory word to describe people who are gay. It has been reclaimed by some lesbian, gay, bisexual, or transgender people who self-identify as queer to show pride in who they are, including their differences.

racism　"system of advantage based on race" (Wellman, 1977, chapter 1). "Any behavior or pattern that systematically tends to deny access to opportunity or privilege to one social group while perpetuating privilege to members of another group" (Ridley, 1989, p, 60).

sexual orientation　an inborn, enduring emotional, romantic, affectional, and sexual attraction to another person; sexual orientation falls along a continuum ranging from exclusively heterosexual to varying degrees of bisexuality to exclusively homosexual (lesbian or gay). Sexual orientation is not determined by behavior (e.g., sexual intercourse between two men, two women, or a man and a woman), but by primary affectional attraction and how one self-identifies.

stigma　a mark of shame or discredit, and an identifying mark or characteristic.

transexual　a transgender person who has undergone or is undergoing sex-reassignment interventions such as surgery and drug therapies.

transformational learning process that results in fundamental changes in how people see themselves and the world. "Transformational learning *shapes* people; they are different afterward, in ways that both they and others can recognize" (Clark, 1993, as cited by Merriam & Cafarella, 1999, p. 318).

transgender a person whose self-identity is of one gender (for example, male), but whose physical gender is different (for example, female).

well-meaning white person (WMWP) (Wolfe, 1995)—one who consciously despises racism, but possesses hidden racist attitudes and fears, which impede the development of authentic relationships with people of color. The WMWPs have an investment in differentiating themselves from blatant racists and oppressive institutions, to support the belief in themselves as "good, concerned, altruistic person[s]" (Wolfe, 1995, p. 44). Despite an expressed commitment to equality and justice, there is little evidence of *anti-racist* practices, and rarely examination or ownership of one's own racism and prejudice.

REFERENCES

Dovidio. J. F., & Gaertner, S. L. (2000). Aversive racism and selection decisions: 1989 and 1999. Psychological Science, 11, 319–323.

Dovidio, J. F., Gaertner, S. L., Kawakami, K., & Hodson, G. (2002). Why can't we just get along? Interpersonal biases and interracial distrust. *Cultural Diversity & Ethnic Minority Psychology, 8,* 88–102.

Herek, G. M. (1990). The context of anti-gay violence: Notes on cultural and psychological heterosexism. *Journal of Interpersonal Violence. 5,* 316–333.

Jagger, A. M. (1983). *Feminist politics and human nature.* Sussex, England: Rowman and Allanheld Publishers.

Kovol, J. (1970). *White racism: A psychohistory.* New York: Pantheon.

Merriam, S. B., & Caffarella, R. S. (1999). *Learning in adulthood: A comprehensive guide* (2nd ed.). San Francisco: Jossey-Bass.

Ridley, C. R. (1989). Racism in counseling as an adversive behavioral process. In P. B. Pedersen, J. G. Draguns, W. J. Lonner, & J. E. Trimble (Eds.). Counseling across cultures (3rd ed., pp. 55–77). Honolulu: University of Hawaii Press.

Rogers, C. R. (1957). The necessary and sufficient conditions of therapeutic personality change. *Journal of Consulting Psychology, 21,* 95–103.

Wellman, D. (1977). *Portraits of White racism.* Cambridge: Cambridge University Press.

Wolfe, N. (1995). The racism of well-meaning White people. In M. Golden & S. R. Shreve. *Skin deep: Black and White women write about race* (pp. 37–46). New York: Doubleday.

Index